THE LAST NOBLE GENDARME

How the Tsar's Last Head of Security and Intelligence Tried to Avert the Russian Revolution

Vladimir G. Marinich

Cover: Major General Konstantin Ivanovich Globachev. Source: Marinich collection.

Published by State University of New York Press, Albany

Printed in the United States of America

For information, contact State University of New York Press, Albany, NY
www.sunypress.edu

Library of Congress Cataloging-in-Publication Data

Names: Marinich, Vladimir, author.
Title: The last noble gendarme : how the Tsar's last head of security and intelligence tried to avert the Russian Revolution / Vladimir G. Marinich.
Other titles: How the tsar's last head of security and intelligence tried to avert the Russian Revolution
Description: Albany : State University of New York, [2021] | Includes bibliographical references and index.
Identifiers: LCCN 2021030161 (print) | LCCN 2021030162 (ebook) | ISBN 9781438485997 (hardcover : alk. paper) | ISBN 9781438486000 (pbk. : alk. paper) | ISBN 9781438486017 (ebook)
Subjects: LCSH: Globachev, K. I. (Konstantin Ivanovich), 1870–1941. | Globacheva, Sofia Nikolaevna. | Russia. Okhrannyi͡a otdi͡elenīi͡a—Biography. | Secret service—Russia—History—20th century. | Soviet Union—History—Revolution, 1917–1921. | Political culture—Russia (Federation)—Saint Petersburg—History—20th century. | Globachev family. | Immigrants—New York (State)—New York—Biography. | Russians—New York (State)—New York—Biography. | Saint Petersburg (Russia)—Biography.
Classification: LCC DK254.G56 M37 2021 (print) | LCC DK254.G56 (ebook) | DDC 947.084/1092 [B]—dc23
LC record available at https://lccn.loc.gov/2021030161
LC ebook record available at https://lccn.loc.gov/2021030162

10 9 8 7 6 5 4 3 2 1

To my Barbara

Contents

Illustrations

Preface

Konstantin Ivanovich Globachev was the chief of the Petrograd Security Bureau (Okhrana) from early 1915 until the February Revolution of 1917. Thus, he was the Okhrana's last chief and he saw firsthand the Revolution as it was happening, and he and his family lived through it.

He wrote his memoirs, in Russian, several years later, between 1920 and 1922 when he was attached to the Russian Embassy in Constantinople. This was, in effect, the Russian Embassy in exile. In his memoirs he describes his years in office, the seething unrest in the capital, and how it grew into a revolution replete with all the mayhem and violence that is known in the history of that event. But he also wrote about his colleagues and his superiors and his relationship to them. It was his superiors to whom he gave detailed information in the intelligence reports his office was responsible for producing, and which were often disregarded, misunderstood, acted upon too late, and sometimes flat out rejected. The warnings of the intelligence agencies were often unheeded.[1] Globachev also covers the turmoil that went on from February through November 1917, and the takeover by the Bolsheviks, which in turn, led to the Russian Civil War that lasted until 1920 (although there were continued uprisings in various parts of Russia until about 1923) when the "White" Russians had to be evacuated, mostly to Constantinople and the surrounding islands. He ends his memoirs in December 1922.

Globachev's wife, Sofia Nikolaevna Globacheva, also wrote her memoirs. She wrote them in the late 1940s, just a few years before her death in 1950. They are personal, and they are filled with her anxiety and fear for her husband's safety, as well as for her children's, and she describes the crises that they lived through vividly. So, this is the story of both Konstantin and Sofia.

Here is the background on how this particular narrative on Globachev evolved. Several years ago I was home in the evening when the telephone rang. I answered and the voice on the other end introduced himself and asked if I knew or had any information on General K. I. Globachev. I responded that I had a lot of knowledge and information about the general since he was my maternal grandfather. There were several seconds of silence. I think that the caller never expected to hear from a person still alive who knew a lot about General Globachev. That began my acquaintance with Jonathan Daly, professor of history at the University of Illinois at Chicago, an expert on Russian history and especially on the tsarist security police. Happily our camaraderie has continued to the present. I told him what I thought I might have for him—some old documentation and a few photos. I said that I would look around some more, and I did. I began to search through family materials, most of which were in boxes that had not been opened in years. There were also some photos and documents that were with my brother Oleg, who lived in Florida. It all turned out to be a treasure trove—photos, letters, documents, some of which were faded with age, but others that were still in good condition, and this treasure trove included an original copy of my grandfather's memoirs, and the memoirs of my grandmother, the wife of General Globachev.

Daly recommended that I contact Professor Zinaida Peregudova, a renowned historian who worked in the State Archives of the Russian Federation (GARF) in Moscow. She is the world's foremost authority on the history of the tsarist political police. When I contacted her she, too, was pleasantly surprised that there was someone still living who knew about the general and his family and had both oral and documentary information on the Globachevs. I exchanged information and materials about Globachev and his wife with Peregudova. At some point she asked me if I would give her permission to publish their memoirs in a Russian history journal. How could I say no to a world-class scholar who shared a lot of information that her sources at GARF had about my grandfather? Both of my grandparents' memoirs were initially published in Russia in 2002 in the Russian scholarly journal *Voprosy Istorii* (Issues in History). They were then subsequently published, again with my permission, in Russia in 2009, as a book, in Russian, with commentaries by Peregudova and Daly, and additional pertinent documentation, all edited by Peregudova. This book is 519 pages long and it includes a comprehensive introduction to the history of the tsarist political police from the middle of the 1800s through Globachev's tenure as head of the Okhrana from 1915 up to the Revolution. This introduction was written by Peregudova and Daly. General Globachev's memoir follows, then his wife's, and following that are various primary source reports (originally classified during Nicholas II's reign) that Globachev produced for his superiors, various archival documents, and letters. The title of this book is *Pravda o Russkoi Revolutsii* (The Truth of the Russian Revolution), the same title that General Globachev had given to his memoirs.

The two original Globachev manuscripts, Konstantin's and Sofia's, were donated to the Bakhmeteff Archives (known to scholars as BAR) at Columbia University. Copies of the manuscripts are also in Moscow, at the State Archives of the Russian Federation.

All of what happened that I share with you, the reader, inspired me to translate both of my grandparents' memoirs into English so that the Globachevs' adventurous and traumatic experiences could be made available to the English-reading public. In 2017 the State University of New York Press published the translated memoirs. The title of the original book was kept. Not all the documents from the original book were translated, but the memoirs, the words of the Globachevs, were.

A note about the endnotes: because the Russian book consists of three narratives—Pergudova's introduction, the general's memoir, and his wife's memoir—endnotes that were necessary to include in this book cite the person who is speaking. Thus, when it is the editor of the Russian book, it is cited as "Peregudova"; when it is the general, it is "Globachev"; and when it is his wife, it is "Globacheva." Also, the pages cited are for the Russian text and for the English translation. Globachev's reports and his testimony before the Provisional Government are not translated, so only the Russian text is cited.

This book is about Konstantin Ivanovich Globachev and his wife, Sofia Nikolaevna Globacheva. It is about their personalities and especially their character, as it shows itself through their experience. In the process of getting to know them there are many individuals with whom they crossed paths. These people, too, are part of the story. Some were Globachev's colleagues, some were his superiors at different times in his life, and some were adversaries.

Wherever possible I have used documented sources, but since this is also about the Globachevs as people, I have relied also on information that is anecdotal and by this I mean that it is oral history. Let me explain this in detail. Even though I was born in New York City, I grew up in a Russian home. I spoke Russian before I spoke English. Our home included my grandparents (who are the subject of this story); their daughter (my mother); her brother (my uncle); my father, who had been a cavalry officer in the Russian army in World War I; my older brother, Oleg; and me. Our home had photos of Tsar Nicholas II, watercolor portraits of Peter the Great, Nicholas I, and Alexander II, all painted by my grandfather. Russian was spoken at home, and discussions were very often about bygone days. When friends and acquaintances of my grandparents and parents came over for dinner, and the menu was quite Russian, the conversations would really go into depth about everything and everyone pertaining to tsarist Russia. I was intrigued by these stories.

Over the years I took courses in Russian history, religion, and literature. I would always talk to my mother, father, and grandmother about what I was learning (my grandfather died when I was very young). My grandmother spoke Russian as she had learned it in Russia. So, my brother and I, who grew up in the middle of the twentieth century, learned the kind of Russian that was spoken in Russia at the beginning of the twentieth century.

My grandmother had a lovely singing voice and played the piano well; often at home she sang love ballads that were popular during her youth and adulthood in Russia. All this was an important part of the oral history that I experienced. In the last several years of my mother's life, when she lived with me, we discussed in detail her early life in Russia and as a refugee after the Russian Revolution, and certainly she shared a great deal of her recollections of her parents. These recollections are invaluable, because my mother described how the Globachevs lived, who some of their acquaintances were, what they looked like, what the vocabulary and idiom was in pre-Revolutionary Russia, and much more. Her memories of the Globachevs' life come close to being the last live witness accounts to events. Today, there are no remaining eyewitnesses to the events described. So, this story of the Globachevs will include such oral history. Citations that I use in this area of oral history will include who gave me the information, but it will not be dated, because a lot of what was discussed or passed on to me happened numerous times over the years.

A few words about words, names, and dates: all of the specific dates, such as month and day that refer to Globachev up to his emigration, are in what is called Old Style, the Julian calendar. The dates that are used once the family is in the United States and later in Paris and back to the U.S. are Gregorian calendar dates. I have used the very accepted method of spelling Russian last names as one finds them in just about all historical books—for example, Dzhunkovskii rather than the older way Dzhunkovsky. In a few instances, however, I continue to spell the name of a major player of the February Revolution, Alexander Kerensky, with a "y" rather than "ii." My reason is basically that most people would probably recognize his name spelled that way. The books that he wrote have his name spelled that way, and he himself spelled his name in English with a "y."

There are quite a few names of Russian persons with whom Globachev interacted, or whom Globachev mentions, sometimes in passing. For the reader who is interested in who these people might be, there is a glossary of names mentioned in the text that has some biographical information, especially what happened to these people. There is also a glossary of terms to make it easier for the reader to stay with the narrative.

The agency that Globachev was the chief of between 1915 and 1917 had the official name of "Bureau for the Public Security, Safety, and Order in Petrograd." There were two other such major offices in the empire, one was in Moscow and the other was in Warsaw. Different authors have translated this lengthy title into "Political Police," "Secret Police," and sometimes put in an added title—"Department." I have chosen to refer to these offices as "Security Bureau" in order to be clear that these were not the Department of Police, which had supervisory authority over these bureaus. In addition, these Security Bureaus also had connection to the city administration where they operated. I have also used the term "Okhrana"(Russian for security) interchangeably with Security Bureau, so that readers will not be confused if they see this word in this or in other books.

The Globachevs came into contact with quite a few people. In identifying these people I use the full name, at least initially; this includes first name, patronymic, and last name. An example is Alexander Pavlovich Martynov. And wherever a name is easily Anglicized, I have done it. Thus, it is Nicholas instead of Nikolai, or Alexander instead of Aleksandr.

Russian cities had administrative heads called *Gradonachal'nik*. In most cases this person was a military man, a general officer. Again, various authors have translated this title in different ways, and that could be confusing. Some of the titles are "commandant," "mayor," "city governor," "urban prefect," and probably even more. I have chosen to use the term city prefect, because the *Gradonachal'nik* was not the commander of a military district, nor was he an elected mayor, nor was he a governor, because there is a very exact title, *Gubernator*, for governor. I have chosen to use the term city prefect because it seems to be a bit less confusing than the other terms. Use of the term city prefect is not my original idea; this term has been used before. I am mindful that Sir Bernard Pares, a highly respected historian in the early part of the twentieth century, used it in his book *The Fall of the Russian Monarchy*.

Acknowledgments

There are several people who made this book possible. The first person that I communicated with at SUNY Press was Michael Rinella. He helped me to understand how everything was going to work, from forms to contract to putting me in touch with other SUNY folks. Thank you, you made things easier. Ryan Morris is the production editor at SUNY Press. She was super helpful in terms of the production process, and she was so patient with me for all my questions. Thank you, Ryan. John Raymond was the copy editor. I marvel at how he was able to wade through all the Russian names of people, their patronymics, the names of places, and the various Russian terms. I truly appreciate his effort, care, and patience. My thanks to David Prout for his care and advice.

My dear Jim and Theo Yardley (I spelled their last name correctly) read the manuscript and offered their observation and advice. Their professional experience allowed them to dig deep in what I was trying to say, and that was really helpful. My deepest thanks to them and I owe an S.O. to Jim.

I live in a family where there is never a day that I don't feel love from my kids and grandchildren. They all support and encourage me. So, to my children, Greg and Cat, Di and Mike, Jim and Theo, Betsy and Drew, Alec and Kelly, and Cole, my love and thanks. My grandchildren are consistently letting me know of their love. Here they are from oldest to youngest: Jack, Nicholas, Meggie, Erin, Olivia, Mick, Ben, George, Jeremy, Eddie, Pax, and Thea. I love you all.

Barbara Livieratos is my wife, my partner, and very definitely my muse. She encourages me when I am in doubt, pushes me to do better, keeps me focused, and she is always there for me. I've said this before, but it is as true now as it was before. Without Barbara this book would not have been written. I cherish you.

CHAPTER 1

Beginnings

The Globachev name begins to appear sometime around the mid-1700s. The earliest ancestor whose name we know was Kornilii Globachev. He lived in Vilnius and was a member of that area's gentry and of the Globach gentry, and was possibly descended from Crimean Tatars. He left Vilnius in 1770 and settled in Ukraine. He had a son, Fedor Kornilievich, born in 1750, who became a priest. Fedor's wife was Agrippina Iakovlevna.[1]

Fedor had three sons. Dmitrii Fedorovich became a priest, and Ioan Fedorovich also became a priest and rose to the rank of archpriest in Odessa. The third son was Antonii Fedorovich, born in 1782, and he too became a priest. His wife was Maria Romanova. All these sons were priests not of the monastic order that required celibacy. They were all part of what was known as the "white clergy," and that required a priest to be married or widowed.

Antonii had a son, Ivan Antonovich. The latter's birth date is not known. His higher education was at the Ekaterinoslav Seminary, which he completed in 1827. He remained in Ekaterinoslav, a city on the Dnieper River. That same year he chose not to continue to pursue a religious career. He applied for a secular job. He initially held a job that is not recorded in his life's record, but after a few years he made his career in an administrative position in the Ekaterinoslav nobility assessment administration. This was an organization that maintained the qualifications for membership in the local nobility, processed applications, and kept records of the membership.

The Ekaterinoslav nobility were Russian. The area that is now known as Ukraine was annexed by the Russian Empire at the end of the eighteenth century. It was generally called "Little Russia" (Malorossia), and over time Russians populated the area and Ukrainians were Russified. The Globachevs were Russian.

Ivan Antonovich was awarded the St. Vladimir Cross, fourth degree, for his good work. In 1869 he was accepted into the Ekaterinoslav hereditary nobility. His and his wife's names were entered into the registry of hereditary nobility. Their sons, Ivan, Konstantin, and Mikhail, were included in the registry.[2] It is Ivan Ivanovich's son who is the subject of this narrative. But first, some information on Ivan Ivanovich.

Ivan Ivanovich Globachev was born in the Ekaterinoslav Province of the Russian Empire in 1835. The major city of that province was Ekaterinoslav; later, during the Soviet era it was known as Dnepropetrovsk; its post-Soviet name is now Dnipro. Then as now it was a major industrial and transportation center on the Dnieper River. Ivan Ivanovich's career included several years in the army, from which he resigned with the rank of staff captain and entered into a career in police work as a local police superintendent of the Fourth Precinct of the Sokolskiii District of the Grodno Province. He married Natalia Nikolaevna somewhere between 1860 and 1865. By 1860 he had become the chief of police of the province, a rank that was equivalent to that of lieutenant colonel, and in that position he reported directly to the provincial governor.[3]

As Ivan Ivanovich's family grew, the names of his sons were entered into the registry of hereditary nobility.[4] This type of award did not bestow property or title to the recipient, but it did raise the family socially and helped to open doors of education and job positions to the family.

By 1870 he and Natalia had three sons: Vladimir was born in 1866, Nicholas in 1869, and Konstantin in April 1870. All three sons were born during the reign of Tsar Alexander II. In other parts of the world, Bismarck was unifying Germany, Emperor Napoleon III of France was taken prisoner by the Germans, Count Cavour and Giuseppe Garibaldi were unifying Italy, and Ulysses S. Grant was the president of the United States.

Since all three of Ivan Ivanovich's sons were of the hereditary nobility, they were eligible to attend the Polotz Cadet Corps, an academy that was open only to male members of the nobility. The function of such an institution was to prepare young males of noble birth for a military career.

The usual age at which a youngster could be admitted to the academy was from eight to about twelve years old. The curriculum was taught by military-ranked instructors, and the length of time that a youngster attended the school was about eight years. The curriculum during a cadet's stay included mathematics (through trigonometry), history, philosophy, literature, science, French, and German.

Ivan Ivanovich died in 1876 at the age of forty-one as a result of an infection that had developed on his foot that may have been caused by his applying a home remedy to a sore on his foot.[5] The funeral was, of course, in the Russian Orthodox Church, in a very typical Russian Orthodox church. The inside probably tended to be just a bit dark since most churches did not have stained glass or other kinds of windows. The walls and columns were covered with frescoes and murals depicting the life of Christ, scenes from the Old and New Testaments, and depictions of saints, prophets, and Russian saints such as Nicholas the Wonder Worker and Seraphim of Sarov. Icons could be seen on walls and on tables or lectern-like stands especially prepared to hold the icon. Around these were candleholders where the faithful could light a candle dedicated to the scene or saint depicted on the icon. The scent in the church was a mixture of incense, candle wax, and, since this day was a funeral, flowers.

Figure 1.1. Konstantin Globachev, age 10.

The service was certainly somber. Ivan Ivanovich was laid in his coffin in the traditional Russian Orthodox manner. There were no cosmetic improvements to his appearance, as was the Orthodox custom. His complexion was somewhat gray, a prayer ribbon was placed across his forehead, and a Russian Orthodox cross was in his hands. The service was in Church Slavonic. Prayers were chanted for his soul, for forgiveness of his sins, and, finally, the priest chanted, "Grant, O Lord, peace to the soul of thy servant Ivan."

Kostia, which was Konstantin's nickname, was six years old, Nicholas was seven, and Vladimir was ten years old. It is difficult to know what such youngsters really understood about the death of their father, but one of the things that stayed with Kostia for the rest of his life was his dislike for the scent of hyacinths, which he somehow associated with his father's funeral. Kostia was admitted to the Polotz Cadet Corp at about age ten, and he graduated from there in 1888. His older brothers were already at the school. It was while the three brothers were at school that their mother remarried a man whose name was Vasilii Axenov, who had two or three sons by a previous marriage. One of these sons, Leonid, became a physician, specializing in ophthalmology.

Kostia was a good student. Upon completion of his years at the Polotz Cadet Corp, he continued on at the Pavlovsk Military Academy,

Figure 1.2. Konstantin as a junior lieutenant, circa 1890.

which he finished with a first-class rating. In 1890 he was assigned to the Life Guards Keksholm Regiment with the rank of junior lieutenant. Both of his brothers were already in that regiment. Three Globachevs in the regiment at the same time was something. The brothers became well known throughout the regiment. They were branded as Vladimir, "the happy Globachev," Nicholas, "the chatty Globachev," and Konstantin, "the handsome Globachev." The regiment was stationed in Warsaw.[6] Konstantin was well liked. He knew how to play the concertina and was quite a good artist. His painting ability would serve him well in later years.

The two older brothers continued in military careers. Vladimir became a colonel and a Politzmeister (police chief) of a district in Petrograd. He died in Finland after the Revolution. Nicholas was a battalion commander in the Russo-Japanese War. He was a regimental commander on the Prussian front during the early part of World War I, and he was promoted to the rank of major general and was commander of the Novogeorgievsk Fortress from 1915 to 1917. Following the Russian Revolution he immigrated to Berlin and lived there until the end of World War II. He and his stepbrother, Dr. Leonid Axenov, who also had immigrated to Berlin after the Revolution, were on good terms. Nicholas was arrested in Germany by the Soviet secret police, the NKVD, shortly after World War II and died in Siberia.

Konstantin's military training continued with an assignment to attend the Nikolaevskii General Staff Academy in St. Petersburg. This was one of the premier upper division military educational institutes in Russia.[7] Upon completion of his educational tour there, he returned to his regiment. One of Globachev's first assignments after his return was as adjutant of the 3rd battalion in the regiment.

In 1899 he was temporarily assigned to St. Petersburg to be part of the greeting party for the Austrian emperor Franz Joseph, who was the honorary commander of the Keksholm Regiment.[8] Globachev received a commendation medal. Back in the regiment he was appointed staff officer of the regimental court. This is where he learned the law, legal procedures and protocols, and the orderly processes that are involved in military legalities, investigations, and military court proceedings. This is where he also developed his understanding of the importance of the rule of law, a concept that would stay with him as his life and career moved forward.

It was during his regimental tour of duty in Warsaw that Konstantin met Sofia Nikolaevna Popova. Sofia Nikolaevna Popova was born in

Warsaw in 1875. She was the daughter of Nikolai Korneleevich Popov, who was a councilor of state for peasant affairs (Destvitelnyi Statskii Sovetnik). She, too, was a member of the Russian hereditary nobility and could trace her ancestry back to Semeon Korsakov (1787–1853), a well-known expert on homeopathic medicine and an early pioneer in building "smart machines" that used perforated cards as sources of information,[9] and Semeon's son, Michael Semeonovich Korsakov, governor-general of East Siberia from 1861 to 1871.[10]

Sofia's parents may have died when she and her siblings were not yet adults. Sofia's daughter, Lydia, stated that a guardian raised Sofia and her brothers and sisters. Sofia had three brothers and two sisters. The brothers were Michael, Nicholas, and Vladimir, and the sisters were Olga and Maria. They all received a very good education. Growing up in Warsaw and attending a girls' educational institute that also had daughters of Polish gentry and nobility as students, Sofia became fluent in Polish and in German because of a nanny that was employed in the house, and French, of course, since any truly educated Russian of those times knew French as their second language. As she was of Russian parentage, naturally she was fluent, literate, and well read in Russian

Figure 1.3. Sofia, circa 1898.

literature. She was an excellent pianist and had a pleasant singing voice. Sofia was also strong-willed. Within the family circle and among friends, she was called Sonia, a very customary Russian diminutive for Sofia. It was probably during her earlier years, when she and her siblings were in the care of a guardian, that she inherited about sixty acres of property in the Warsaw area. It is not known whether, or how much, Sofia's siblings might have inherited.

Sofia was attractive—not beautiful, but striking. Her posture was such that she gave the appearance of being taller than she actually was, which was about 5'4". She had very expressive gray eyes. She carried herself very well, was sociable, had a good sense of humor, and was a good conversationalist in any of the languages in which she was fluent. Konstantin, too, was educated, cultured, and pleasant in appearance. He was well into his twenties, had good posture, was trim, about 5'10", had already developed the customary handlebar moustache, and generally had a calm disposition. Konstantin was attracted to Sofia, and she to him. While he took his position as an officer seriously, he did not take himself seriously. He did not promote his importance, and his modesty was an attractive quality.

Figure 1.4. The newlywed Globachevs, 1898.

Sofia and Konstantin were married in Warsaw on January 9, 1898. He was twenty-seven years old and she was twenty-two. He could not have married earlier, because there was a regulation in the army that an officer had to have a certain sum of money in savings before he could marry. Regardless of being of the hereditary nobility of Ekaterinoslav Province, he did not own any property and his financial status was modest.

Sofia and Konstantin soon started their family. They had three children. Sergei, the first child, was born around 1900, and died around 1902–3 from typhoid fever. The tragedy of Sergei's death was made even worse when one of Sofia's sisters told her that Sergei's death was God's punishment for some unspecified sin that Sofia must have committed. Sofia never spoke to that sister again. Many years later, when Sofia would mention Sergei in conversations, she would be sad and wistful. Lydia was born in October 1901, and Nicholas was born in 1903.

Sofia's brother Nicholas saw action in the Russo-Japanese War and later became a colonel and regimental commander of the Brest Infantry Regiment during World War I. Following the 1917 October Revolution, Nicholas and his family became separated and he wound up either in Latvia or Lithuania. The night before he was to be reunited with his wife and daughters Tamara and Alla, he died of a heart attack.

Sofia's brother Michael joined the army and served most of his career in the east, possibly near the Chinese border. He was married to a German woman by the name of Anna, and they had a son, Boris, and three daughters, Olga, Tatiana, and Vera. The third brother, Vladimir, became an artillery officer stationed in Riga during the war. He and his wife, who was known as "Aunt Musia," had three children, Olga, Nina, and Alexander. According to Konstantin's daughter, Vladimir died of a heart attack during the Revolution when he was about thirty-six years old. Sofia states in her memoirs that one of her brothers (she does not mention his name, but it must have been Michael) was captured and shot by the Bolsheviks during the Civil War.

Konstantin continued his life in the regiment and his married life in Warsaw. This was ideal for Sofia. She loved living in Warsaw, where she was born and grew up, and her memories of those early married years in Warsaw were ones of happiness and peace.

Konstantin was promoted to captain and was transferred in 1900 from his duties in the regimental court to being in charge of the regimental training command. This was his first experience in a leadership position, and he spent the next three years responsible for the orientation of new military personnel, their basic training, professional development, and education. He was also responsible for keeping all regimental staff updated on policies, strategies, tactics, and any other such matters. However, it was not clear what the future held in store for him once his duties with the training command ended and he would be reassigned to another job in the regiment.

Globachev loved the regiment, but regimental life did not entirely fulfill his ambitions, nor did it quite suit his character. In addition to its military role, a life guard regiment had a number of other responsibilities, including providing security to visiting dignitaries, being a presence and participating in ceremonial events, and participating in parades. This was not something that Globachev thought brought out the best in him. Some of the social life of a regiment also was not in keeping with Globachev's personality. Gambling and drinking, as could be found in some regiments, was not something that interested Globachev. But the experience that he had while being attached to the regimental court, and his leadership while with the training command, gave him a sense of direction. In spite of some of the perceived shortcomings of being

Figure 1.5. Globachev as staff captain.

in the regiment, he continued to have fond memories of, and pride in, having been a member of the regiment. He had made friends in the regiment that he would keep for the rest of his life, and serving with his two brothers in the same regiment certainly added to his fond memories. Even after the Revolution and his subsequent life as an émigré, he always wore his regimental pin on his lapel.

In 1903 he applied to enter the Special Corps of Gendarmes. His application was accepted and he got a good recommendation. The review of his application was very favorable. It stated that he was of "high moral character, highly competent, and dedicated to duty. He had a good reputation among his superiors and comrades, and he has a theoretical knowledge of French and German and he speaks Polish."[11] There are a number of reasons why Globachev chose to enter the Corps of Gendarmes. A few have been given above, such as those regarding some of the regimental culture but, as he stated, he chose this move as a matter of conviction. A major responsibility of the Special Corps of Gendarmes was to investigate suspicious political activities and crimes against the existing laws of the empire. The work was more exciting than some of regimental life, it was broader in its operations geographically, and more profound in its impact on the empire. Promotions could happen faster too. He was accepted into the Corps of Gendarmes at his captain's rank.

The headquarters of the Special Corps of Gendarmes was in St. Petersburg. This is also where the training facilities were located. Each person entering the corps had to go through a three-month training program. The curriculum included criminal law, railway regulations, and investigative procedures. At the end of three months the officer trainees took a written final examination.[12]

Between May 1903 and September 1905, Globachev was assigned to various provincial gendarme administrative offices. This was undoubtedly part of his orientation and training. His first assignment was as adjutant in the provincial Gendarme Administration in Peterhof where he served from September 1903 until April 1904. He was then reassigned to the Gendarme Administration in Baku where he spent only about a month, after which he was assigned to the Gendarme Administration in Grodno Province, whose headquarters was in the city of Bialystok. This was a small security agency operation. His posting there was from May 1904 to September 1905. Globachev's official service record shows only that he was assigned to the Grodno Gendarme Administration.[13] It is not known whether he was chief of the administration, or in some other role. Globachev's daughter stated that her father never had a subordinate role once he was in a line position in the Corps of Gendarmes. Globachev's wife states in her memoirs that he was "in charge" of the Bialystok agency. Globachev's personal resume states that he was the head of the Bialystok Okhrana.[14]

Bialystok was the largest city in the northeastern part of Russian Poland. In the last years of the nineteenth century, the population of the city was about sixty-six thousand, and about 63 percent was Jewish. The city was a center of textile manufacturing. The mix of population included industrial factory workers, peasants, students, artisans, and many unemployed poor, as well as professional anarchists. This is the environment into which the Globachevs moved. He was responsible for security and order. Sofia came with their three-year-old daughter and one-year-old son. She writes, "it was with our arrival in Bialystok that my life became anxiety-ridden and tormented, since not a day went by that I could not be sure that my husband might not be killed by the revolutionaries."[15] She recounts various killing incidents, such as when terrorists stalked an orderly and shot him in the street. Young and old civilians were killed. Raiding terrorist hideouts was a very dangerous enterprise. Globachev's wife describes how her husband, as head of the agency, participated in one such event. A terrorist bomb maker's hideout was made known and was raided. He was captured before he could detonate the bomb.[16] The Globachevs had armed guards who escorted them whenever they left their home.[17] Sofia Globacheva's anxiety was well founded.

The Globachevs were in Bialystok for one year only. In September 1905 Globachev was assigned to the Lodz District Gendarme Administration. His service record shows that he was appointed chief of that office.[18]

While Globachev was at these postings in various parts of Poland, Russia was involved in a number of crises. The Russo-Japanese War lasted from February 1904 to September 1905, and in January 1905, right in the middle of the war, St. Petersburg experienced Bloody Sunday, a peaceful demonstration by workers that turned into a massacre. Russia's Revolution of 1905 was felt in Poland, especially in Lodz.

Lodz was a major industrial city about eighty miles southwest of Warsaw. It was also a very polluted city. "Approaching the city, one could see from several kilometers away a huge cloud of thick, black smoke permeating the city."[19] In 1905 the population of Lodz was almost 344,000. The security situation in Lodz was very similar to that in Bialystok. There were strikes, killings by anarchists and revolutionaries of

Figure 1.6. Globachev as lieutenant colonel.

various ideologies, and, in general, the never-ending task of the gendarme office of keeping track of suspicious people and behavior, and of arresting those who were identified as political criminals. The importance of this assignment led to Globachev's promotion to lieutenant colonel in April 1906 (the rank of major in the armed forces had been abolished in 1884, thus the promotion system was from captain to lieutenant colonel), and that same month he was awarded the St. Vladimir Cross, fourth degree, for meritorious service.

Life for Sofia was never without some anxiety for Konstantin's safety, but there were some moments that the family could get away from Lodz. Sofia and her young children were able to spend summers in Spala, and Sofia took the family's German nanny and a servant also. Spala was approximately thirty miles southeast of Lodz. Spala was the park where the Tsar's hunting lodge was located. The lodge, with its accompanying cabins, was available to senior governmental staff. Globachev was in that category as head of the Lodz Gendarme Administration.

During Sofia's summer stays Konstantin was able to take some short time off to join Sofia and the children. There were many activities available at this resort. There was bowling, bicycle riding, horseback riding, walks in the woods, visits to the nearby village, and lapta. Lapta was a game with a ball that has sometimes been loosely compared to baseball. The children of the various dignitaries who were on vacation had many activities too, and the Globachev nanny and the nannies of other vacationers watched the children as the adults indulged in their activities.

CHAPTER 2

Warsaw, Nizhni Novgorod, and Sevastopol

The Globachevs spent four years in Lodz, and then came a major career appointment. Globachev's career in the Corps of Gendarmes had progressed nicely. His leadership while in Bialystok was followed by his appointment to head the Lodz office. His performance was recognized in St. Petersburg and he was appointed to head the Warsaw Okhrana in December 1909, just six years after his transfer to the Corps of Gendarmes from his infantry regiment. He replaced Colonel Pavel (Paul) Pavlovich Zavarzin, who was transferred to head the Moscow Okhrana office. Globachev's posting to Warsaw was definitely an important promotion. The three most responsible and prestigious security offices in the empire were Moscow, St. Petersburg, and Warsaw. A member of the Corps of Gendarmes had to stand out in his performance to get an appointment to one of these three major posts. Within four months of his appointment, Globachev was promoted to the rank of full colonel.

Sofia was delighted with the move: "I was happy to live in Warsaw once again, a city that I knew very well. It was here that I had completed the Alexander-Marinskii Institute and where I had been married. After all, I had lived in Poland almost from birth, and those Poles whom I knew since childhood, both adults and children, with whom we were friendly, treated us very well and amicably notwithstanding the fact that we were Russians."[1]

The tour of duty in Warsaw lasted three years. Despite Sofia's delight at being back in Warsaw, these were difficult years for Globachev because Warsaw was a dangerous place. It was a hotbed of revolutionary forces that were very strong and very well organized in terms of conspiratorial operations.[2]

Globachev's job was quite complex. As chief of the Warsaw Okhrana, he was also responsible for security operations of the entire region—meaning much of Russian Poland. He not only reported to the Department of Police in St. Petersburg but also directly to the assistant to the Russian governor-general of Poland.

Globachev's transfer to Warsaw in 1909 happened at the same time as the Department of Police was conducting a major investigation and review of the personnel of all the offices involved in political investigation (Okhrana offices and Corps of Gendarme offices) that came under the supervision of the vice director of the department. Thus, Globachev's operations were reviewed in the early months of his tour of duty. Sergei Evlampievich Vissarionov was the vice director of the Department of Police at this time. Born in 1867, he was university educated in law, and between 1889 and 1908 he held various positions within the judicial system. He had not been in the military and was not a career gendarme officer.

The review that Vissarionov embarked upon was quite in-depth. Not only were there the fairly routine matters to be looked at, such as the education of all employees (including chiefs), their debts, family situations, knowledge of departmental rules and regulations, and so forth, but also whether the employee who was responsible for investigations knew the history of revolutionary movements and revolutionary groups within the empire. A major matter of review was to determine how many secret agents these employees had personally brought into the system and with what parties these recruits were affiliated.

In the spring of 1910 the Warsaw Okhrana operations were reviewed, and the result was documented in a report that pointed to several deficiencies in the operation of the Warsaw office. Globachev was criticized for having met with only eleven of the thirty-seven agents and because secret agents were under the supervision of two of Globachev's subordinate officers. Globachev concurred with the report, but as he had been on the job for only five months, the report acknowledged that fact and scheduled a second review for some months later. The second review was conducted in February 1911 and it was reported that over the year that Globachev was now in office he had been unable to turn things around. The report stated that the operation of the secret agents was weak, that Globachev was slack as a leader, and that some of his subordinates criticized him for lacking energy, being too soft, and for not being interested in his work, but some of the very same subordinate officers of Globachev's were criticized for being "inactive in the area of political investigation, were not familiar with procedures, and some behaved consciously negatively toward Globachev."[3] Vissarionov sent a negative report on Globachev to N. P. Zuev, the director of the Department of Police in St. Petersburg. This was a major mark against Globachev.

Vissarionov's system-wide review led to fourteen chiefs of Gendarme Administrations being fired, among whom were the heads of Moscow, Nizhni Novgorod, Smolensk, Riazan, Minsk, Kherson, and other security offices. Globachev was not among those fired. While the negative evaluation he had received was serious, he had very strong backing from the governor general of Poland, General M. Kaznakov, and from the general's deputy for police matters, Lieutenant General Lev Karlovich Utgof. Utgof's professional background had a strong foundation in supporting Globachev. Utgof had been the chief of the Petrokovsk Province's Gendarme Administration, and in 1905 he was the chief of the Warsaw Province Gendarme Administration. He not only questioned some of Vissarionov's criticisms, but also went on the offensive and wrote directly to the director of the Department of Police, who at that time was Stepan Petrovich Beletskii, who had recently replaced Zuev. Utgof recommended that Globachev be awarded a decoration as soon as possible, and he reminded Beletskii of Globachev's promotion to the rank of colonel in 1910 for meritorious service. Utgof went on; "Since Colonel Globachev carries an excessively difficult responsibility for the Security Bureau [of Warsaw] and for the entire region, I consider the award of a decoration not only for his service but as a necessary incentive to a person who is heavily burdened in his work."[4] Not only did Utgof's strong defense of Globachev counter Vissarionov's negative review, but recently a historian concluded that Vissarionov's review of Globachev was biased.[5]

Vissarionov's review of security offices and operations was followed with memos and orders to the various offices to tighten their operations and particularly to increase the recruitment of secret agents. This produced an interesting result. Some security chiefs, having experienced this system-wide review and wanting to avoid any further inquiries and investigations, recruited friends, local clerks, leaders of rural communities, old people, and so forth just to increase the numbers; they padded their quotas of secret agents. Globachev did not do this.[6] It is possible that Globachev's refusal to pad the numbers of recruited agents in his Warsaw bureau antagonized some of his staff by putting them in a bind and by not going along with them.

The Department of Police decided to transfer Globachev to another post. At first a recommendation was made in June 1912 to assign him as head of the Gendarme Administration in Yaroslavl,[7] an industrial city on the Volga that was approximately 160 miles northeast of Moscow, but several months later, in November, this was changed and Globachev was transferred from Warsaw to Nizhni Novgorod, as chief of the regional Gendarme Administration.[8] His transfer from Warsaw may be related to more than just the negative evaluation he had received. He had been in Poland for a long time and his superiors may have decided that it was time for a change.[9]

In a way this was somewhat of a demotion. Being the head of the Warsaw Okhrana, with its widespread responsibilities, was a feather in any gendarme officer's cap. Warsaw was, after all, one the three major Okhrana postings in the empire. However, Nizhni Novgorod was a big city and the Tsar would be coming to visit in the next year. Thus, toward the end of 1912 Globachev took up his new post. In that year, in southeastern Europe the First Balkan War was in progress, and farther off, in the United States, Woodrow Wilson had just been elected president.

Nizhni Novgorod was a major commercial, industrial, and transportation center that was at the confluence of the Oka and Volga Rivers. Like so many other cities in Russia it had its ancient fortress and its Kremlin looking over the river. A very important institution of the city was its market, and especially the summer trade fair that brought tradesmen from as far away as Central Asia in the east and Europe to the west. This made the Gendarme Administration a key government agency, and the year 1913 was the 300th anniversary of the House of Romanov and Nizhni Novgorod was on the Tsar's itinerary of touring some major Russian cities. The Gendarme Administration thus had the added task of coordinating security operations even more than usual with the local constabulary of the city, with the Tsar's personal security, and with the chief of staff of the Corps of Gendarmes, who was responsible for railway security. It must also be mentioned that as part of the anniversary celebrations, the Tsar gave amnesty to many political prisoners. That added to the city's Gendarme Administration workload, since those given amnesty still had to be kept under surveillance.

Upon his arrival in Nizhni Novgorod, Globachev quickly asserted his authority. Documents of the Moscow regional Okhrana (within which Nizhni Novgorod fell) showed that Globachev got to know his subordinates and local gendarmes quickly, and his reports to his superiors demonstrate his activity and grasp of the region's revolutionary parties and the mood of the population.[10]

Preparations for the Tsar's stop in Nizhni Novgorod in May 1913 included an earlier inspection visit in March by General Vladimir Fedorovich Dzhunkovskii, who was the assistant minister of the interior for political matters. He was, in effect, in charge of all security matters. His inspection visit included meetings with the governor and with various other heads of agencies and of local government. One of those whom he met with was Globachev. Dzhunkovskii's assessment of the city's Gendarme Administration was that "it was organized in an excellent manner, thanks to Colonel Globachev, who was in every way an honest and irreproachable officer."[11] He further comments on Globachev: "He impressed me greatly and that was fully confirmed as I got to know him better. He was an outstanding officer in every way, he understood fully investigative matters; he was calm, he had a gentle disposition, honest, modest, and did not try to stand out. I later promoted him to the responsible position of Chief of the St. Petersburg Okhrana, a position he held until the very revolution. When I met him for the last time in 1918, this was still the honest and noble person that I had known before."[12] Globachev's daughter attested to this view of her father. She often commented on her father's modesty. Unlike some other Russian

Figure 2.1. Colonel Globachev and staff of the Nizhni Novgorod Gendarme Administration.

officials who would often look to take credit for some decision or event, or even take credit for someone else's accomplishment, Globachev did not indulge in pomposity or hypocrisy.[13]

Globachev's relationship with his superiors in St. Petersburg, who were now a different set of persons, was not only back on track but was also one where he was trusted and respected. His career was back on track too. He was doing his job well in Nizhni Novgorod, but Sofia was not enamored with the city: "I did not like Nizhni Novgorod. Although it was the main city on the Volga, it was sleepy and boring. The view of the Volga, however, was remarkably beautiful with loaded barges and huge, grandiose, richly appointed passenger ships scurrying about all the time. The city came to life during the Fair, which was held on the opposite side of the Volga and seemed to be something from a fairy tale, especially at night when it was awash with lights. Merchants and industrialists gathered here from all over Russia, deals worth millions were concluded. All the nationalities of Russia brought their finest merchandise and crafts, and there was nothing that you couldn't get there. Your eyes would wander all over trying to take it all in; life and merriment was in full swing. Theatres, the most luxurious restaurants, and various forms of entertainment opened during this trade fair."[14]

Globachev's tenure as head of the Gendarme Administration in Nizhni Novgorod was only about a year but, as mentioned, 1913 was very active for him and it was significant in several ways. The preparation for the Tsar's tour with his family, and the rest of the Tsar's retinue, required a lot of work, as did the responsibilities of running a security operation. The Tsar's visit and the celebrations that accompanied it went well and without incident. Globachev did not attend the various celebratory events due to his office's total involvement in maintaining security and counterintelligence operations at all times. Sofia was a part of the social circle of Nizhni Novgorod given that she was the wife of a senior government official. She attended various events, and was one of the few ladies who were presented to the Empress Alexandra Fedorovna and her children.

The Gendarme Administration was functioning effectively and things were going well for Globachev in general, but his year in Nizhni Novgorod was not without incident. A little later that year an inspection was made of Globachev's operations by the Moscow Security Bureau. The administrative structure was such that Nizhni Novgorod fell within the jurisdiction of the Moscow region. Consequently there was some oversight of Nizhni Novgorod by Moscow.

Figure 2.2. Celebration of the 300th anniversary of the House of Romanov in Nizhni Novgorod, 1913.

Lieutenant Colonel Alexander Pavlovich Martynov was head of the Moscow Okhrana in 1913. He, too, came from the hereditary nobility just like Globachev. He, too, had two brothers. To some extent Martynov's career paralleled Globachev's. And they had some similar experiences. Born in 1875, he attended the Moscow Corps of Cadets followed by further education at the Alexandrovsk Military Academy. He then entered an infantry regiment, followed by an assignment to a grenadier regiment. In 1899 he transferred to the Special Corps of Gendarmes, and in 1901 was appointed adjutant to the St. Petersburg Gendarme Administration. Over the next decade he had tours of duty in gendarme offices in various cities—Petrokovsk, St. Petersburg, and Saratov. He was appointed chief of the Moscow Okhrana in August 1912 on the recommendation of the director of the Department of Police, Stepan Beletskii. Martynov was a lieutenant colonel. Globachev was a colonel.

A year into his position in Moscow, Martynov went to Nizhni Novgorod in August 1913 to investigate Globachev's administration because of a report that Martynov had received about the questionable activities of one of Globachev's agents. Martynov's report to his superiors in St. Petersburg was apparently very critical of Globachev.[15] Beletskii, who was Martynov's superior and had appointed Martynov to his position, responded to Martynov's report in November with a seven-page memo. In his response, Beletskii quotes Martynov's attack on Globachev—"In this entire matter there is a fundamental absence of any control over secret agents." He further recommends that Globachev initiate more effective procedures to deal with agents.[16] Beletskii then assesses Globachev's record and concludes that the policies and procedures that Martynov had recommended Globachev initiate were in fact in place prior to Martynov's investigation. The director of police further criticized Martynov's methods, motivation, and attitude, and concluded that this unjustified investigation was bad for the department and for Martynov's career.

On December 13 the assistant minister of the interior, General Dzhunkovskii, who was Beletskii's superior in St. Petersburg, wrote to Martynov and reprimanded him very severely, accusing him of arrogance in attacking a more senior officer who had greater experience than he, for being too hasty to judge, and for being misleading. Dzunkovskii's final sentence in his communiqué to Martynov is his "extreme displeasure in this matter."[17] Prior to his appointment as assistant minister of the interior in 1913, Dzhunkovskii was governor of Moscow from 1908 to 1913, so he was acquainted with Martynov. He and Martynov did not like each other. While it could be argued that Dzhunkovskii's criticism of Martynov could have been based on their prior relationship, the fact that Beletskii, who was Martynov's sponsor, was highly critical of Martynov's attitude and motivation does speak to Martynov's reputation, and even earlier in his career Martynov had been reprimanded for not having been sufficiently careful in his job.[18]

Within a year of his appointment to Nizhni Novgorod, Globachev was transferred to be the head of the Sevastopol Gendarme Administration. His appointment was effective February 1914, but it was another month or so before he actually took charge in Sevastopol. The city was a major commercial and naval port on the Crimean Peninsula. Globachev arrived there just before World War I began.

By August the war had begun and Sevastopol, being a major port city, would be involved. Two German warships, the battle cruiser *Goeben* and the light cruiser *Breslau*, had been patrolling the Mediterranean Sea, and at the outbreak of the war they bombarded ports in Algeria. Chased by British ships, the German cruisers made their way to Constantinople and were transferred to the Ottoman Empire, although still under German command. On September 28–29 the German warships under the Turkish flag shelled Odessa, Sevastopol, and Novorossisk.[19]

Globachev's work was really cut out for him. Inspection and other visits by members of the royal family led Globachev to become acquainted and work with Colonel Alexander Ivanovich Spiridovich, who was in charge of the Tsar's and the royal family's security. The war and the shelling of Sevastopol required security cooperation with Spiridovich and intelligence work and coordination with army and navy intelligence agencies. While Globachev and Spiridovich worked well together, and

Figure 2.3. German battleship *Goeben*.

would for the next year, their relationship was professional and courteous, but not one of close friendship. Spiridovich's background was typical of the many men who went into the Special Corp of Gendarmes. He was born in 1873, was a member of the hereditary nobility, and graduated from the Nizhni Novgorod Corps of Cadets in 1891 and the Pavlovsk Military Academy in 1893. For the next six years he was assigned to an infantry regiment, and then in 1899 he was accepted into the Special Corps of Gendarmes and assigned to the Moscow Okhrana.[20] In 1906 he was appointed to be in charge of the Tsar's security. After the assassination of Minister Peter Stolypin in Kiev in 1911, there was some blame that Spiridovich did not provide enough security to prevent the assassination. He was not prosecuted and continued as head of Nicholas II's security detail.

CHAPTER 3

As Petrograd's Chief of Security

Globachev served in Sevastopol for only one year. That changed on New Year's Eve 1914. Sofia writes: "We were still in Sevastopol when we met the 1915 New Year. About thirty people had been invited to our home to celebrate the New Year. Precisely at midnight, as we were congratulating each other, my husband received a telegram appointing him head of the Okhrana in Petrograd. All of the guests congratulated him on this appointment, but I felt some sort of heaviness on my soul. I didn't want to go to Petrograd, as if having a premonition of all that we would have to live through there, and I expressed this. The guests tried to convince me that I had no right to try to talk my husband out of this, thereby harming his position, and that in general an appointment cannot be refused."[1] Globachev's reputation was very favorable and he was respected, especially by General Dzhunkovskii, who had met Globachev two years earlier in Nizhni Novgorod, and it was Dzhunkovskii who recommended Globachev for this senior position.

Yes, the name of the capital had been changed from St. Petersburg to Petrograd. After all, Russia was at war with Germany and Austria, so how could the Russian capital's name have the German suffix of -burg?

Sofia had every reason to be anxious for her husband. After all, in the past ten years there had been at least four political murders, assassinations: the Grand Duke Sergei, Prime Minister Peter Stolypin, Minister V. Plehve, and closest to what Globachev was being promoted to was the 1909 murder of the chief of the St. Petersburg Okhrana, Sergei Karpov, who was killed when his apartment was bombed.

Globachev went to the capital to report to his new superior, Nicholas Alexeevich Maklakov, the minister of the interior. Upon arriving in Petrograd, Globachev was informed that his wife, who had stayed in Sevastopol to get ready for the move, had come down with typhoid fever. Globachev was given leave and he rushed back to Sofia. She recovered and joined her husband for their life in Petrograd. Sofia wrote: "With our move to Petrograd our life became a real nightmare with all the emotional upheaval due to the failure of the war and all of the growing internal revolutionary mood among the intelligentsia. This was not the case at the front and officers, arriving on leave, tried to return [to the front] as quickly as possible from this somber mood of rumors and gossip."[2] This was Sofia's assessment, even though Globachev's assignment was a promotion—he was the head of security for the capital—and that made their social status higher now. Their apartments were in the Oldenburg Palace; they had servants and chauffeured automobiles. Sofia's acquaintances were now the wives of colonels, generals, senior ministerial staff, and educated professionals. One of the acquaintances that Sofia made, and with whom she became friends, was Julia (Lili) Dehn, who was a friend of the Empress Alexandra. Theirs became a social world that included balls, theatre, opera, and, on Orthodox holy days, attendance at the ministerial church, one whose parishioners were senior governmental officials and their families. Sofia also hosted dinners and other events in their home. Whenever Sofia had to go somewhere in the city, she was chauffeured. None of this relieved her anxiety, though. And in two years, all this physical and social comfort would be gone, and gone quickly, gone irrevocably, and replaced with fear for the family's life.

Petrograd was the largest city in the Russian Empire and its capital. All of the major government offices were there, as were all the ministers of the interior, assistant ministers, and directors of the Department of Police with whom Globachev had to interact, often on a daily basis, and to whom he had to report. And it was an industrial city that would have occasional strikes, demonstrations, active clandestine revolutionary groups, such as the Social Democrats (Bolsheviks and Mensheviks), the Socialist Revolutionaries, various anarchist groups, and a State Duma, some of whose members openly propagandized against the government during sessions of the Duma, and at other times criticized the government when visiting various towns and army bases. And there had been assassinations, as mentioned, like the one of Globachev's predecessor, Colonel S. G. Karpov. Sofia had cause to worry about her husband, and about Russia.

Further, the Ministry of the Interior and its subordinate units became the targets of all kinds of criticism. "N. P. Muratov, a senior official, wrote that under Interior Minister Makarov the minister's office had lost its awesomeness; under Maklakov it had lost its seriousness; and under Shcherbatov it had become a ludicrous place where one only brought papers to have them signed."[3]

Globachev stepped right into the reality of the politics and intrigues of Petrograd, which was "a city full of intrigue, with a stifling bureaucratic atmosphere."[4] The new Okhrana chief makes the following observation: "Over a two-year period I was witness to the preparation of the riots against the sovereign power, unstoppable by anyone, bringing Russia to unprecedented shock and destruction."[5] But there was more than Globachev just seeing how things were developing: "In my two years of service in Petrograd I had direct contact with six Ministers of the Interior and I must point out one characteristic that they all had: they understood little of the revolutionary movement in Russia and were little interested in it. Recalling that the minister of the interior had a deputy who was responsible for political matters, it would seem that they would have shown some interest in these issues. Each newly appointed minister devoted all his efforts and energies to strengthening and holding on to his job, and that really created some serious problems in light of all the influences and intrigues that were involved."[6] In addition to what more than one historian referred to as ministerial leapfrog,[7] Globachev also saw six assistant ministers of the interior come and go, and five different directors of the Department of Police. Several of these individuals had no background in political investigations and intelligence operations. Since they were all in the direct chain of command over Globachev, he had to constantly review with each new superior what was going on, and in the case of those who had no background whatsoever, he would have to orient them on the various revolutionary groups, their ideology, their organization, their strength, activities, and strategies.

In addition to the frequent changes of ministers of the interior, assistant ministers, and directors of the Department of Police, other ministries had similar problems. During Globachev's two-year tenure in Petrograd, Russia experienced four prime ministers, four ministers of war, three foreign ministers, and four ministers of justice. As one historian summed up these ministers, "A few were competent; most were craven and inept."[8]

Some of the functions of the Okhrana were to maintain surveillance over suspicious people and revolutionary groups, and to conduct searches, confiscate illegal materials, and arrest revolutionaries, and it all had to be done within the law. Globachev certainly understood this and abided by it. But politics sometimes got in the way. Globachev is quite clear about this in his memoirs. He acknowledges that arresting and neutralizing revolutionary and underground groups required the approval of either the assistant minister or the minister himself: "This approval was easily given when the matter concerned underground organizations, workers' groups, or unimportant individuals, but it was an entirely different matter if, among those designated to be arrested, were individuals who held whatever government position or were in a socially high position." Globachev goes on to say how sensitive and complicated the need for a legitimate arrest could get if the suspect had connections or was a member of the Duma.[9]

This was not a normal two-year tour of duty. There were politics and intrigues that some of these individuals tried to draw Globachev into, but they were unsuccessful. It was no wonder that Sofia was not happy with the move to Petrograd.

One of the first individuals whose position and decisions affected the Okhrana, and therefore Globachev's operations, was General Vladimir Fedorovich Dzhunkovskii, the same official who had praised Globachev two years earlier when the latter was the chief of the Nizhni Novgorod Gendarme Administration, and it was he who promoted Globachev to the Okhrana position in Petrograd.

Dzhunkovskii was appointed assistant minister of the interior for police matters in January 1913. He was in charge of the Department of Police, the Special Corps of Gendarmes, and the various Okhrana (Security Bureau) operations. He had previously been the governor of Moscow. He was selected for the assistant minister position by Nicholas Alexeevich Maklakov, the minister of the interior, who appointed Dzhunkovskii with the Tsar's full approval. Dzhunkovskii had been a member of the Preobrazhenskii Life Guards Regiment and was known and liked by the Tsar. He was connected. The new assistant minister loved and respected the army, but considerably less so the security forces.[10]

Very soon after assuming his position Dzhunkovskii began to initiate a set of reforms—a number of them to make the various police institutions more respectable. Since the gendarme officers had to come from the ranks of the army, they wore their traditional army uniforms. He directed that gendarme officers should wear the very recognizable blue gendarme uniforms. He closed a number of smaller Okhrana offices and

Figure 3.1. Major General V. P. Nikol'skii, chief of staff, Corps of Gendarmes (left); General V. F. Dzhunkovskii, deputy minister of interior (center); V. A. Brune de St.-Hyppolite, director of Department of Police (right). About 1913.

incorporated them into the provincial Gendarme Administrations. Thus, his thinking went, he did away with inefficiency and the bureaucratic ambitions of the leaders of these local offices. But probably the most important of his reforms was abolishing the use of police informants in the military. He issued the directive that put this into effect on May 15, 1913. He made the decision based on moral principles.[11] He was very clear on this. "I considered it a depravity and a breakdown of the entire army to have soldiers themselves within the military as secret agents, and this could no longer be tolerated."[12] He also abolished the use of informants in secondary schools. While there were some who found these decisions to be benevolent, there were others who felt that he was doing significant harm by doing away with the tools that were necessary for national security. Globachev disagreed with what Dzhunkovskii had done. "From that moment on, the investigative agencies were able to pick up intelligence only in passing and by chance, and what they learned was superficial."[13] When Globachev took up his post in Petrograd, there had been no agents or informants in the army or navy for almost two years. This was one of many challenges that the chief of the Petrograd Okhrana had to deal with, and would have to contend with over his two years in the capital.

CHAPTER 4

And Then, There Was the "Mad Monk"

Figure 4.1. Rasputin.

His name was Grigorii Efimovich Rasputin. He was reportedly born somewhere between 1864 and 1869. Given Douglas Smith's thoroughly researched biography of Rasputin, 1869 will be the date accepted in this book. He was born in the village of Pokrovskoe, which is in the Tobolsk

Province of Siberia. He was of peasant stock. Rasputin's father, Efim, spent much of his early life in various jobs of physical labor, but finally was able to purchase some land and get into farming. Little is known of Grigorii Rasputin's early life. But there are many myths. "Rasputin's entire youth, indeed the first thirty years or so of his life, is a black hole about which we know almost nothing, a fact that helped make possible the invention of all sorts of tall tales."[1]

In the twentieth century Rasputin picked up the epithet of "Mad Monk." He was neither mad—that is, he was not insane—nor was he a monk. Indeed, he had no clerical position whatsoever. The combination of his religious preaching, his reputation for being a healer, his customary black attire, and his close association with some priests and bishops all helped to create the appearance of some special religious position. Among those who were his friends and followers he was often referred to as *starets*, a Russian word that was used to describe religious elders and leaders.

It was around 1897 that Rasputin had a religious experience while he was visiting a monastery, and he began to be known as a mystical individual who had some kind of religious power. His reputation as a religious pilgrim and healer spread. He made his way to St. Petersburg around 1904–5 and became acquainted with, and accepted by, a number of members of the senior clergy of the Orthodox Church. And it was around 1906 that he met Tsar Nicholas II and his wife, the Empress Alexandra. His reputation as a *starets* who had powers impressed the royal couple. They were searching for anyone who could help their son, the Tsarevich Alexei, who suffered from hemophilia. Alexandra was especially taken with what she saw as the holy persona of the *starets*. Rasputin soon became young Alexei's "healer," and the royal couple, especially Alexandra, considered him a true friend and a holy man. The Empress's lady-in-waiting, and a close confidante of the Empress, Anna Alexandrovna Vyrubova was also a very devoted follower of the *starets*. Controversial as he was, his influence at court increased over the next several years, and the Empress was particularly loyal and supportive of him, as was Vyrubova. Rasputin had considerable influence at the palace. He also had supporters among the clergy, both priests and bishops. Not everyone, however, saw him as a saintly presence. Some recognized him as a source of influence on the Tsar and his wife and therefore sought his favor to promote their personal gain. There were position seekers who curried Rasputin's favor, opportunists of all kinds, society ladies who saw their positions enhanced by their closeness to the *starets*, and those who already had important government positions, but wanted to ensure the security of their jobs. These people were referred by him as "ours" and as "friends." Others saw him as a danger to the throne and to Russia because of these corrupt relationships and because of his licentious behavior. There were members of the clergy who were in this opposing camp, and they were known as "not ours."

In June 1914 a woman named Khionia Guseva, who had been stalking Rasputin, finally caught up to him in Pokrovskoe, Rasputin's native village, and stabbed him in the stomach. Rasputin was in critical condition requiring surgery, but he recovered. Guseva was judged to be insane and was committed to an asylum. She was released in 1917 during the Revolution. The result of the assassination attempt was that Tsar Nicholas ordered his minister of the interior, Nicholas Alexeevich Maklakov, to provide constant security for Rasputin immediately. Nicholas's message to Maklakov was direct and to the point:

> *Nikolai Alexeevich.*
>
> *I learned yesterday that in the village of Pokrovskoe in the Tobolsk province an attempt was made on the starets Grigorii Efimovich Rasputin, a man much honored by Us* [*sic*], *and he was wounded in the abdomen by a woman.*
>
> *Fearful that this attack was the doing of a clique of foul people with evil intentions, I hereby instruct you to keep a vigilant watch over this matter and to protect him from any further such attacks . . .*
>
> *NICHOLAS*[2]

Maklakov directed his deputy, General Dzhunkovskii, to investigate this matter and to provide immediate security to Rasputin. Dzhunkovskii obeyed and assigned four agents, two of whom would operate in the open, and two who would operate under cover, to provide security for Rasputin and to maintain surveillance of Rasputin's comings and goings and those of just about everyone with whom Rasputin was in contact.[3] The official responsibility for this security was assigned to the St. Petersburg Okhrana, effective July 1914. This, then, was Globachev's responsibility when he was appointed chief of the Petrograd Okhrana in early 1915.

Rasputin was not happy with agents hovering about him. Globachev comments, "Rasputin understood that in addition to protecting him I was maintaining surveillance over him. This occasionally constrained him and he complained about me to Tsarskoe Selo. So, I had to explain to him that he was being protected by order of higher authority. He reconciled himself to this, but I had to honor his wish to replace one of the agents assigned to him."[4] By Tsarskoe Selo, this meant that Rasputin complained to Anna Alexandrovna Vyrubova, the lady-in-waiting who was a very close confidante and friend of Alexandra's, and very much a devotee of Rasputin. She believed in Rasputin's goodness and godliness, as did the Empress. The *starets* had a conduit to the royal family.

The Okhrana chief's assessment of Rasputin is detailed in the memoirs that Globachev wrote after the Revolution and the Civil War that drove the White Movement out of Russia: "My official duties caused me to cross paths with Rasputin, since all the external surveillance over him for the last two years of his life crossed my desk. I became acquainted with him in 1915 when he was at the height of his influence." Globachev was quite clear about Rasputin's definite influence in governmental affairs. "In general, he made a fairly pleasant impression on me. His appearance was rather rough and serious. His movements tended to be jerky, he had a soft pleasant voice and his speech was that of a common peasant, but a smart one. The only thing that was not pleasant about him was that when he spoke to someone, he did not look him or her in the eyes. His deep-set gray eyes darted back and forth across the room. He did not impress me as a person endowed with some special gift of prophesies, as some people said. There is no doubt that this was a man with a strong will who was able to subordinate others to his will, but still he seemed to me to be an ordinary, but smart, peasant. Rasputin had no formal education whatsoever. His early learning of grammar, dogma, and church doctrine, that he liked to show off, was developed during his lengthy pilgrimages and wanderings, even before he became a firm presence at court."[5]

But it was not just security and surveillance over Rasputin that Globachev had to supervise; he also tried to minimize Rasputin's scandalous behavior, whether it was his recklessness while driving cars or getting into brawls.[6] There were also the intrigues that surrounded Rasputin or that he participated in that created challenges for the Okhrana. To say that Rasputin was a controversial figure is an understatement. Newspapers attacked Rasputin and the royal family too. Vyrubova got death threats

Figure 4.2. Rasputin's obvious influence—the *starets* seated between two senior officers, Colonel Dimitri Lotman and General Count Mikhail Putiatin.

in the mail and was afraid to leave her residence at the Summer Palace compound to go to Petrograd. She was nervous and asked the head of palace security, General Alexander Ivanovich Spiridovich, to provide her with security when she went to the city. He informed her that his duty was strictly palace security, but that she could be assured that "General Globachev (head of the Petrograd Okhrana) can be trusted."[7]

Rasputin's continued presence in Petrograd, and his considerable influence at the palace, particularly with the Empress Alexandra Fedorovna, increased newspaper attacks on him, on the royal family, on those associated with the royal family, and on those who owed their careers to Rasputin's recommendations to the Empress—or to Vyrubova, who transmitted Rasputin's requests to the Empress. Criticisms of all this and of the government in general could be heard in the State Duma.

General Dzhunkovskii, in his capacity as assistant minister of the interior in charge of police matters, got regular reports on Rasputin's comings and goings, who he saw, and information on his behavior. In June 1915 Dzhunkovskii submitted a report to the Tsar that described Rasputin's licentious behavior at the Yar Restaurant in Moscow back in March. There was much false information in the report, if not just about all of it. Dzhunkovskii hated Rasputin for the threat that the latter posed to the royal family and to Russia as a whole. The Tsar listened to Dzhunkovskii's report, thanked him, and asked for a copy. Nicholas shared this information with Alexandra who became incensed and wanted the general fired. The general was dismissed as assistant minister of the interior, and was assigned to a command position at the front.

The general's dismissal must have been met with relief, if not with pleasure by some. Colonel A. P. Martynov, the chief of the Moscow Okhrana, mentions Dzhunkovskii in his memoirs, and his assessment of his former superior is blistering: "This was, if I may express myself briefly but accurately, an utter but polished fool, but an arrogant fool, susceptible to flattery and an absolutely talentless person."[8] He goes on further. As in many government offices the portrait of a superior officer would hang in a prominent place in the building. Martynov relates how Dzhunkovskii's portrait was removed from Martynov's office after the former had been dismissed from his post as assistant minister of the interior. The portrait was moved to the surveillance agents' assembly room. Martynov's final slap at the general used a play on words, and it was vicious: "If one had to find a more appropriate place to hang General Dzhunkovskii's portrait, it should not go into the assembly area [*sbornuiu*], but into the toilet [*ubornuiu*], since he would be in his proper place, fully answerable for his well-known sexual tendencies."[9]

General A. I. Spiridovich was head of the palace security from 1906 to 1916. He knew Dzhunkovskii. The latter worked with and appreciated Spiridovich's competence; however, Dzhunkovskii felt that Spiridovich was morally lax, and the latter had very little use for Dzhunkovskii. He was quite explicit that "Dzhunkovskii promoted the development of the Russian Revolution through his unprofessional actions."[10]

Globachev's opinion on Dzhunkovskii's dismissal is not known. Personally, he liked Dzhunkovskii and thought him to be a gentleman.[11] Globachev's memoir gives the assistant minister some credit. "Dzhunkovskii was on the job for only two years, but he began to realize that you could not judge all the agents from this point of view and that the foundation for coping with the revolutionary movement was in having intelligence that was acquired by internal agents. But thanks to his views in 1913, Dzhunkovskii was able to . . . remove agents from the military and secondary schools." Globachev continues, "It was self-evident that this directive untied the revolutionaries' hands in terms of their ability to propagandize and agitate among the youth and the army's rank and file."[12]

Since it was Dzhunkovskii who appointed Globachev and held him in high regard, it is not known whether Globachev felt that he had lost a patron who would support the chief of the Okhrana should the need arise. In any event, not only was Dzhunkovskii gone, but the minister of the interior, Nicholas Alexeevich Maklakov, was also dismissed (he was not one of Rasputin's "ours"), and replaced by Prince Nicholas Borisovich Shcherbatov, whose only professional background and experience had been as the director of the State Horse Breeding Agency. His tenure as minister of the interior lasted from June 15 to September 21, 1915. Shcherbatov left little impression in his short tenure in office. Dzhunkovskii, who had been fired recently, stated that Shcherbatov was "sneaky and insincere."[13] Perhaps the kindest criticism of Shcherbatov is by Globachev: "Shcherbatov lasted in his job for three months and he brought neither harm nor good to it. I think that he was dismissed due to pressure from Rasputin's people because at that time the name of Alexei Nikolaevich Khvostov, who had been a member of the Duma, was being promoted for the position of Minister of the Interior."[14]

Sofia was involved also in the confluence of society and politics. As the wife of a highly placed government official, she entertained dignitaries and their families in the Globachevs' Petrograd home, had the general's staff for occasional meals and teas, and frequented the theatre with her society lady acquaintances. But Sofia was also the wife of the head of the Okhrana, and it was the Okhrana that protected and maintained surveillance over Rasputin. So, who better than the head of the Okhrana's wife to ask about Rasputin? The *starets* was a constant topic of interest in Petrograd, especially among the social circles. Even though Sofia had never come into contact with Rasputin, had never seen him, she was asked about him. One day, after Sofia and some acquaintances had gone to see an opera at the Marinsky Theatre, they were on their way home in a chauffeured automobile that Sofia had access to. Her companions began to ask about Rasputin. They were particularly interested in knowing whether the rumor was true that Rasputin was authorized to have a specially armored automobile assigned to him, one that had machine guns attached inside the car on both sides.[15] Sofia let her acquaintances know that there was no such vehicle, and, indeed, after the Revolution no such vehicle could be located.

CHAPTER 5

The Opportunists

There is a Russian word, *avanturist*, that is generally translated into English as "adventurer." This word in our language does not carry any negative connotation and, quite possibly, it can create an image of bold and romantic attributes. From a Russian dictionary one of the definitions of "avanturist" is of an unprincipled individual who indulges in shady deals, obviously for his own benefit. The single English word that seems to me to come closest is opportunist, but it could also include conspiracy.

Alexei Nikolaevich Khvostov was appointed minister of the interior on September 25, 1915, the day after Shcherbatov was dismissed. Khvostov's appointment had been decided upon well before Shcherbatov's departure. The Empress's lady-in-waiting, Anna Vyrubova, and Rasputin recommended Khvostov to Empress Alexandra Fedorovna for the position, and she, in turn, made her wish known to the Tsar. "I do hope Goremykin will agree to your choice of Khvostov—you need an energetic minister of the interior—should he be the wrong man, he can later be changed—no harm in that."[1] Nicholas approved the appointment.

Khvostov was a member of a rich landowning noble family that had properties in Vologda, Voronezh, Orlovsk, and Tula. He was born in 1872 and graduated with honors from the Imperial Alexandrovsk Lycee in 1893. At the start of his career and over the next several years he held several government positions, including assistant prosecutor in Tver and then in Moscow. By 1904 he was vice-governor of Tula, then governor of Vologda, and in 1910 he was governor of Nizhni Novgorod, an important position in a major city. He gave up that position in 1912 when he was elected to the Fourth Duma, representing a right-wing

Figure 5.1. A. N. Khvostov, minister of the interior, September 1915–March 1916.

faction. Khvostov became acquainted with Prince Michael Mikhailovich Andronikov. They were close to the same age, Andronikov having been born in 1875. Andronikov was of noble birth and he was much more than a man-about-town. He was an intriguer, gossipmonger, collector of information on people, and schemer. His motivation for this behavior was for personal gain, and he had access to Vyrubova and Rasputin. Khvostov was "vain and ambitious, he distinguished himself in the Duma with his fierce anti-Germanism and his fondness for flaunting his right-wing attitudes and showy patriotism."[2] Globachev was clear on his view of Khvostov: "Khvostov always seemed to me to have a criminal side."[3] Spiridovich, who was in charge of palace security, also had something to say: "Khvostov was an ignoramus in politics as well as in police matters."[4] Khvostov's lack of competence was an opportunity for Andronikov to promote the cause of a friend, Stepan Petrovich Beletskii, to be appointed assistant minister of the interior. This was the same Beletskii who was fired by Dzhunkovskii from his post as director of the Department of Police back in 1912.

Figure 5.2. S. P. Beletskii, assistant minister of the interior, September 1915–February 1916.

Khvostov did not get involved in the intelligence and police work of the Okhrana. He left that to Beletskii. That was fully understandable. Khvostov had little knowledge of political police functions, whereas Beletskii's past experience as assistant director of the Department of Police between 1909 and 1912, and then as director of the Department of Police until 1915, made him ideal to oversee those operations.

At the beginning of his tenure in office, Khvostov curried the favor of Rasputin, since the *starets* did have influence in getting Khvostov his job. The latter was beholden to Rasputin, much more than Khvostov counted on. The minister's attitude toward Rasputin at first "was one of good will, based on the principle that Rasputin was the personal business of Their Majesties into which the authorities should not meddle."[5] It did not take long for Khvostov's attitude toward Rasputin to sour. One of the reasons was that both Khvostov and Beletskii owed their positions to Rasputin's influence at the palace. Rasputin knew that too. The *starets* became more demanding for payment in promoting the cause of individuals who were office seekers, and he began to communicate with Khvostov by sending him notes and letters addressed directly to him with various demands. The *starets* became downright insolent. Khvostov was smart enough to know that Rasputin's behavior meant that the *starets* was in control and that he had power over the two he had recommended for high office to the Empress. Rasputin's arrogant demands were a threat to the minister's position. Khvostov and Beletskii began to discuss ways to rid themselves of Rasputin. A different assessment of Khvostov's developing distance and intrigue against Rasputin was because Khvostov wanted the *starets* to recommend him to replace the aged Ivan Logginovich Goremykin as chairman of the Council of Ministers. Khvostov wanted to be prime minister. And Rasputin did not show any interest in recommending Khvostov for this big career advancement.

The state of things got to the point that Rasputin's removal by any means was Khvostov's primary objective. But, in order to do this, Khvostov and Beletskii needed to get closer to Rasputin. They needed someone who would be their private agent, reporting directly to them. Around October 1915 Beletskii recommended an individual whom he had known from past association. This was Colonel Mikhail Stepanovich Komissarov. He was a gendarme officer. Komissarov's reputation and professional record were well known in the Ministry of the Interior, and especially within the Corps of Gendarmes. V. V. Brianskii, who was the secretary to the city prefect of Moscow, stated, "even among the gendarmes, Komissarov's reputation was that of a thorough scoundrel and even a crook."[6] In 1908–9 Komissarov seems to have taken it upon himself to print anti-Semitic posters and documents using the Department of Police presses. His activities were discovered and he was transferred to the Yenisei Province as head of its Gendarme Administration—a clear demotion. Over the next few years he was able to advance his career, though, and between 1912 and 1915 he was the head of the Saratov Gendarme Administration. Saratov was a major port city on the Volga River. Komissarov's "disreputable career flourished because his behavior changed with the prevailing political climate."[7] Globachev certainly knew of him.

Komissarov was considered capable, smart, unscrupulous, and very much into "intrigue and willing to enter into any relationship that served his interests."[8] In 1915, however, Dzhunkovskii, who had a keen sense of honesty and was an honorable man, reassigned Komissarov to be the head of the Gendarme Administration in Viatka, a small city located almost nine hundred miles east of Petrograd, far away from the capital.

Again, this was a much smaller posting than he had before—another obvious demotion.

When Komissarov became aware that Beletskii had been appointed assistant minister of the interior he began to lobby Beletskii to appoint him chief of the Petrograd Okhrana, the position held by Globachev. Beletskii needed Komissarov to be his and Khvostov's personal agent, but not to be in a position of administrative authority where they would not be able to count on his personal loyalty to them. So, Beletskii was not about to get rid of Globachev.

Komissarov was given a fictitious position in an inactive gendarme office. He was appointed chief of the Warsaw Okhrana sometime in the latter part of 1915, but that office and its entire operation had been closed when Warsaw was taken by the German offensive on August 5, 1915. However, since the Warsaw Okhrana was no longer in operation,

Figure 5.3. Colonel M. S. Komissarov, personally appointed agent of Beletskii and Khvostov.

Komissarov was assigned personally to Khvostov and Beletskii, especially to Beletskii. Thus, Komissarov came to Petrograd, a city he had been posted to before, and where he was known. The palace head of security, General Alexander Spiridovich, certainly knew Komissarov. The latter's drinking and womanizing prowess was known in many of the Petrograd restaurants and clubs.[9]

Komissarov's job was to report directly and personally to Beletskii. His assignment was to establish surveillance over Rasputin that was parallel to the official security and surveillance by Globachev's Okhrana staff. Komissarov was authorized to recruit some agents to maintain a constant surveillance of Rasputin, to chauffer Rasputin on his various visits in Petrograd and its environs, and to report on everything that Rasputin did and everyone he saw. Globachev was not to be informed of any of this.[10] Beletskii introduced Komissarov to Rasputin and to Vyrubova and convinced them of Komissarov's good standing. He was to engage Rasputin and get on Rasputin's good side.[11] In this way Khvostov and Beletskii would get detailed information on Rasputin's habits, his whereabouts at any time, and any other information that would help them plan to get rid of the *starets*.

Beletskii's agent frequented Rasputin's apartment very often, mixed with the other visitors there, and plied Rasputin with drink. But, while this was happening, Khvostov began to distance himself from Beletskii. The assistant minister writes, "At this time I noticed that Khvostov was getting close to Komissarov and was asking for regular reports and meetings with the Chief of the Okhrana, Globachev."

Komissarov was playing both sides. He reported both to Khvostov and to Beletskii, and when he met with Beletskii he made sure that he criticized Khvostov. The situation was getting out of hand. Beletskii began to mistrust his superior even as they both continued to plan Rasputin's murder. The assistant minister had to find out whether Globachev was involved in any way. Thus, there was a very real danger that Globachev faced.

As the head of a security agency Globachev was knowledgeable and experienced in dealing with and handling sensitive and even sinister situations. There were almost always issues surrounding clandestine surveillance, the use of secret agents, and the need to operate according to the law in all such situations. He also knew that his position and reputation could be compromised easily. An example was an incident when Globachev was head of the Gendarme Administration in Nizhni

Novgorod and the chief of the Moscow Okhrana, Colonel Martynov, attempted to discredit him. On another occasion, after the directive was issued that prohibited secret agents in the military, an army officer made an appointment to speak to the Petrograd Okhrana chief. This officer, knowing the rule about agents in the army, offered to spy on his own regiment for money. Globachev refused. Even in later years, he spoke of this officer's offer with disdain.[12]

Matters pertaining to Rasputin had to be carefully handled by Globachev. Sometimes situations involved someone in Rasputin's circle of "friends," and not the *starets* himself. Nevertheless, things could be murky.

Ivan Fedorovich Manasevich-Manuilov was one of Rasputin's "friends," and a confidant. He has been described as "an infinitely protean, chameleon-like figure . . . unprincipled, unscrupulous, [and] venal."[13] Manuilov had a common-law wife, but he had become infatuated with an artist named Lerma.[14] She was twenty-four years old and he was forty-seven. Lerma was taking horseback riding lessons from a riding instructor whose last name was Petz. Manuilov was jealous and afraid that Lerma might drop him in favor of Petz. Manuilov approached Beletskii and asked him to separate Lerma from Petz somehow.

Manuilov knew that Beletskii should be able to help him. After all, Manuilov saw the assistant minister as being in the category of "friend." The latter said that he could do nothing unlawful, to which Manuilov responded that Petz was a depraved individual who was being investigated by the army for allegedly selling horses to the Germans. Beletskii consulted with Khvostov and the minister saw the situation as one that could be a favor to Manuilov and therefore it might make Rasputin's and Manuilov's behavior to Beletskii and Khvostov friendlier.

Based on the allegation about Petz and some corroboration from the army that there was an investigation going on, Globachev was given the order to arrest Petz. Globachev did so and informed Beletskii that the Okhrana had to initiate an investigation of the charges. The results of the Okhrana's investigation concluded that neither Petz nor anyone in his family were involved in any illegal, revolutionary, or treasonous activities. Globachev informed Beletskii that the law required Petz to be released.

Petz was not released, however. Beletskii and Khvostov decided that Manuilov should be kept unsure of Petz for a while longer. Manuilov's anxiety would have the two ministers in a position of advantage. Beletskii told Globachev to keep Petz detained longer because of Rasputin's relationship to Manuilov. The general knew that this was beyond the legality of how long a person could be detained. This would make Globachev responsible for the detention, but it was an order from his superior. Globachev accepted the order, but he wrote that the assistant minister of the interior ordered Petz's continued detention. Since Globachev did not put his name to the order, Beletskii was smart enough and experienced in how the law worked, so he understood that Globachev would not be held responsible for Petz's continued detention. The assistant minister also did not want to be responsible for this action, which was of more than questionable legality. Beletskii wanted Khvostov's name on the order. It is not known if Khvostov even saw the order. Globachev told Beletskii that this entire matter needed to be resolved, meaning that Petz either had to be charged or released. Petz was released soon after. The only help that Manuilov got out of this entire chicanery was that Beletskii suggested to Petz that he stay away from Lerma.[15]

The Rasputin matter was different. Rasputin, as incredibly controversial as he was, was a nationally and even internationally known figure who was close to the royal family. And the conspirators who were thinking seriously of getting rid of Rasputin were very highly placed government officials. Initially Globachev only knew that something more dangerous was in the works. How else to explain Komissarov's unofficial position and recent closeness to Rasputin, Globachev being bypassed and not being kept informed of matters that were clearly in his purview, and being told to cooperate with Komissarov but not interfere with the latter's activities?

Globachev's suspicion heightened even more when he met with Beletskii in the assistant minister's office during one of Globachev's regular meetings to give Beletskii an intelligence report. Beletskii brought up Rasputin in the conversation and inquired of Globachev how to rid Petrograd of the *starets*. The conversation was apparently very general and hypothetical, but Globachev understood its meaning. Beletskii described how Rasputin was a danger to the monarchy and to the nation. Beletskii mentioned what Khvostov was thinking to Globachev. Beletskii found out quickly enough the Okhrana Chief's position. "In Globachev's astonished look, I saw that he would not join Khvostov in this matter."[16] Globachev would not be a partner in this conspiratorial enterprise.

Globachev states that quite soon his eyes were opened to Komissarov's real role in Petrograd: "On one occasion he approached me with the Minister's approval with the request that I lend him my horse and a sleigh without a driver for the entire night. The reason that was given was that my horse was fast. The request was verified by telephoning Khvostov and, based on his confirmation, I fulfilled the request. I was very surprised when my horse was returned the next day all lathered and the sleigh had a broken shaft. It became perfectly clear to me that if Rasputin was found killed or thrown through an ice hole and my carriage was to be found, all the blame would be on me. Because of that I talked my way out of all of Komissarov's subsequent requests to borrow sleigh or horse by saying that my horse was sick and the sleigh was in repairs."[17]

At first Komissarov established a close and seemingly friendly relationship with the *starets*, which would have made Rasputin more vulnerable in trusting someone who had ill intentions toward him. But soon Komissarov did the opposite. He would come to Rasputin's apartment and act rudely, use foul language, and yell, even in front of other visitors at the apartment. He spread gossip about Rasputin. So, how could Komissarov's strange behavior be explained?

Khvostov and Beletskii were now at odds with each other, and each was looking to protect himself and his job. Komissarov's erratic behavior may have been initiated because both he and Beletskii were trying to distance themselves from Khvostov's near obsession with getting rid of Rasputin. The matter was too dangerous, so Komissarov may have found a way out for himself. By insulting Rasputin he could incur the disfavor of the *starets* and simply be transferred out of Petrograd and be free of all this intrigue.

Khvostov reported dissatisfaction with his assistant minister to the Tsar, and both Beletskii and Komissarov were removed from office. Beletskii was appointed governor general of Irkutsk and Komissarov was sent to Rostov as city prefect, from which position he was fired within six months. Khvostov lasted only a month longer. Khvostov's nefarious activities and his "base character, finally reached Alexandra in the first days of March." On March 2 Alexandra wrote to Nicholas saying how badly she felt that she had actually approved of Khvostov's appointment to the Ministry of the Interior.[18] Khvostov was dismissed on March 3, 1916.

Earlier that year, in January, the Tsar was considering replacing his prime minister, Ivan Logginovich Goremykin, who was seventy-seven years old. Nicholas wrote to his wife, "I think incessantly about a successor for the old man. In the train I asked the fat Khv. [Khvostov] what was his opinion of Sturmer. He praises him, but thinks that he is too old also, and that his head is not as clear as formerly. Incidentally, this old Sturmer has sent me a petition to allow him to change his surname and adopt the name of Panin. I replied, through Mamant[ov], that I could not grant permission without the previous consent of the surviving Panins."[19] So, the Tsar was told that Goremykin was too old, and that was true for the time. In 1916 the life span of a male in the United States was not quite fifty years of age, and it probably was lower in Russia.

Nicholas appointed Boris Vladimirovich Sturmer as prime minister. Sturmer came from landed hereditary nobility. He had graduated from university with a law degree and served in a number of government capacities, including governorships of Novgorod and Iaroslavl. His family name was of German descent, so he wanted permission to change his last name to Panin, a very well-known Russian name on his mother's side. Neither Nicholas nor Alexandra approved the change. Sturmer was sixty-eight years old. Globachev was forty-six.

After Khvostov's and Beletskii's dismissals, Sturmer took over as minister of the interior in addition to his position as prime minister.

CHAPTER 6

1916, Leading to the End

Just as they had done in previous years, the Globachevs greeted the New Year on December 31, 1915 in their apartments in the Prince Oldenburg Palace on the Mytnenskii Embankment. This building was also the headquarters of the Petrograd Okhrana. The Globachev apartment included a large dining room that could easily seat twenty-five to thirty people, and next to it was the reception area that could easily accommodate even

Figure 6.1. Major General Konstantin Ivanovich Globachev.

more. In the center was a massive chandelier, and on one of the walls was a life-size portrait of Sofia painted by her husband. The colonel and his wife had invited many of their friends and acquaintances to celebrate the New Year. Around midnight Colonel Globachev was called to the phone. It was the minister of the interior congratulating Globachev on his promotion to major general.

The promotion was based on his past work at colonel's rank as head of Gendarme Administrations that he had led, and on the evaluation of his first year as chief of the Petrograd Okhrana for which he was given high marks. The celebration went into high gear as the newly appointed general was surrounded and congratulated by his friends. Some of these friends and acquaintances were Globachev's immediate subordinate officers, some colleagues of equal rank to the new general, such as Major General Vladimir Pavlovich Nikol'skii, who was chief of staff of the Corps of Gendarmes, civilian acquaintances who held responsible positions in the government, and close friends of Sofia, such as Lili Dehn, who was a lady in waiting at the court and a personal friend of the Empress. The Globachevs traveled in fairly high social circles.

There was an increase in social events with dinner parties at home, dinners with other high-ranking personnel, and attendance at church services at the Ministerial Chapel, a church particularly "reserved" for highly placed officials. And there were new customs. While he was a colonel, Globachev was addressed by his name and patronymic (Konstantin Ivanovich) by fellow colonels, but now he had to be addressed as "Your Excellency."

There was another customary practice that existed for generals. Globachev's daughter recalled how she was in a restaurant with her parents and a junior officer approached her father, the general, and asked Globachev for permission to dine at the restaurant. Globachev gave his permission, but he never felt comfortable with this custom. Indeed, as Globachev's daughter told it, her father was rather flustered and embarrassed the first time that he experienced such a thing.

But now, 1916 was going to be tumultuous in many ways. The situation in Petrograd was getting worse, if not by the day, then by the week. Of the six ministers of the interior that Globachev served under, four of them held the position in 1916. They were Alexei Khvostov, Boris Sturmer, Alexander Khvostov (Alexei Khvostov's uncle), and Alexander Protopopov. The first minister served from September 1915 to March 1916. Sturmer's tenure as minister of the interior lasted four months, from March to July 1916. Alexander Khvostov served for roughly two-and-a-half months, July to September, and Protopopov from mid-September to the February Revolution. This meant that Globachev had to orient each minister to the operations of the Okhrana and interact with each of them in terms of their personalities, experience, and understanding of the various revolutionary groups. In most cases they did not understand much about the revolutionary groups, their ideologies, organization, or tactics. Some of the ministers were not clear on the differences among the various groups. And almost always permeating the ministers' lives was their relationship to Rasputin.

Globachev had worked under Khvostov from September 1915 until March 1916, so the first new minister in 1916 was Sturmer, and Globachev's assessment of his new boss was quite critical: "He was old, incompetent, stubborn, and unable to fathom the most basic issues." In addition, he "was thoroughly useless by seven in the evening," and would doze off at meetings.[1]

Boris Sturmer, who was chairman of the Council of Ministers and not yet minister of the interior in January, organized a meeting in his office to discuss economic and political issues, but there were no concrete results from the meeting.

Figure 6.2. Boris Sturmer, chairman of the Council of Ministers and minister of the interior, 1916.

The frustrating part of Globachev's job was the constant presence of Rasputin and his involvement with the palace and with all kinds of officeholders and office seekers. Khvostov and Beletskii had been preoccupied with the *starets*, and after they both were gone from office so was the next minister of the interior, Boris Vladimirovich Sturmer. Globachev observed, "Sturmer was not interested at all in either the political situation or the mood of Russian society, but he was extraordinarily interested in Rasputin and in court circles."[2] Major issues and problems during Sturmer's tenure went unresolved.

Conditions in Petrograd had been bad since the beginning of the year. Globachev's reports continued to detail the activities of revolutionary groups, workers' strikes, and the unreliability of the Petrograd reserve troops. His reports became more frequent, lengthier, and more detailed. To give his superiors a sense of the economic crisis that the capital was facing, his report of January 27, 1916 was to A. N. Khvostov, the minister of the interior. Classified "Secret," the twenty-eight page, single-spaced typed report was primarily a report on the economic situation and its effect on the population in Petrograd, which Globachev enumerated with charts on how the cost of living had skyrocketed. The report had very little on revolutionary groups or organizations that were launching criticism against the government. Globachev compared prewar prices to current prices. In many cases prices had increased by 100 percent and in some instances even more. The details in Globachev's report were comprehensive. He listed many items that were affected by price increases ranging from coal and firewood to meats, butter, flour, chocolate, and even candy. The report stated that the problem was not one of lack of goods; rather, it was primarily an issue of corruption. The report included information about price fixing, profiteering, and speculation by individuals who were leaders in businesses that could, and did, control prices by controlling the transportation and distribution of goods. The general named such individuals and recommended that there be a lawful way to have the government control the distribution of goods and thereby keep prices within reason.[3]

A serious problem occurred in the early summer of 1916. The population in the capital had increased greatly as a result of the war. People fleeing from the German advances in the west had fled to Russia's big cities. From a prewar population in Petrograd of not much more than a million the number jumped to almost three million.[4] The crisis in population also included the growing number of Russian reserve forces, and the necessary establishment of more hospitals, clinics, and medical staff. Living accommodations were inadequate for the mass of humanity that was now in Petrograd. There was the lack of provisions for this increased population, prices had increased, and discontent and antigovernment propaganda was on the rise, especially among the reserve units, and it would get worse.

A meeting called by Sturmer to address the problem included Globachev and General Nikolai Evseevich Tumanov, commanding general of the Petrograd Military District. The question was how to relieve the crisis in the capital. Globachev was asked to present his views. After presenting a survey of the social, economic, and political situation in Petrograd, he recommended, and insisted on, the removal of "all reserve troops and unnecessary medical units from Petrograd."[5] His argument was twofold. There were several battalions of reserve units, each of which had between nine thousand to twelve thousand troops. Their evacuation would relieve the problem of living accommodations, prices, and provisions for the population of the capital. And Globachev had acquired intelligence that the reserve troops could not be relied upon in a crisis.

General Tumanov disagreed with Globachev, not on the latter's information and position on the matter, but because Tumanov's conclusion was that it would be too expensive to move all the reserve troops out. Globachev countered by saying that the capital's security was more important than the expenses that might be involved. Sturmer ended the meeting with no conclusion or decision. Sturmer did not address the problem again, although Globachev would bring the matter up again subsequently.[6]

On other matters the minister, however, was very concerned. Anything having to do with Rasputin had Sturmer's full attention. On one occasion the minister got a report that a beggar woman who spotted Rasputin leaving the Kazan Cathedral shouted that the *starets* was a murderer who should be strangled. Sturmer summoned Globachev urgently and said that Rasputin's life was threatened. "I had to try really hard to calm him and assure him that there was no threat to Rasputin from this beggar woman." On another occasion, while Globachev was away from his office on some necessary official business, Sturmer called the Security Bureau three times demanding that the chief of the Okhrana come to Sturmer's office immediately. When Globachev later arrived at the minister's office, Sturmer started with "Do you know what happened at Tsarskoe Selo yesterday?" When Globachev said he did not know, Sturmer, who was in an agitated state, wanted to know why he was aware what had happened but Globachev was not. Globachev said that his responsibility was for security in the capital and that palace security personnel were responsible for security at Tsarskoe Selo, and that Globachev would not necessarily have received a report. Sturmer said that he did not know that. The incident that upset Sturmer so much was that two drunken naval officers had appeared at Tsarskoe Selo and wanted Rasputin's address. Sturmer saw this as a threat to Rasputin's life. Globachev recollected, "I calmed Sturmer and told him that there was no threat to Rasputin in this drunk escapade. In case of any real necessity to get Rasputin's address, they would not have gotten it this way. In addition, almost everyone in Petrograd knew that Rasputin lived at 64 Gorohovaia Street." Sturmer was also unhappy with the press. He felt a particular animosity toward a journalist by the name of Kliachko, and he informed Globachev that he suspected Kliachko of being a German spy. He wanted Globachev to arrest him. The Okhrana chief stated that this could not be done without evidence. Such a matter needed to be turned over to the military counterintelligence agency. The matter was dropped soon after.[7]

But the serious work of the Petrograd Okhrana still had to be addressed in addition to all the minutiae surrounding Rasputin's comings and goings and the chicanery and incompetence of ministers and assistant ministers. Combatting terrorist and left-wing revolutionary groups was a never-ending job. Sofia Nikolaevna, Globachev's wife, attested to this:

"My husband, his subordinate officers, and all others who served worked day and night, not even having some rest on holidays, neither at Christmas nor on Easter. My husband got up at nine in the morning and would go to his office by ten. At that time the officers and other personnel arrived. At two o'clock I would send a servant to ask my husband to come for lunch, but he rarely did because he could not get things done in peace because the chairman of the Council of Ministers or the minister of the interior would want to see him, or there was an emergency and he would have to go to the Department of Police or to the City Prefect. He would come home around seven in the evening and sometimes he was able to lie down for an hour before supper, after which he went back to his office to read reports and give orders for the next day. It was the same every day to five in the morning. I sometimes had the opportunity to invite his officers for some late evening tea. They all complained bitterly that they were working so hard for no results because the powers that be did not pay attention to my husband's daily reports in which he pointed to the inevitability of a terrible revolution unless immediate necessary steps were taken."[8]

The stressful responsibilities of the Okhrana increased in 1916, even more so in the second half of the year. Throughout 1916 both the Petrograd and Moscow Okhrana offices issued warnings to their government superiors of the imminence of the coming revolution.[9] According to a report by Alexander Blok, "The reports of the Okhrana in 1916 give the best characterization of the public mood; they are filled with alarm, but their voice could not be heard by the dying regime."[10]

As summer was replaced by fall, the work of the Okhrana increased. Globachev continued to have to contend with ministers of dubious competence and other officials of questionable ethics. But of greater significance were conditions in Petrograd. Popular discontent had increased sharply by September. There was anger and vicious criticism of the government in the Duma, in the newspapers, in factories, and among the reserve troops. Revolutionary groups fanned these flames. Certainly a major problem was also the worsening economic condition in the capital. There was hunger, erratic distribution of foodstuffs, lack of most essential retail items, the low salaries of workers, and inflation—all woven into the tapestry of the massive increase in the capital's population.

Globachev's assessment of the overall situation was that "at the present time we have definite and accurate information that allows us to conclude categorically that this entire movement has an economic basis and is not tied to any purely political program. It will take only this movement to express itself in some specific act (a pogrom, a major strike, a massive confrontation between the public and the police, etc.) at which time it would become purely political."[11]

Even though the activities of the various revolutionary groups were slowed considerably by the Okhrana, Globachev's reports at the end of November still voiced apprehensions. "It would seem that even though the results of earlier repressive measures against the Social Democrat organization left it in an 'awful condition,' and the SRs were absolutely 'broken up,' Globachev insisted on further arrests of the 'organizing body' (Mensheviks) on September 13 and the terrorist anarchist organization on September 17. Bolsheviks were arrested from December 9th to the 19th and the night of January 1, 1917. As Globachev reported the next day to A. T. Vasiliev, the director of the Department of Police, the steering committee of the Bolshevik faction of the Social Democratic Party remained intact and presumably was attempting to initiate demonstrations on January 9, the anniversary of Bloody Sunday."[12]

While all this was going on, that is, the authorized work of the Okhrana, Globachev had to work with a new minister of the interior and try to get him to understand the function of the security agency and the current conditions in the capital. This new minister was Alexander Dmitrievich Protopopov, appointed by Tsar Nicholas around the third week of September 1916.

His "appointment had been in the works for a long time by Rasputin and his clique."[13] Protopopov was known to meet with the *starets*, and to consult occultists. It was also rumored that he was insane as the result of suffering from syphilis.[14] Globachev presents his observation of the new minister from the perspective of administrative competence: "As the head of the Ministry of the Interior, Protopopov did not have service competence, administrative experience, nor aptitude, and he did not want to learn anything."[15] Nevertheless, Globachev had to present the best intelligence to the minister. This was not always easy. Protopopov was preoccupied, as were past ministers, with Rasputin and his activities, and the minister usually did not understand details. This became very clear to Globachev early on, and became critical by the end of the year.

Figure 6.3. Alexander Protopopov seated between two subordinates.

It was early in Protopopov's tenure as minister of the interior that Globachev presented two major issues to his superior and to Sturmer, who was now the chairman of the Council of Ministers. Sofia writes that her husband constantly advised Protopopov and Sturmer that it was necessary to have a constitution issued as soon as possible to prevent a revolution. Globachev also argued for the abolition of the Pale of Settlement, which Protopopov apparently agreed to. The Pale, a large area in Russia within which Jews had to live, was to be abolished at Easter 1917. Globachev also insisted that he should submit reports personally to the Tsar. Protopopov apparently agreed, but nothing came of it. And the general informed the minister of the unreliability of the Petrograd garrison. Globachev also recommended that the city's reserve garrison be exchanged with a cavalry unit that was at the front. In this way the unreliable units in the city would be gone and in their place would be battle-hardened veteran soldiers who could be trusted.

The Tsar reviewed this information and agreed, but the corps commander of the front-line unit that would be affected resisted. Tsar Nicholas dropped the matter.[16] This was not the first time that this concern was raised by the Okhrana chief. Earlier, in the summer of 1916, Globachev had called upon General N. E. Tumanov, the current commander of the Petrograd Military District, to remove the reserve units of the capital's garrison. Globachev argued that the troops were unreliable and had been influenced by revolutionary propaganda. General Tumanov refused to remove these troops from the city.[17] Globachev would raise this issue again.

There was also something else going on. Around November, the city prefect of Petrograd was Major General Prince Alexander Nikolaevich Obolenskii. He had held this position since July 1914, but now he was transferred to command a brigade on Russia's western front. His departure was not voluntary. He was not liked by either Empress Alexandra or by Interior Minister Protopopov. "Rasputin was not pleased and wanted [him] replaced. His main grievance was the growing food crisis in the capital and what Rasputin saw as Obolenskii's ineffectiveness in dealing with it."[18]

The position of city prefect was now vacant and a new official had to be appointed. Protopopov presented a list of four candidates to Nicholas and Alexandra. All were major generals. The candidates were P. P. Meier, the city prefect of Rostov; A. I. Spiridovich, the city prefect of Yalta; K. N. Khogondokov, governor of the Amur military district; and

Alexander Pavlovich Balk, formerly the deputy to the police chief of Warsaw. Nicholas rejected Meier because he thought that the candidate's German name was a problem. Khogondokov did not impress Alexandra, and as far as Spiridovich was concerned, Alexandra said, "Let him stay where he is."[19] The last candidate was Alexander Pavlovich Balk. He and Protopopov had known each other for many years and had been classmates at a cadet academy. Protopopov promoted Balk's candidacy, extolling the latter's good points. Rasputin also approved of Balk's candidacy. Balk got the job effective November 10, 1916.[20]

In the United States, Woodrow Wilson was reelected president in November 1916. The United States would enter the war in several months.

As winter continued to roll in, Globachev's agents continued to maintain surveillance over Rasputin and provide him with security. Unfortunately, because of Rasputin's complaints about agents hovering over him, Rasputin was able to dismiss his bodyguards if he was going to be staying at home in the evening, and so "on the tragic night of December 16, 1916, at 10 p.m., he told his guards that he was going to bed."[21] That night he was murdered by three conspirators. They were Vladimir Mitrofanovich Purishkevich (age forty-six), a member of the State Duma; the Grand Duke Dmitri Pavlovich (age twenty-five), a first cousin of Tsar Nicholas; and Prince Felix Felixovich Yusupov (age twenty-nine), who was married to Nicholas's niece. All three saw Rasputin as being a major threat to the royal family and especially to Russia. The major investigation of the murder was carried out by the Petrograd police and the palace police. The Okhrana was not involved in the investigation in any major way.

The assassination certainly did not help Russia. While there were many in Russian society who applauded the death of the "Mad Monk" and his evil influence over the royal family, there was also dismay that the murder was committed by members of the high nobility and, not only that, that none of the conspirators were charged or stood trial for murder. All were put under house arrest for a short time and then Prince Dmitrii Pavlovich was sent to Persia to join a Russian brigade that was stationed there. Yusupov was exiled to his country estate, and Purishkevich left the city for a while. Nicholas II virtually did nothing other than to declare that murder was wrong.

Rasputin's admirers saw him as a martyr, but the high social status of the murderers undermined much of Russian society's respect for the throne. Globachev's assessment of the murder was that "the murderers did not gain popularity, but instead lost the respect of many. Rasputin's close relationship to the throne was a major evil, but an even greater evil was his murder under such circumstances."[22]

Rasputin's demise did not relieve Globachev and his organization of an evil nuisance. Rather, evolving circumstances now required the Okhrana to step up its surveillance and intelligence collecting because of the country's and the capital's heightened anxiety and disarray. There was turmoil as the war continued to go badly for Russia amid growing antigovernment and antithrone sentiment in the capital.

The winter of late 1916 and early 1917 was much colder than the past several seasons had been. "In Petrograd, the temperature in the first three months of 1917 averaged 12.1 degrees below zero centigrade (10 Fahrenheit) compared to 4.4 (40 F) degrees above zero the same time the previous year. In February 1917 it dropped to an average of minus 14.5 degrees (6 F)." This led to major problems in providing the capital with supplies, food, and fuel. As an example, much of the railway "stood immobilized by the weather; during the winter of 1916–17, 60,000 railroad cars loaded with food, fodder, and fuel could not move because of the snow."[23] The weather helped to produce food shortages and the associated price increases. Globachev's reports throughout January 1917 addressed secret meetings of State Duma factions, student disturbances, rumors of possible terrorist attacks, newspaper articles focusing on food shortages and price increases, and activity by revolutionary groups.

On January 5, 1917, Globachev sent a top secret report to his superiors that outlined conditions in the capital. Unlike his report of a year before that dealt with economic issues this one was entirely on the social and political crisis that was present and continuing to evolve in Petrograd. His report dealt with student disorders that could lead to terrorism, members of the Duma who were considering a palace coup, and how the Kadets might force the government to transfer power to the more progressive bloc of the Duma. A copy of his report found in the records of the Department of Police had a number of Globachev's most critical statements underlined.[24]

On January 9 Globachev reported to Minister Protopopov on the results of the Okhrana's success in neutralizing several revolutionary groups: "I reported to Protopopov that on this day about 200,000 workers went on strike in Petrograd and the Security Bureau liquidated [neutralized] three underground organizations, seizing three illegal printing presses and a lot of illegal printed materials." In Globachev's presence, Protopopov telephoned the chairman of the Council of Ministers, Prince Golitsyn, and reported that "January 9 went well, there were no strikes—just trifles—we arrested three armed workers' detachments and seized a lot of material." In addition to Protopopov's behavior on this occasion, it became clear to Globachev that the minister did not read the reports that the Okhrana and the Department of Police sent to him on a daily basis.[25] Protopopov's personality and behavior were much in question by many more than just Globachev. "Interviews in 1917 with Protopopov's servants and colleagues indicated that the new interior minister had an erratic, even chaotic, but fertile mind frequently smitten with something like manias." He was also described as speaking endlessly, not being able to concentrate on a topic, and not understanding the role of the ministry for which he was responsible.[26]

Globachev also had doubts that intelligence information that was reported to Protopopov ever got to the Empress, who would get such reports when the Tsar was absent from the capital and was at military headquarters in Mogilev. After the Revolution Globachev was told "by one of the Empress' ladies-in-waiting that Protopopov never reported to the Empress on the seriousness of the political situation in Russia, and particularly in Petrograd, and the Empress thought right up to the revolution that everything was fine."[27]

Globachev continued to keep tabs on the reserve units in Petrograd as best his organization could, given the ongoing prohibition on having secret agents among the troops. Nevertheless, what intelligence he had still indicated that the reserve troops would be unreliable in the event of a popular disturbance. "I took the initiative to bring up the matter of the unreliability of the troops of the Petrograd garrison," Globachev writes. "I presented all the data on the make-up and mood of the garrison, repeating everything that I reported earlier to Sturmer. It was the same as before, nothing changed. Thus, at the moment of the imminent workers' disturbances, Khabalov, who was the new commander of the Petrograd Military District, having replaced General Tumanov, had to count on the unreliable garrison that was ready to revolt any minute." Globachev continued to push the issue. Khabalov called a meeting that was held at the headquarters of the Petrograd Military District. All the capital's police chiefs were there, as well as Globachev, City Prefect General Balk, and Lieutenant General Alexander Chebykin, the commander of the city's reserves. The Okhrana chief gave a report on the political situation, and how events were coming to a head. At the end of his report, he turned to Chebykin and asked him if he could vouch for his troops. The commander responded, "I can vouch for them completely, and even more, the best of our crack troops from the training command will be assigned to put down the disorders." The results of this meeting were reported back to Protopopov and Khabalov. According to Globachev, both were absolutely relieved. The Okhrana chief was far from relieved.[28]

Globachev submitted a "top secret" report to the Department of Police on January 19, 1917,[29] with copies to his superiors in the chain of command. The report was based on information that the Okhrana had received from a secret agent who worked for the Okhrana. The readers at the Department of Police underlined the most important points that were being made in Globachev's report. Every page of the report, which was approximately twelve typed pages, had multiple underlining.

The report was very clear in its presentation of how dangerous conditions had become in Petrograd. Globachev's report begins with the activities of the State Duma and how the speeches of some of the Duma leaders were attracting more and more of the capital's population to support the Duma in its defense against being dissolved by the government. Rumors and gossip were spreading throughout the city such as the Duma's development of a petition that demanded the removal of three hundred of the highest government officials including the entire Council of Ministers—with the exception of the naval minister. The radical members of the Duma considered the petition insufficient. The report further addresses the Duma's refusal to work with the administration, and the report suggests that should the government dissolve the Duma, the support of the population for the Duma will then lead to more workers' strikes, more demonstrations, violence, and possibly terrorist events.

A week later, on January 26,[30] General Globachev issued a report to the director of the Department of Police. Once again it was "top secret" and again the police readers underlined many key phrases and sentences on each of the several pages of the report. The report, as before, was based on information acquired by a secret agent. Members of the liberal opposition in the Duma were more sure than before that a power takeover was nigh, and, given that, had begun planning about who the leaders of a new government should be and how the various factions within the Duma might participate in the new government. Globachev mentions a number of the leaders by name, such as Alexander Guchkov, Alexander Kerensky, Georgii Lvov, and others. Guchkov and Lvov were particularly hopeful that the army would support them whether the change in power happened by popular revolution or by a palace coup.

Neither the report of January 19 nor the one of January 26 dealt with the various revolutionary groups—the Socialist Revolutionary Party, the Bolsheviks, Mensheviks, or various anarchist groups. As mentioned above, most of these organizations had been pretty well neutralized by the Okhrana. The issue at this time was what role the population would play as things were getting worse by the day in terms of availability of food products, living expenses, the psychological exhaustion of a lengthy war that was going badly, and the very active antigovernment position and speeches by Duma members who were inciting the population and the army.

February 23, 1917 was International Women's Day. Spontaneous gatherings and demonstrations by women began. The women were making their concerns known, and these concerns were economic, not political. Banners and posters were about food and family needs, asking for bread and for rations for the families of soldiers who were fighting on the front. There was no organized illegal underground band of revolutionaries behind this movement, and that is why the government agencies were caught off guard. The Okhrana had been effective in neutralizing the Socialist Revolutionary (SR) and Social Democratic (SD) organizations, but Globachev did not have any prior intelligence information that a demonstration might be in the works. Z. I. Peregudova provides detail on how events on February 23 were intensifying by the hour:

Figure 6.4. Demonstration on International Women's Day, 1917.

"February 23, 1917 saw the start of massive disturbances. 78,443 workers did not show up for work. The next day this number increased to 107,585, and on February 25, the figure was 201,248, although department records indicated 240,000 people. A possible explanation for the somewhat sudden big demonstration was because the weather had improved with higher temperature.

"Petrograd's City Prefect, Balk, who was appointed in November 1916 by Protopopov, later claimed that Globachev was not in a position to explain the reasons for the popular disturbances of February 23. Balk states in his diary that 'neither the Department of Police nor the Okhrana could answer my question as to the motives for this occurrence. At the evening meeting, the Chief of the Okhrana, Major General Globachev did not have information to explain that day's events.' Even though Globachev reported on the mood in Petrograd on a daily basis, and for months he sounded the alarm about impending disturbances, the events of February 23 seemed unexpected."[31] The huge numbers were the result of not only the women and workers who showed up but also female students and children. The government was caught off guard.

On February 24, General Khabalov, the commander of the Petrograd Military District, took command of the security of the capital. He had the agreement of the city prefect, General Balk. This meant that the city police were relieved by the city's garrison troops. These were the military units that Globachev had reported many times as being unreliable. The turmoil in the city intensified.

CHAPTER 7

Turmoil and Arrest

In the evening of February 26 Globachev reported to General Khabalov, the commander of the Petrograd Military District, that troops were not maintaining order throughout the city. Indeed, many of the soldiers and mounted units were chatting with demonstrators, allowing people to pet and feed their horses, and letting people pass through the lines. Globachev again warned of the unreliability of the troops who, after all, were reserve troops who had been called up for active duty very recently. Khabalov was irritated and said that the troops were just young soldiers who had not been fully trained.

That same evening Globachev got a call from the director of the Department of Police, A. T. Vasiliev. The latter asked Globachev to come to his apartment, but to know that Protopopov would be there too, and the minister wanted to see Globachev. The Okhrana chief arrived and gave a report on what was going on in Petrograd and the seriousness of the situation. As he spoke, Protopopov and Vasiliev were having coffee. On completion of his report, instead of delving into the issues, the occasion seemed to be a social evening with Protopopov chatting about his relationship to the Empress and how intelligent and sensitive she was. Globachev left not knowing the point of his having been there.

By the morning of February 27 all hell broke loose with strikes spreading throughout all the capital's districts. What happened throughout the day is vividly described in Globachev's last dispatch to the Department of Police:

Secret

27 February 1917

At approximately 3 o'clock in the afternoon a crowd gathered in the Znamenskii area of the Alexander Nevskii Monastery and troops fired several volleys on them. There is no information on whether there were any wounded or killed.

At the same time a large crowd gathered on the Nevskii Prospekt near the City Duma and two infantry companies arrived and fired three volleys of blanks at the crowd. After this, the crowd dispersed. At 3 o'clock a crowd of approximately 6,000 gathered at the corner of Nevskii Prospekt and Sadovoi Street. Upon refusing orders to disperse, there were some futile shots fired.

At the same time a crowd of approximately 10,000 gathered at the corner of Nevskii and Vladimirskii Prospekt. In spite of the request that the crowd disperse, the crowd stood in place, and because of this the troops fired a series of shots as a result of which several people were killed and wounded. After this the crowd dispersed.

At 4:30 troops opened fire on crowds that refused to disperse at the Znamenskii area and Goncharnyi and Likovskii streets. There is unsubstantiated information that 40 people were killed and a like number were wounded.

At 5 o'clock in the evening a crowd was fired on at the corner of Suvorov Prospekt and Rozhdestvenskii Street for refusing to disperse. Ten people were killed and several were wounded.

At 6 o'clock in the evening Company 4 of the Life Guards Pavlovskii Regiment, commanded by a junior officer, left its barracks to join with the academy command of the same regiment that had been firing on the crowd. The company met a ten-man mounted patrol of the city police near the Church on Spilled Blood and a confrontation ensued, and shots were fired. One city police officer and his horse were killed and one city police and his horse were wounded. After this the troops returned to their barracks.

In a short while Colonel Eksten arrived and according to witnesses some rebellious troops cut off his hand. A company of the Life Guards Preobrazhenskii Regiment arrived soon and quickly disarmed the rebellious troops and secured the area.

At 7 o'clock in the evening police officer Lashchinskii was wounded at the corner of Suvorov Prospekt and Rozhdestvenskii Street. He had his Nagan pistol and sabre taken from him. Police supervisor had four fingers of his hand hacked off.

At 8 o'clock in the evening police supervisor Botov was disarmed at the house at No. 3 Korpus Street.

At 8:30 in the evening five policemen were approaching Apraksin Lane where there had been some shots fired by the public. Another five policemen followed the first group and returned fire. After that the policemen headed for their police station. As they neared the station they were again fired on by the crowd. None of the policemen were harmed in these two shooting incidents.

Industrial enterprises were closed today in keeping with the holiday.

I am respectfully dispatching this information to Your Excellency.

There were no arrests made.

Signed: Chief of the Bureau Major General Globachev

Witness: Captain Dubrovin[1]

By this time there was no regular delivery of mail, memos, and other documents. Things had broken down, so General Globachev's aide, Captain Dubrovin, personally delivered the dispatch to the apartment of Colonel Vasiliev of the Department of Police.

Globachev's detailed report of what had happened hour by hour was based on reports by agents, Okhrana personnel, local police, and so forth. While the dispatch is factual, Globachev presents a broader picture of what went on in his memoirs: "By the morning of February 27, strikes spread throughout the capital's districts, and the strikes became one general strike. Crowds of workers began to move toward the State Duma; it became clear to anyone that it was the revolution's center. About noon four regiments rebelled and went over to the workers: the Volynsk Life Guards, Preobrazhenskii Life Guards, Litovskii Life Guards, and Sappers. The barracks of all four of these were in the district of the Tauride Palace and they became the first strongholds of the revolution."[2]

Within a short time during the day, General Khabalov finally understood that the reserve troops were no longer under his control. In fact, the general only had his staff that he could depend upon.

Colonel Paul Zavarzin, who had been the head of the Okhrana offices in Moscow and Warsaw, was between assignments and was in Petrograd at this time. He phoned the director of the Department of Police and the city prefect to get some sense of the level of danger of the moment. This was probably during the last week of February. Both the director and the city prefect seemed concerned that things were not going well because of the frequent demonstrations in the streets. Zavarzin then phoned his friend and colleague General Globachev, and from him he got a very clear assessment of the danger, especially if the troops were to try to restore order by firing on the demonstrators.[3]

Zavarzin was staying in another part of the city and by February 27 the situation there was getting worse by the moment. Throughout the day crowds increased, there was gunfire, and people were wounded and killed. And, even more, there were riots, looting of stores that sold firearms, and breaking into liquor stores. Chain gang convicts were being freed by demonstrators. City police officers were caught and killed in the streets.[4]

Globachev had posted his men around the city to watch and report to Okhrana headquarters on unfolding events. The Okhrana chief tried to keep the palace commanders of Tsarskoe Selo apprised of what was going on. As the crowds of civilians and soldiers grew larger, Globachev's lookouts had to retreat back to Okhrana headquarters. Globachev had moved his headquarters from the Oldenburg Palace to a secondary Okhrana office. Some of his retreating staff were wounded in all the violence that was going on, and one died of a head wound. The gunfire had subsided during the night and Globachev spent the entire night in communication with Tsarskoe Selo. Earlier that evening, the Council of Ministers dissolved the State Duma and fired Protopopov. In effect, the government collapsed. But, by next morning, February 28, gunfire began again, and was even more intense than the day before. Armed workers and soldiers attacked several buildings. The city's major telephone station was taken and the Okhrana headquarters building was ransacked and looted. Communication with Tsarskoe Selo was broken off.

Globachev had already been informed that crowds were moving toward his position, "and so as not to endanger people to excesses or needless loss of life, I ordered all the staff who were present to leave immediately and go to their homes. Having done that, I locked all the entrances to the building and left with my closest subordinates."[5] Thus ended the general's role as chief of the Petrograd Okhrana.

There was one last possibility to stop the chaos, soldiers rebelling, looting, and killing that was going on in the capital. There were several thousand troops at Tsarskoe Selo whose function was to defend the village where the Summer Palace was located and to protect the palace. If some of these troops could be sent to Petrograd, they might be able to stop the turmoil in the city, at least so thought Globachev. He and one of his subordinates decided that they should make their way to Tsarskoe Selo, which was about fifteen miles south of Petrograd.

With all the turmoil and danger in the capital over the past few days, and the crowds that were advancing on various buildings, including the headquarters of the Okhrana that were also the apartments of the Globachevs, Sofia decided to join Konstantin at the headquarters that he had set up at the Security Command Building. She had taken her son, Kolia, who was thirteen years old, to some friends who would watch him. Her daughter, Lydia, was still in Moscow at the Catherine Institute, a private boarding school for girls. Leaving the Globachev apartments Sofia had to gather as many belongings as she could carry. In addition to clothes, Sofia was able to take some keepsakes with her that included photographs, some of Kostia's medals, and an icon that Kostia's subordinate officers in Sevastopol had given him in 1915 as a going away gift when he was promoted to his Petrograd position. Sofia was also able to take several thousand tsarist paper currency rubles that the Globachevs had withdrawn from their savings bank in January and kept at home. They certainly had a premonition of things to come.

Sofia was going to go with Konstantin to Tsarskoe Selo. They would have to take a train to Tsarskoe (as it was often called). The train station was the Tsarskoe Selo Railway Station that connected the capital to the summer residence of the Tsars. As they planned to go, there were "armed workers, soldiers and sailors intermingling with all kinds of rabble; they were all firing, rushing about, but I do not think that they themselves knew what they were doing. Armored cars drove about noisily, and machine-gun fire could be heard."[6] A group of these armed people were getting too close to the Command Building. The Globachevs and two of the general's subordinates had to get out of the building by a back stairway. The station was a distance from the Command Building, so Konstantin, two of his subordinates, and Sofia would have to go on foot to the station. All public transportation had ceased to function, so they would have to tread along streets, side streets, and courtyards to avoid angry crowds and the gunfire that was going on. Something that would have taken less than half an hour by trolley or cab took them four hours, as they had to zigzag through the city.

The danger was real. Even though Konstantin and his subordinates were in civilian clothing, they could be mistaken for profiteers, if for no other reason than that they were dressed better than the crowds. And, if anyone recognized the general, he would surely be killed. Sofia knew all this. She was frightened of the gunfire, worried for Konstantin, worried for her son, and she was exhausted. As they moved along toward the railway station, Sofia began to lag behind Konstantin, her nerves were frayed, and as gunfire grew louder and bullets whizzed by, she pressed herself against a wall and cried. Konstantin saw that she had lagged and came back for her. They continued to the station. The station was quiet. There was no turmoil there as there was in the center of the city. One of the general's assistants left them at the station to stay in the city. Konstantin, his assistant, and Sofia were able to get a train to Tsarskoe Selo and get to the palace grounds.

It was early afternoon when they arrived at Tsarskoe Selo. Globachev "was struck by the order and calm that reigned at Tsarskoe. His

Figure 7.1. Chaos breaks out in Petrograd, late February 1917.

Majesty's escort guards were at their posts, the palace police continued to carry out its duties, and it seemed that the life of the town was proceeding normally. Even so, there was a sense of anxiety and anticipation of something inevitable coming; this was seen in the serious and gloomy faces of the staff."[7] The general was able to contact Colonel Gerardi, who was the head of the palace police. Globachev told him what was going on in Petrograd and informed Gerardi that he should expect insurgent mobs to show up at Tsarskoe within the next several hours. The palace police chief answered Globachev, telling him that the palace was safe and that the five thousand troops of the palace garrison were loyal and could repulse any attack.

Gerardi's assessment of all the turmoil in the city was that it would subside, because the real matter at hand was that there would very probably be a palace coup involving the removal of the Tsar in favor of his younger brother, the Grand Duke Michael Alexandrovich, who would take the throne. Globachev tried to point out that what was going on in Petrograd was very different, but the palace police chief seemed to think that Globachev did not understand the situation.

Toward evening, around 6 p.m., Globachev met with Gerardi again, and this time the palace police chief was depressed. There was information that crowds were moving toward the palace and, within a short time, the entire garrison joined with the crowd. Those who were officers and senior civilian personnel of the palace left before the crowd took over. The Empress asked that there should be no resistance offered so that no blood would be spilled. No harm came to her, but she was now a prisoner in her own palace.

It was late. Getting a train back to the capital would be difficult and dangerous. Konstantin, his assistant, and Sofia were able to find a dacha that was outside of the town of Tsarskoe,[8] where they could spend the night because there was already rioting and looting going on. They were exhausted. Sofia was so tired that she could hardly stand. They got little or no sleep that night as gunfire could be heard in the distance. In the morning it was decided that Konstantin and his assistant would stay at Tsarskoe to monitor events, and Sofia would return to Petrograd to make sure that their son Kolia was all right, and to assess how things were in the city. She would then return and join Konstantin. But at some point she overheard whispering between Konstantin and his assistant. The conversation was in low tones and Sofia heard words that upset her. She was afraid that if things got worse, however that might be,

Konstantin and his assistant might commit suicide. Before she headed back to the city, she made Konstantin promise that he would not do anything to harm himself. He promised.

Sofia got to Petrograd and went to her acquaintance's home to get her son. Her friends told Sofia that their place had been entered and searched twice during the night and therefore it was not safe. Sofia took Kolia to some other friends where it would be safer. Sofia also found out that the newly formed Provisional Government had issued an order that all tsarist officers and senior civilian government personnel should report to the State Duma Building within three days. In effect, the point of this order was submission to voluntary arrest. Sofia had to get to Konstantin to make him aware of this order. Again, she had to get through streets on foot to get to the train station. Sofia trekked this distance distraught, exhausted, with her feet bleeding and bullets whizzing by. To her great relief, Konstantin and his assistant had returned to the city and met Sofia at the station.

Nicholas II had already abdicated and his train, which was to take him back to Tsarskoe from military headquarters in Mogilev, had been stopped by rebelling troops not far from a place named Dno. Dno is also the Russian word for "bottom" or "depth."

There was mayhem and violence in the Petrograd streets. There were no law enforcement agencies any more that could maintain order. Individuals who were suspected of being part of the old regime, or might just look like they had been, were beaten and killed by roaming crowds, and this applied especially to people who were former police personnel or members of the Corps of Gendarmes.

Globachev's choices were very limited, and whatever he chose was fraught with great danger. If he attempted to hide out, there was almost no place to do so other than with friends, and that would put them in danger. And, if he was found out and caught, a violent death for him and those who had helped him was almost certain. His other choice was to obey the order of the Provisional Government to report, meaning to surrender, to the State Duma that met in the Tauride Palace. That was the choice that Globachev made, but in order to get to the State Duma he would have to walk along the street to that building.

Fortunately, Globachev and an assistant who was with him were in civilian clothes. That somewhat minimized the danger of being attacked. Still, and in Globachev's own words, "In such a situation, in light of an absence of refuge in Petrograd, and in order to avoid personally being

Figure 7.2. "Days of the Revolution. The arrival of the arrested at the State Duma."

the victim of the brutal excesses of the raging mobs, I decided to go personally to the State Duma. I asked an officer acquaintance of mine to take me there as if he had arrested me. It was hard to get into the Duma, notwithstanding that it was already relatively late, and crowds of drunken soldiers and workers surrounded it. I got inside the building with some difficulty, and it was only thanks to identifying myself by rank and profession to a student who was at a control desk that he handed me over to a member of the State Duma, Papadjanov, who was responsible for the control and disposition of those arrested. He had me wait for at least two hours and finally had me sent under escort to the Ministerial Pavilion, where I was settled in as under arrest of the revolutionary order."[9]

Mikhail Papadjanov, the representative of the new government, questioned persons who came to the State Duma on March 1 and were now under arrest. Individuals who were determined as not being a threat were released. Others were assigned to different detention areas of the State Duma building. Globachev was assigned to the Ministerial Pavilion. This part of the building was assigned to those prisoners who were arrested for more serious offenses. This type of decision was not based on law, rather the seriousness of the detention had to do with the type of authority and responsibility the detainee had in the tsarist government. The Ministerial Pavilion included a meeting hall, two large offices, a general public area, and a toilet. One door led from the meeting room to a lobby and another door led to a garden. The detained individuals were placed into the meeting hall and offices with guards at the doors.

After being searched, Globachev was led to the hall and seated at the long conference table along with other detainees. Globachev lists them in his memoir, every minister, staff general and admiral, gendarme and police chief, all his colleagues and superiors. He names thirty-two individuals, "and others." The detainees were ordered to sit at the table or, if all the chairs at the table were now taken, they sat on sofas and armchairs around the periphery of the room. They were not allowed to talk. A guard escorted those who had to use the toilet, and several times a day the detainees marched around the table, in an ordered manner, for exercise. They slept, fully dressed, sitting at the table or in the armchairs or sofa. They were fed decently enough and were given tea. This lasted for three days and on the third day Kerensky came to see all the detainees. He informed them of Nicholas's abdication, the Grand Duke Michael's rejection of the throne, and the formation of the Provisional Government. He also spoke of the goals of the government in promoting justice, truth, and fairness. Although Globachev was not particularly impressed with this meeting, "the best result of Kerensky's visit to us was that from that day on we were allowed to talk to one another."[10]

The psychological state of the detainees was quite mixed. The rigid rule of sitting all day and not being allowed to speak or move about produced incredible tedium, but included with that was certainly anxiety, depression, and fear. Some were calm, but still dispirited. Here were individuals who had held high government positions of responsibility and authority, "now it was sad to look at them—they looked so lost."[11] Some of the detainees lost their composure and there was an incident of an individual very frightened that he would be executed and another incident when an admiral attacked a guard and tried to get the guard's rifle.[12] The worry was how the Provisional Government would deal with them. Were they to be charged and tried for various offenses and punished? At this time they were detained but not charged. This alone increased the detainees' confusion and anxiety. And, with all the wild crowds just outside the Duma Building, was there the possibility of an incited mob breaking in and going on a killing spree?

Within several days some of the detainees were transferred from the Ministerial Pavilion to the Peter and Paul Fortress. This place had been used as an arsenal and as a prison for political prisoners. It was still guarded by soldiers who were assigned there during the tsarist regime, as were some of the officers in charge, but who accepted the new government. The regimen at the fortress tended to be very strict and many detainees who knew of the place did not want to be incarcerated in that dismal place. Globachev was not sent there. He remained at the Ministerial Pavilion for the remainder of March.

CHAPTER 8

Sofia Springs into Action

Sofia Globacheva was living with her son at the apartment of some friends. Her home in the Oldenburg Palace no longer existed, and she had only the clothes and belongings she was able to save and, as mentioned already, some memorabilia and money. Now, two days later her husband had surrendered to the Provisional Government, and it was the third day that he was being detained, and Sofia had no word or information about him, none whatsoever. She knew only that her husband had been successfully delivered to the State Duma, as she was told by Globachev's subordinate who had escorted him. She was worried and frightened. Sofia's past anxieties about Kostia's safety were nothing compared to now. By the third day of not knowing anything, she sprang into action. She decided that she had to go to the Duma to find out about her husband. She had her son stay with her friends and she left for where the general was detained.

"I was very worried and because I didn't know what [had] happened to him, I decided to go to the Duma myself to find out. There was no transportation available, so I had to go on foot and crowds of people were going about their business in the streets. I joined these crowds, but since I hardly ever had to walk about Petrograd, always having a vehicle available, and because my orientation was always bad, I did not know how to get to the Tauride Palace where the State Duma was located. There was some officer who was walking next to me, so I turned to him and asked if he could tell me the way. He told me that he was going there and that I should follow along. I asked him if there was any way that I could get into the building, and I found out that he worked there and

Figure 8.1. Sophia Globacheva, 1917–18.

that he had an entry pass."[1] There were two checkpoints to get through. With the help of this officer, a stranger to her, she was able to get into the building, but trying to find somebody to help her was so unnerving that she began to cry.

Here she was in a large hall with masses of people shouting, pleading, and arguing. Finally, she was able to get some help. A member of the Duma saw her and approached her. She told him who she was, who her husband was, and asked to see her husband. This member of the Duma did some checking, and finding out where Globachev was detained, he arranged for Sofia to see Konstantin and even got her a pass to come to the Duma any time.

Sonia found her Kostia to be depressed, so much so that after leaving him after her visit, and fearing that Kostia might do something to harm himself, and since her suspicion and fear of him possibly committing suicide had already entered her mind earlier, she phoned the commandant of the guards when she got back to her friends' apartment and asked him to look in on Kostia and let her know if Kostia was all right. The commandant checked on Globachev and let Sofia know that her husband was all right and not in any danger. Sofia visited Konstantin, according to the rules of the new government, twice a week and often brought their son and daughter with her. Their daughter had been brought home to Petrograd from a girls' boarding school in Moscow, out of fear that communication might break down with Moscow as a result of the possibility that the city might still fall to the Germans.

Somehow Sofia had to see someone in authority who could get her husband released. It took a lot of running around to find the proper office and person who could answer the concerns of Sofia and other wives who were in the same anxious predicament. Sofia and the other wives wound up going to see the prosecutor of the Provisional Government's Judicial Court. This was N. S. Karinskii. The latter did not know what the disposition of the detainees was or when they might be released. Understandably, this was totally unacceptable to Sofia. She would go to the government's senior prosecutor, Pavel Nikolaevich Pereverzev.

Sofia, along with some other wives of former tsarist officials, did indeed meet with Pereverzev. Sofia hoped that some kind of positive results could come from such a meeting; after all, she had known Pereverzev socially before the Revolution. However, the latter was not much help, and the wives were passed on to Nicholas Konstantinovich Muravev, who had been appointed to head the Provisional Government's Extraordinary Investigative Commission. All the wives who were trying to get their husbands released found Muravev to be a hateful man.[2] Sofia would not be stopped. She sought out Alexander Kerensky, who in the first months of the Revolution was the minister of justice. It was not easy to get through to Kerensky. She first had to figure out which building held his office. Once she located where his office was, the hall leading to his office was crowded with all kinds of people who wanted to see him. A clerk outside the minister's office suggested that Sofia should first try to see an assistant minister.

Sofia refused and sat down to wait for Kerensky, who was in some other location in the building, to return. As Kerensky returned to his office all the people who wanted to see him were milling about. But not Sofia.

"I never would have thought that I would do what I did, but I jumped out of my chair and ran toward him. Kerensky was taken aback, but he stopped.

'I need to speak to you,' I said.

'What is your name?' he asked.

'Globacheva,' was my answer.

'I will not approve your seeing your husband,' answered Kerensky.

'I did not come about seeing my husband; I want to talk to you.'

He thought for a moment and said, 'Alright.'"[3]

Sofia wanted to know why Konstantin had been arrested and when he would be released. Kerensky said that the general was needed to provide certain testimony and that once the threat of possible violence from crowds angry at former tsarist officials subsided he would be released. But Kerensky relented somewhat and said that Sofia would be allowed to see her husband. As she was leaving Kerensky's office, she turned back to him and told him that she and her son had no place to live. The minister called his assistant and told him to take care of this matter. Sofia got authorized identification cards that would allow her easier access to government buildings and to the various prosecutors who were handling Konstantin's case.

In between visits to Konstantin, Sofia's attempts to get him released had her shuttling from one office to another. Her visits to her husband and her shuttling about were all on foot. She had considerable distances to walk, and her feet bled. When Sofia met again with Pereverzev, she insisted that Konstantin should be released since he had not been charged with anything. The prosecutor told Sofia that the Soviet of Workers' and Soldiers' Deputies would be opposed to the prosecutor making such a decision unilaterally. Sofia was advised to get a document from the Soviet approving the general's release. Sofia was brazen by now. She wanted Pereverzev to promise her that if the Soviet gave her such a document, that he would release the general. Pereverzev agreed.

After spending time again going from one office to another in the Tauride Palace, Sofia finally found someone who seemed to be in authority. This was Nicholas Semenovich Chkheidze, one of the major leaders of the Soviet. Sofia told him about Konstantin being held without being charged. She did not mention her husband's name or his past role in the Okhrana. That could be dangerous. She just mentioned that he was a general. Chkheidze sent Sofia to the secretary of the Soviet of Workers' and Soldiers' Deputies. Here she was told that other wives had made the same complaints, and they were all refused. Sofia insisted that she get a document. The secretary told her that the Soviet would be meeting the next day and the request would be brought up. Sofia returned three days later and was told to file a formal request to the Soviet. The request—really an application—required the name, rank, and organizational affiliation of the person on whose behalf the application was presented to the Soviet. The secretary of the Soviet looked at the document, and seeing the heading, "he turned red and shouted, 'How is it possible that there are no charges against the head of the Security Police? It is not possible.' I kept my calm at his outburst and said, 'It may seem strange to you from your perspective, but there are no charges that can be produced, other than that he honestly carried out his duties and responsibilities.' Little by little he calmed down, took my application, promised that he would hand it over to the Soviet of Workers' and Soldiers' Deputies for their decision and said to come back in a week for an answer."[4]

Sofia waited out the week, and then went to Tauride Palace to the office of the secretary of the Soviet. He handed Sofia the document that stated that the Soviet did not object to Globachev's release and left the matter to the Provisional Government. Sofia was elated. The next day she went to Pereverzev's office and gave him the document.

"'Here is the paper, now you must release my husband,' I said.

'I cannot release him,' replied Pereverzev.

'Why?' I was indignant.

'Because he was the Chief of the Petrograd Security Bureau,' was his answer.

'But you gave me your word that you would release him as soon as I brought you the paper from the Soviet of Workers' and Soldiers' Deputies.'

'Well, that was then and things are different now,' answered 'Justice Minister' Pereverzev.

'Have you any other charges, other than that he held that position?' I asked.

'No,' was his reply."[5]

While Sofia was literally running around from office to office, again and again, trying to get Konstantin released during his detention in the Ministerial Pavilion, Globachev and other detainees were questioned from time to time by various representatives of the new government, and in some cases by nongovernmental people such as journalists of various revolutionary papers and magazines. In one case the interrogator was V. I. Burtsev, a radical journalist who had been arrested several times during the tsarist regime and had written negative articles about the Okhrana. In meeting with Globachev, he wanted to know the names of the various secret agents who had worked for the Okhrana, and he wanted Globachev to write his impressions of the Revolution. The general refused both requests.

One of the visitors who came to see Globachev was Kerensky himself. Their exchange was short and testy. Here is the general's recollection of that meeting:

"On one of his visits he called me out and began the following conversation: 'It is definitely clear to me that you were involved in placing machineguns and are guilty of the bloodshed of the people.' I told him that I absolutely reject such an accusation, but that I witnessed machine-gun fire when I walked along the streets between February 24 and March 1. Then Kerensky announced to me, 'We have witnesses who can testify against you.'

'Who are these witnesses?'

'I will not tell you who they are, but the matter will be investigated.'

'And I am asking you to do just that, and when you have investigated you will see that it was workers who placed the machine guns.'

'Don't tell me that, these are fabrications,' said Kerensky, and then he asked me, 'Is it true that there was a tunnel under the Neva that led from the Okhrana to the Winter Palace? I ordered a sapper company to verify this.'

'I answered him that I did not know of such a tunnel until now, but with the assistance of a sapper company one could be built.'

'Kerensky got angry and said, 'If you are going to answer like that, then we have nothing more to talk about,' to which I answered, 'As you wish,' and I added, 'Pay attention to the notice in the newspaper that the Okhrana had a rooftop radio telegraph and an armored car in the garage; that is about as true as the tunnel story.'

For some reason Kerensky said, 'Well that is nonsense.' Then he asked me one more question; why did I, who had graduated from the General Staff Academy, join the Special Corps of Gendarmes, and when I answered him, 'By conviction,' he became completely angry and rushed out of the room. After that I never had occasion to speak to him again."[6]

Life in detention was not easy. While there were some guards who treated the detainees with some sense of respect and kindness, there were others who were indifferent to the detainees, were rude, and verbally threatening. There was hardly ever any physical abuse, but there was danger. The guards and their supervisors were soldiers who were officially under the authority of the Provisional Government, and here was the rub: the Provisional Government was represented by members who had been leaders in the State Duma. A number of these leaders had been representatives of Russia's major industries, landholdings, and wealth.

The Soviet was more grassroots and was peopled by soldiers, sailors, industrial factory workers, and everyday workers in stores, bakeries, and so forth. The Provisional Government did not represent them, and so the Soviet stood apart from the Provisional Government and represented the working, impoverished class; at best, the relationship between the two was a tenuous coalition.

The Ministerial Pavilion guards were more loyal to the Soviet than to the Provisional Government. As conditions in Petrograd were not improving and the mood among soldiers and workers could be angry, there was the possible threat of them breaking into the prisons and other places of detention and seeking vengeance on former tsarist officials for past wrongs. The anxiety of the detainees was twofold—how would the Provisional Government pursue lawful justice for the detainees, and how would the common folk outside the prisons seek justice for past wrongs?

Detention in the Ministerial Pavilion was temporary. It had only been meant to be in operation as a place of detention until other facilities became organized. Toward the end of March, Globachev was informed that he was to be transferred to the Peter and Paul Fortress, not at all a pleasant prospect. The fortress was old, dank, and the cells were crude and dark. Fortunately several days went by and the transfer was delayed because the fortress was being repaired.

Globachev's detention in the Ministerial Pavilion, with its made-up rules and flung-together facilities for the detainees, was worrisome enough for Sofia, but now the general would be transferred to a real prison where there were already criminal convicts that were to be mixed with the political detainees. And, around the prison there were, as elsewhere in the city, demonstrators who wanted punitive justice for the detainees or freedom for the convicts. None of this calmed Sofia in even a small way, rather the bleak prospects for her husband undoubtedly heightened her anxiety and fear for his safety and survival.

CHAPTER 9

Incarceration

Globachev had spent almost the entire month of March at the Ministerial Pavilion where he and the other detainees were allowed to do almost nothing, got little exercise, and slept seated in chairs and whatever armchairs and sofas there were in the Pavilion rooms. It was not even as comfortable as being in a prison. So far, none of the detainees had been charged with any specific crimes, nor had they been questioned other than the short visits of various government officials, and their detention in the building that was the headquarters of the new government probably did not help the administration to keep order outside the building, which, throughout March, still had crowds milling about, demonstrating, and demanding justice for the former tsarist officials.

The experience of being detained like this for almost a month was incredibly enervating and worrisome for the general and the others who were being held. They were in the dark about what might happen next. So was Sofia. She was on the outside, but her nerves were frayed too. She feared for Konstantin's safety, she had to run about trying to find officials who could give her accurate information, and she had children to worry about. The one fortunate thing was that Lydia had come home from the famous Catherine Institute for Girls in Moscow. Even so, March was a tough month.

Finally, on March 23 Globachev and five other former tsarist officials were ordered to get ready to be transferred to the Vyborg Prison, better known by its popular name, "The Crosses." The Russian name was "Kresty." The prison got its name because each of the three stone buildings was in the shape of a cross. At the time of its construction it seems to have been based on the American Auburn model of prison architecture. Each of the buildings had 100 cells, and prison personnel standing in the middle of each building could see in all directions. So, this was a real prison.

The guards made a big show of the transfer of these six individuals. The six detainees "were put in a small bus with two armed guards; two other guards were on the rear door's running board, one on each front fender, and two on the roof. In order to make the transfer longer and to show how important criminals were transferred, we did not go straight down the Shapalerov Boulevard to the Liteiny Bridge but made a big swing along the Kirchnoi."[1]

The prison was crowded not only with former tsarist officials but also with convicted criminals such as petty thieves, pickpockets, and robbers. The officials did not want to mix the political detainees with the convicted criminals. Globachev and several other political detainees were assigned to be held in the prison infirmary where there were about ten beds. There were more detainees than there were beds, however. This meant that several lucky individuals got beds and others had to sleep on the floor and in chairs, much like before. Just before Easter, which fell

Figure 9.1. Vyborg Prison, also known as "The Crosses."

on April 2 in 1917, a number of prisoners and detainees were released, and this gave those who remained in detention a little breathing room, not much, but better than before.

The daily regimen was easier in the Kresty. The guards were members of the Moscow Life Guards Regiment who had been prison guards before the Revolution. Most of them had bought into the revolutionary movement, but they did not bother the detainees. As a matter of fact, the guards were pretty lax in watching over the detainees. Cells were kept open so that the detainees could mingle in the corridors or visit each other in cells. The cells were not guarded, but there were soldiers stationed in the corridors.

Globachev describes the daily routine in the prison in some detail. "The daily routine was that we got up at six in the morning, washed either in the bathroom or kitchen, and got hot water to make our breakfast. In addition, each cell had to be cleaned, and this was the responsibility of the person assigned to be the duty officer of the cell. Each cell had the duty in its turn to keep the corridor, kitchen, and toilet clean (the criminals handled these chores for us for an agreed-upon price). We also had yard exercise where we walked about for half an hour under the surveillance of the guards, but we were not allowed to talk. Our lunch was brought to us at noon. The first course was a bucket of hot water in which an uncleaned herring that had gone bad floated, or some cabbage. The second course consisted of undercooked lentils. It is understandable that almost nobody was able to eat this stuff. So, our meals simply consisted of black bread and tea or canned food that our relatives or friends brought. At six o'clock our dinner was brought in. It consisted of watery gruel that nobody touched, since it was about the same quality as the lunch. At nine o'clock we were locked in for the night." The prisoners were allowed to have relatives visit, receive packages of food and clothing from them, read newspapers, and even enter into conversations with the guards.[2] But, for all of these improvements, the confusion, anxiety, and fear of being incarcerated without being charged did not go away. There was also the anxiety that demonstrators and activists could break into the prison to get at the representatives of the tsarist regime, and added to all this was the incredible boredom of incarceration.

It was now April and on the world stage the United States entered the Great War on April 2, 1917, when President Wilson sought a declaration of war from the Congress. Within a few days, the United States was at war. It is not known how, or when, or even if at all that the detainees were informed of this or of anything else happening in the war. They were allowed to read newspapers, but these were all Russian newspapers and dealt more with news of what was going on in Russia.

It was around mid-April that the Extraordinary Investigative Commission of the Provisional Government was established. On April 24, Globachev turned forty-seven years old. The Commission's purpose was to investigate the abuse of power and illegal actions taken by senior military and political leaders of the tsarist regime. The Commission questioned these individuals. "The work of the Commission was entrusted to trained jurists of high standing. Those who gave evidence before it were ordinarily not examined as under any kind of prosecution . . . they were questioned with great courtesy and consideration, but plainly and exhaustively."[3] Globachev was one of the many officials who testified before the Commission, and while the courteous behavior of the questioners is a matter of record, Globachev was not impressed with the quality or qualifications of some of the questioners.

While the conditions of detention had improved in terms of relatives being allowed greater freedom to visit the detainees, bring food, changes of clothing, and other noncontraband items, the future was still unknown to the detainees and their families, and this led to a constant state of anxiety. The Globachevs had to deal with how Sofia and the children were to live an everyday life under these conditions. On May 18 the Globachevs were allowed to develop a document, signed by a notary, that gave Sofia the legal rights to all the Globachev possessions, accounts, funds, and so forth. The general was in detention and Sofia had to function and take care of the children. So, it was done.[4]

The Provisional Government had moved its headquarters from the Tauride Palace, where the State Duma used to meet, to the Winter Palace (now the Hermitage) on the embankment of the Neva River. The Vyborg Prison was across the river and northeast of the palace. The Investigative Commission operated out of the Winter Palace and the testimonies of various detainees were conducted there. This included Globachev.

When it was the general's turn to be questioned, he was escorted by two guards, and they walked from the prison, along an embankment, across the Liteiny Bridge, then along the Palace Embankment to the Winter Palace. It took somewhere between thirty minutes to an hour to make that walk. Globachev wrote that "going to these questioning sessions was pleasant in only one way: it allowed me to breathe fresh air and it gave me some diversion from the tedious prison regime."[5]

On June 1 the general was escorted to a vacant room in the prison and there was Pereverzev. This was not going to be an interrogation. The minister was there to seek Globachev's advice! The new government was having major problems with the growth of anarchist organizations and actions. The anarchists were involved in robberies, raids, looting, and even in taking over the summer home of a former minister of the interior, P. N. Durnovo. Globachev's advice was that the Provisional Government should try to find whatever Okhrana documents had survived that had the names and addresses of anarchist activists and these activists should be arrested. Another of Globachev's suggestions was that the Provisional Government should establish a system of agents who would conduct surveillance and arrests and would operate within the law and under the supervision of a court investigator. The general noted that the Okhrana's experience was that anarchists were close to common criminals in their thinking and in their behavior.

Pereverzev's position was that the Provisional Government could not pursue such methods as they were against the government's democratic values. When asked by Globachev how the government would handle the situation, the minister had no realistic ideas.[6]

Even though the prison's regimen was not all that tough, it was still a prison. There was another place of detention that would be better for the general. This was the building on Furshtatskaia Street. It had been the headquarters of the Special Corps of Gendarmes and there were already some tsarist officers and officials in detention there. It was not a prison and there would not be any common criminal convicts around, as there were in the Kresty. Sofia never let up on trying to help her Kostia. She pushed for Konstantin to be transferred to Furshtatskaia Street. She did not trust Pereverzev anymore, but she did work through a deputy prosecutor in Pereverzev's office. This was a man whose name was, coincidentally, Popov—the same as Sofia's maiden name. He was able to get approval to move Globachev. The general and some other past tsarist officials were transferred to Furshtatskaia Street in early June 1917.

Some of the other tsarist officials who were at Furshtatskaia Street under detention had been under arrest at the Ministerial Pavilion. There was General Sergei Khabalov, the commander of the Petrograd Military District; General Mikhail Beliaev, the war minister; Lady-in-Waiting Anna Vyrubova; Justice Minister Nikolai Dobrovolskii; General Alexander Balk; the Petrograd city prefect; some naval officers from Kronstadt; and some army officers.

The regimen there was pretty easy; it was more like being under house arrest. There were several individuals per room, they could walk about in the yard without guards, and they were allowed visitors who could bring parcels every day. They could receive food, clothing, newspapers, and cigarettes.

Globachev was questioned several times between April and October 1917. These testimonies were very detailed. The general was asked about the organizational structure of the Okhrana and its general method of operating, the Okhrana's use of secret agents, many questions about his superiors and their relationship to Rasputin, and the Okhrana's actions against illegal underground revolutionary groups. The Commission was particularly interested in the Okhrana's use of covert agents. In prior years there had been examples of covert agents infiltrating revolutionary groups and instigating them to do something unlawful so that they could be arrested. They were called agent provocateurs. Some agents had been double agents also, and some actually were involved in the assassinations of government officials.

Globachev's testimony on this matter was very clear and to the point. He stated, "When the activities of a known illegal revolutionary group became clear, the group was 'liquidated,' that is, the leaders and senior personnel of the group were arrested. Agents were absolutely forbidden to have any active role in the work of the group. During my tenure in the Petrograd Security Bureau we never resorted to provocation and none of my superiors ever gave me any indication or orders to have agents take any provocative measures. I would not have done this under any circumstances."[7]

When he was not giving testimony at the Winter Palace, officials of the Provisional Government visited Globachev and the other detainees. Often enough these visitors might have asked some questions, but they also visited to promote the Revolution and castigate the old regime. One particular individual who came to see the general was Paul Nikolaevich Pereverzev, the same person that Sofia had sought out. He had been appointed prosecutor at the start of the Revolution, and in April he was appointed the government's minister of justice. This meant that he had responsibility and authority over detainees and whether detainees would be charged. Thus far, Globachev and his many colleagues and superiors had not been charged.

During Globachev's first month at Furshtatskaia Street, a number of gendarme and police officers were released, but not the general. His former position as head of security and intelligence in the capital was perceived as more responsible than that of some other officials. The Provisional Government had introduced a new law that authorized "extrajudicial arrests." This explained the detention of various individuals without charges being brought against them. It also explained why some were released but Globachev was not. According to the general, "My crime was considered more serious, and so the prosecutor of the Petrograd Judicial Court, N. S. Karinskii, assigned V. D. Stavrovskii to the most serious cases and to bring me to trial under Chapter 2, Page 342 of the Penal Code. That is, in exceeding or in criminal negligence of my authority. The basis for these charges was supposedly that I used secret agents, or as they were now called 'provocateurs,' illegally. As part of the evidence against me, there were two volumes of the Bulletin of the Provisional Government in which 152 named individuals were exposed as secret agents."[8]

Globachev, therefore, was in a more serious situation in a number of different ways. He was detained while some others were released. He was probably going to be charged, particularly on the matter of having used secret agents, and perhaps worst of all, the Bolsheviks were gaining strength in the Soviet and within the population. If they came to power while the general was detained, he would certainly be executed.

During one of Sofia's visits with Kostia, he told her that his case had been handed over to a special prosecutor, Stavrovskii. Kostia asked her to go and try to meet with this prosecutor. Sofia rose to the occasion immediately, as she always had. She went straight to see Stavrovskii. The latter told Sofia that his immediate superior, Karinskii, had turned some papers and the case over to Stavrovskii and that he should proceed with charging Konstantin, especially on the matter of the Okhrana chief's use of secret agents. Sofia insisted that she be shown the paperwork. Some of the documents seemed official, but others were newspaper clippings. Sofia went on the attack and pointed out that all security institutions everywhere used secret agents, and furthermore, the newspaper clippings were worthless as evidence. The prosecutor said that he would go and see the general the next day. And so he did.

The prosecutor met with Globachev, and the general again referred to the laws under which he had to operate as head of the Petrograd Okhrana. Stavrovskii told Globachev that he could not find any evidence of crimes on the general's part, but he did ask Globachev to testify on what he told the prosecutor. Globachev agreed.

On October 14, 1917 the case against Major General Konstantin Ivanovich Globachev was closed, but with an order that he not leave the city. The general agreed, in writing, and he was released.[9] Karinskii was upset, but he could not overturn Stavrovskii's investigation and conclusion that the general had not abused his office as Okhrana chief.

Eleven days later, the Bolshevik Revolution took place. Globachev was released just in time. Some of the other tsarist officials were not as lucky.

CHAPTER 10

Release, Fright, and Flight

The first several days of freedom were not at all easy for the Globachevs. Just about all their possessions were gone. The Okhrana headquarters and the adjoining Globachev apartment within the Oldenburg Palace were gone. "Everything right down to the smallest item was plundered and stolen, and what was too big to be taken was broken, ruined, soiled, and turned over to the guards who now occupied my former apartment for their use."[1] While the Provisional Government was still hanging on to what little power it had, Globachev, upon his release, enlisted in the Petrograd Military District Reserves. This allowed him to draw a salary, but not for long.

The first few weeks that followed the Bolshevik Revolution of October 25 are commented on by Globachev: "At that time it really did not matter to me whether Kerensky or Lenin ruled Russia, but if one looked at the entire issue from the point of view of a citizen, then I must say that at first the new regime lightened the burden of the citizenry. This was due to the fact that the new regime acted decisively against robberies, and this made life more tolerable for the citizens. This was only in the early days."[2]

The general and his family were now in small quarters, living in an apartment building that was run by a committee approved by the new Bolshevik government. The Provisional Government was gone, the Bolsheviks were gaining in power, and this meant that everyone was being watched. This in itself was stressful. Upon his release Globachev was not well. The eight months of detention, with its physical and psychological stress, led to his loss of weight, loss of energy, and his being bedridden for a short time, but it was not long before he recovered his physical and mental strength.

The Bolsheviks got organized fairly quickly, but not all areas of their new ruling administration ran smoothly. It sometimes happens in revolutions that new regimes keep some competent officials of the overthrown regime to help the new government to get under way. But, within a month of coming to power, the Bolsheviks abolished the Military District Reserves and all military personnel over a certain age were dismissed.[3]

The Bolshevik government also replaced many of the officials and bureaucrats of the old regime with Bolshevik commissars who were considerably, if not in some cases totally, inexperienced in governmental administration. It was in these early days of the new regime that anti-Bolshevik activity began, and Globachev was part of it.

Over the next several months the Globachev family was involved in survival. The Bolshevik government began to create various collective operations. Both men and women had to participate in communal work such as cleaning streets, shoveling snow, being on committees that managed apartment buildings, and keeping those buildings clean and in working order. All these activities were under the watchful eyes of Bolshevik supervisors, and the Bolsheviks had roll calls to make sure that people were showing up for work. Sofia was ordered to be on the street cleaning detail, which she refused. The supervisor threatened to report her, and said that she could be shot for such insubordination. She responded, "Let them shoot me, but I will not unquestioningly submit to the wild orders of the Bolsheviks." The head of the house committee gave Sofia a dismissive wave of his hand and did not bother her again.[4] Freed of this requirement, her efforts were nevertheless time and energy consuming. The family had to be fed. It often took her hours to get food.

Food products began to diminish in the latter part of 1915, shortages of food intensified in 1916, and by 1917 the problem was very serious. Sofia notes how during the time of the Provisional Government there was still some availability of food such as cereal and potatoes at the markets. However, once the Bolsheviks came to power the situation became even more grim. The new government prohibited private trade. Merchants were outcast, their goods were confiscated, and they were often arrested. A black market developed and prices were high. In order to get any kind of food one had to have money or ration cards, and even then these resources were not enough to get decent meals. Sofia gives an example of what the family's meals were like. A two-day ration was a quarter of a loaf of bread for the four of them and tea with no sugar. On a few occasions they could get a little cod, but its taste was foul.[5] Sofia's brother helped the family with money, and friends helped by providing ration cards, as best as these friends could under the circumstances.

The Globachev children, Lydia, now sixteen years old and called Lialia, and Nicholas, fourteen and known as Kolia, attended a local school. Sofia made sure that no matter how dire the circumstances, her children would not be denied education. But both of the children were also required to do some occasional work in the apartment cooperative.

Konstantin did the communal work. This allowed him to play it as safe as possible, but this was not where he put his energy. He was working for the anti-Bolshevik underground. The general was able to get agents who could provide the secret organization that he was a part of with information on Soviet activities. Some of his agents were even inside the Cheka, the Bolsheviks' notorious secret police. Globachev's colleague, Major General V. P. Nikol'skii, who had been the chief-of-staff of the Corps of Gendarmes, confirmed that Globachev's agents were able to penetrate even the offices of M. S. Uritskii, the head of the Petrograd Cheka, and Globachev was able to get information on the activities of English and German counterintelligence operations.[6]

This was incredibly dangerous work, and on one occasion there was an event that could have cost the general his life. The Bolsheviks were beginning their roundup of former tsarist officials, members of the nobility, members of the church, and anyone else who was seen as a threat to the new regime.

The Globachevs were staying in the apartment of General Kaznakov and his wife. This was the same Kaznakov who had been the governor general of Poland some years before. The Bolsheviks had developed a program of searches that could happen anytime. Sofia recounts how the general was sick in bed when the Bolsheviks entered the apartment, primarily looking for weapons, but while they were at it they also ransacked the apartment and took whatever documents they found that looked official or questionable. And this time they took some of Globachev's documents that contained information about some former tsarist officials who were now employed by the Bolsheviks. Those documents had to be retrieved immediately.

Sofia rose to the occasion once again. "The next morning I set out for the regional commissariat to get them back."[7] The commissariat was crowded and noisy, with people milling about, and Sofia had to find a clerk or official who might know where the documents were. She finally did find out that the documents were in the building, but would be on their way to Cheka headquarters soon. She was able to accompany the delivery clerk to Cheka headquarters and on entering the building she approached a clerk and demanded to see the Bolshevik commissar of Petrograd, Moisei Solomonovich Uritskii. Sofia was told that Uritskii was in a meeting that might take a long time. The general's wife said that she would wait. She had arrived at Cheka headquarters at 9 in the morning.

She was still waiting at 8 p.m. Finally, she got to see Uritskii. Sofia told him that there was a packet that she needed returned, and that she could not take any more lengthy waiting for the return of her documents. Uritskii sent for the packet and began to go through the papers, but very superficially and quickly. Sofia was on edge lest the commissar find some of the information about Globachev's notes on people who were in Uritskii's organization. He did not notice any of them. He returned the packet to Sofia. He apparently had not recognized her last name, nor had he asked her about her husband. Sofia's aggressive pursuit of the documents paid off. She had lucked out.

Over the next several months the Soviet government grew stronger, its security organization, the Cheka, became more efficient and effective in hunting down anti-Bolshevik organizations and people. The consequence of getting caught was most often summary execution—no due process and no trial. Globachev had to get out of Petrograd.

The general would have to move fast. He and Sofia agreed that he would leave Petrograd first, and alone. There were several possible escape routes that people took. For Konstantin south was the best direction. By now, the early part of 1918, many people who hated, feared, or saw no advantage to staying within a Soviet system headed south where an anti-Bolshevik movement had begun to get organized—the White Movement. Another factor that came into play for Konstantin was that he had been born in Ekaterinoslav and that made him legally a Ukrainian citizen, and his passport showed that. One of the two passports in his possession showed his Ukrainian citizenship. Even though this was a legal passport, it had his real name on it and, if any inspector recognized the name, and therefore the general's former position, Globachev would surely have been shot on the spot. The other passport was a forged one with a different name that he had just in case. Even so, the situation was dangerous. Even though he could claim Ukrainian citizenship, if he was recognized as the former chief of the Okhrana, that could be his end.

Anyone who wanted to leave the city had to get approval to get a railway ticket, and that approval had to come from the Soviet government. Konstantin lucked out. He was able to buy a ticket from a young man who had planned to leave the city, but apparently changed his mind. Konstantin was able to bypass having to go to a government office for approval to leave Petrograd.

Sofia escorted Konstantin to the railway station and they agreed that as soon as he got to the city of Orsha he would send Sofia a telegram—but addressed to a friend of theirs, that he was all right. He would also send a second telegram once he got across the border into Ukraine. He was off to Orsha. This was around May or June 1918.

Orsha was an industrial city on the Dnieper River some sixty miles southwest of Smolensk and not quite four hundred miles from Petrograd. It was on the railway track from Petrograd, and on the border of Ukraine, which between February and October 1918 was occupied by the Germans. The Dnieper River was a means of transportation to Kiev. Orsha was a possible spot for getting out of Bolshevik-held territory. A Russian historian provides an excellent description of the limited choices that tsarist officials had in terms of fleeing the Bolsheviks:

"Fleeing as the red terror was beginning they only had two directions: north to Finland or south to Ukraine which had recently declared its autonomy from Russia. The Finnish border, very near to Petrograd, was heavily guarded. It is enough to say that even such a capable political operator of the old regime who had an opportunistic character, such as the famous I. F. Manasevich-Manuilov, using forged documents to get across the Finnish border, was recognized by vigilant revolutionary soldiers and shot on the spot.

"Fleeing south from Soviet Russia seemed more promising and most people preferred to put their fate at the boundary of Ukraine, where Bolsheviks generally allowed people with Ukrainian documents to pass. Thus, Gerasimov and Vasiliev were able to take advantage of this situation. Less fortunate was General V. F. Dzhunkovskii: in October 1918 he was removed by watchful police agents from a hospital train in Orsha . . . on which he was hiding trying to get to Ukraine, and he was arrested and sent to a Moscow prison under guard."[8]

There were some other reasons to go through Orsha. The Great War was still in progress, and Ukraine was occupied by the Germans, but with a local Ukrainian government in operation. One side of the border was patrolled and guarded by Bolshevik forces, and the Germans guarded the other side. Getting across the border required papers, and

Globachev had some, but they were fake documents with a fake name. In order to get across to the Ukrainian side he would have to show up personally to a Bolshevik border office. He could be recognized, and if that were to happen, he would be shot. The flight south was fraught with risk and, indeed, was downright dangerous.

The train ride to Orsha was tedious, tiring, and frightening for the general. And, of course, the entire route was full of danger. The overloaded train made a number of stops—Gatchina, Pskov, and Bialystok—before it got to Orsha. At each one of these points and more, Soviet railroad agents and soldiers would check passengers' papers. There was any number of times that Globachev could be caught.

He had boarded the train with some luggage and he quickly realized that this slowed him down. He had no seat assignment, but he was able to get a seat in a compartment with two women who were also heading south. He asked them to watch his suitcase and to include it with their belongings when they crossed over into Ukrainian territory. Here are Globachev's own words: "Truly, by the time that the train got to Orsha there were 10 times that documents were inspected and luggage was searched by young soldiers who were armed to the teeth and who were very thorough. Thanks to the fact that I had no belongings, and that I did not have an assigned seat, I was able to employ various ruses to avoid this unpleasantness, and I calmly got off the train at Orsha."[9]

Some of the ruses that he employed to avoid Soviet guards were to go from car to car to avoid being asked for papers, and to hide in restrooms and in the sleeping car. It took the train almost thirty hours to get from Petrograd to Orsha. When the train finally arrived at Orsha the general got off without incident.

Now, he had to figure out a way to get across the border. The passenger station in Orsha was on the Soviet side and there was a cargo station on the Ukrainian side. There were Soviet guards at various points at the border and the boundary between Soviet Russia and the German-occupied Ukrainian side was clearly outlined with a barbed wire fence. There was a guard booth on the Ukrainian side with a Ukrainian guard and a German officer in charge. Globachev spent two days reconnoitering the border crossing point. He needed to use all his knowledge and experience. He observed how the Soviet guards functioned, how they were armed, who was in charge, when and how the guards changed, and when would be the best time for him to try to get across. The general made his choice on when to risk getting across. "Having seen enough how the border crossing operated, I showed up early in the morning, at least an hour before the customs office opened. It was right at the border crossing and it was heavily guarded. I asked one of the customs clerks to let me go to the Ukrainian border guard, but not to cross into Ukraine. The Ukrainian border booth was about 300 feet from the Soviet side and had barbed wire strung along the border. I was asked to produce authorization from the Soviet Deputy, but I explained that I was not planning to cross the border since my luggage was still loaded at the admissions area waiting to be examined, and that I would be returning for it, but that I had to make some necessary inquiries at the Ukrainian border-crossing booth. After some hesitation, I was given permission, but of course I did not return, for I had no luggage. At the Ukrainian booth I told the Ukrainian commissar who I was and I asked that I be allowed to enter Ukraine. A German officer who was present and noted that I had no luggage gave me authorization to cross and personally escorted me past the barbed wire fence."[10]

Sofia recounts what Konstantin had told her later, and in her memoir she says that when Konstantin got across the border he identified himself to the German officer, and he was saluted by the German officer and escorted personally to the train that was bound for Kiev.[11]

Sofia and the children stayed in Petrograd for about another two months after Konstantin's flight south. Sofia had to get the proper authorization to leave Petrograd because she, Lydia, and Nicholas needed passports to get to Ukraine. While she went from one office to another and the weeks went by, the news in mid-July was that the former tsar Nicholas II and his entire family had been executed in the town of Ekaterinburg in the Ural Mountains. It was not long afterward that rumors began to spread of failed attempts to rescue the Tsar, possible escapes of some of the family, and other often outlandish tales appeared, and they would continue for many years.

Getting approvals to leave Petrograd required getting passports from the Ukrainian committee of the newly established independent Ukrainian People's Republic, and the approval to leave the city from the Commissariat of Internal Affairs, a Soviet government agency. Getting the approval presented some danger. Globachev's name was known, and it was possible that Sofia and the children could be detained, or worse. So, she chose to risk leaving the capital without applying for approval.

She and Lydia and Nicholas were able to get tickets. "Within half an hour of our train's departure, the Bolsheviks came through the train checking passports. A [commissar] came into our compartment with two soldiers and demanded our papers. I gave him our Ukrainian passports. He asked me if I had any other documents, and upon my saying, 'No,' he declared that he would not give me back my passports and we would be removed from the train at Dno, where the train was scheduled to arrive in a while. I became very worried and asked him who he was that he was holding on to my passports. 'I am a commissar,' he answered. 'Show me your papers to prove it,' I said. He dutifully got out some paper and handed it to me and I put it behind my back and told him that I would not return the paper to him. He lost his composure and turned to the soldiers and said, 'Comrades, what the heck is this?' The soldiers looked vacantly and apathetically at all this and did not answer. I thought better of it and handed him back his papers and lay down to go to sleep. My children were worried and I calmed them down assuring them that if I could sleep everything would be all right." When the train arrived at the Dno station Sofia got off and headed for the Bolshevik commandant's office, where the commissar said he would

Figure 10.1. Sofia Globacheva.

take the Globachev passports. On the way there the commissar hurried up to Sofia, gave her back the passports, and told her that she and the children could move on.[12]

Sofia was lucky, but this was just the start of one nightmare after another. The next railway stop they came to was Vitebsk, which was about three hundred miles south of the capital. Sofia and the children were famished and were only able to buy some bread from a peasant woman who was carrying a basket of bread past them. The train continued and finally arrived at Orsha. Again, there were the Bolshevik border guards and the searching of belongings.

The Soviet border guards began to search through Sofia's and the children's baskets. Both Sofia and Lydia had some of the general's clothes hidden in the bottom of their baskets and covered up with their own clothes and, in Lydia's basket, with some schoolbooks on top. As one of the guards reached into one of the baskets he pulled out a man's boot. Sofia was in trouble! "'What is this?' he asked.

"'As you can see, it is a boot,' I answered calmly. He then pulled the other boot out and reached his hand to the bottom where the overcoat lay. To tell the truth I was really frightened, and some instinct came out in me and I began to yell at them that they were ransacking the whole basket and it would be me, not they, who would have to repack it again and all there was were books and children's things. This obviously got a reaction, because a more senior Bolshevik who had been watching over this inspection told his comrade not to disturb things so much, and to repack everything accurately. They closed the basket, gave me back my key. So I was not wrong, my luck held out."[13]

They spent the night in town in a small hotel and could not get a good night's sleep because Bolsheviks were searching rooms for someone they were after. The next morning Sofia had to get permission from the Bolshevik border committee to cross the border into Ukraine, but she did not have the authorization paper that she was supposed to have to allow her and the children to leave Petrograd. She would have to make something up. She went to the border committee building.

The secretary of the committee told Sofia that he could not help her, but that she might be able to get approval from the Ukrainian border detachment commander to join his group and cross the border with the detachment. Sofia ran out and headed for where the detachment was almost ready to leave. She asked to join, but the head of the detachment told her that he would need for her to get approval from the Bolshevik committee. She hurried back, and once inside she was told that the committee was in a meeting and could not be disturbed. She broke into the meeting room. There were about a dozen members of the committee there and the secretary of the committee, who Sofia had spoken to earlier. She told the group about the Ukrainian's deferring to the committee and asked for some kind of formal approval to be allowed to join the Ukrainian detachment. One of the committee, and the only woman, stated that Sofia and her children should be returned to St. Petersburg. Sofia was exhausted, her nerves were frayed, but she was angry. She verbally attacked the woman, accused her of being heartless, and how could she send back a woman who was without money, with children, to a place where there would be no place to live. A doctor who was a member of the committee suggested that Sofia and her children be allowed to join the detachment, but that the committee should contact Petrograd that such incidents not happen again. As Sofia was leaving, she turned to the woman and told her how much more sensitive the men were.

There was another border checkpoint that had to be crossed and the guards looked like they were very thorough in looking through luggage. They were more than thorough; in some instances they required people to undress because the travelers might be hiding something on their bodies.

As Sofia and the children stood in line, they must have been quite nervous, but some kind of Bolshevik festival was starting, so the guards stopped their searches and left. The detachment crossed the border and began walking toward a village that was on the Dnieper River, where they were to catch a boat to Kiev. They spent two nights at this village waiting for the boat. On the third day the travelers were told that there would be no boat and that they would have to walk a number of miles to a cargo depot where they would get overland transportation.

Sofia was relieved. She writes, "It was a beautiful autumn day when we got on the road—the day was clear and the air was fresh. Our caravan of carts moved slowly and creaked. We walked through the woods and the sun's rays came through the treetops to light our path, and the yellowing leaves rustled under our feet. It was a picture of tranquility, and for the first time I felt a calm in my soul."[14]

Lialia and Kolia were helpful to Sofia all along the flight from Petrograd to this point, and they would continue to be helpful. While there were some scary moments for them, Sofia's children took it all in as an adventure.

The detachment arrived in the town of Gomel and spent a night before boarding a train to Kiev. The distance from Gomel to Kiev was about 140 miles. The train moved slowly, made several long stops, and most of the people on the train had not had any food for quite a while. There were some soldiers on board who had some provisions, and Sofia was able to buy about half a loaf of bread from a soldier for three rubles. She, Lialia, and Kolia shared half a loaf.

The train finally arrived in Kiev after an arduous and very lengthy trip, and Sofia and the children were reunited with Konstantin. Their relief and joy at being together after months of separation, anxiety, and danger were real. This was sometime in September 1918 and they were out of danger. Little did they probably know, because communication was almost nonexistent, but back in Petrograd, and in Moscow, the Bolsheviks had already publicly executed most of Globachev's former superiors and other officials and clergy.

The Globachevs felt safe and secure. They were living with Konstantin's stepbrother, Leonid Axenov, a physician, who was in Kiev at the time. Conditions during the first month or so, at least prior to November 1918, were not too bad. But the relief, sense of safety, and any sense of personal comfort were all temporary,

Konstantin had made it to Kiev a few months before his family, and was able to get a job in the newly formed Ukrainian People's Republic. With the collapse of the Romanov dynasty and months of a shaky Provisional Government, Ukraine claimed independence from the now nonexistent Russian Empire. The new leader in Ukraine was Pavel (Pavlo) Petrovich Skoropadskii, who was a member of a wealthy family in Chernigov Province. He had been educated in the Corps of Pages and had become a cavalry officer in the Tsar's army. He saw action in the Russo-Japanese War and rose through the ranks before the Revolution to lieutenant general. In 1917 he became active in Ukrainian political matters and with the independence of Ukraine he became the hetman in Ukraine. This position was somewhat that of a head of state. However, the hetman's power and survivability depended on German support, because Germany occupied much of Ukraine—not a good foundation for long-term stability.

Konstantin's job was as an official in the Department of Government Security. This department was organized similarly to the prerevolutionary Department of Police. Its several functions included criminal investigations, surveillance of political groups, and supervision over local and railway police.

While the Globachev family experienced an improvement in their living conditions, it was relative to what they had lived through just months before. Lialia and Kolia were in school, and living with Leonid gave them some physical and psychological comfort even though the quarters were a bit cramped. Within a short period they were able to move into a hotel. Food was readily available in the city, but it was expensive. "As the value of money plummeted, white bread sold for three hundred rubles a pound, the same weight of sugar cost more than twice that amount, and a pound of lard sold for even more. That winter, shortages of fuel oil and coal halted trains and shut down factories."[15]

Although the surface appearance of Kiev initially looked favorable to the Globachevs, it did not take long for them to see things for what they were. The economic and political situation was far from stable. The hetman governed in an autocratic manner, was clearly reliant on German support, and suppressed political opposition. Ukrainian nationalist separatist parties were against Skoropadskii, who they saw as a German puppet. Some of the members of the opposition parties were Ukrainian Bolsheviks. There were also speculators and profiteers who exploited the city. It is no wonder, then, that an opposition leader emerged. This was Simon Vasilievich Petliura.

His opposition had led to his arrest and detention for about four months, but he was released and his leadership of Ukrainian separatists grew. The hetman's power became even more unstable.

World War I came to an end on November 11, 1918 when the armistice was established and German control over Ukraine ended. The war was over and Ukraine was no longer under German occupation, so Skoropadskii was no longer under German protection. And now Petliura made his move openly against the hetman. It was war between Petliura's separatists and what forces Skoropadskii could raise to defend his position. The Russian general L. N. Kirpichev was able to organize a force of about three thousand volunteers, most of whom had been tsarist officers. Globachev's job changed. He was now on the staff of General Kirpichev and responsible for intelligence and investigation, as a counter to the activities of Petliura and of the Ukrainian Bolsheviks.

It did not take long for Petliura's forces to defeat the Officer Corps and to enter Kiev on December 14, 1918.[16] Petliura was now the leader and head of the Ukrainian Directorate. He began a program of repression almost immediately. The main targets of this program were those who had been associated with Skoropadskii's government and those who had been in the Officer Corps that had tried to defend Kiev. Those targeted were killed in the streets as they were caught. Konstantin had to get away as fast and as soon as possible. His first move was to get out of the public hotel and to move in with his stepbrother Leonid again. It was just a little safer for the moment. Sofia, Lialia, and Kolia stayed in the hotel. That did not last long. Petliura's men barged into the hotel at night and ordered Sofia and the children to get out immediately to make room for Petliura's staff. Sofia was still in bed. Some of the men were in Ukrainian uniforms and others in Russian ones. It was confusing. The Ukrainian officer was the first to make demands of Sofia. "It was night and the arrogance of this officer raised my indignation. I jumped out of bed, tossed on a peignoir and slippers and rushed out to him. As I passed a mirror and saw myself in it looking as I did, I could not help but smile bitterly. I argued with him heatedly that I couldn't be tossed out into the street with my children and belongings. The officer in the Russian uniform tried to convince the Ukrainian one not to insist on the immediate eviction. The Ukrainian put on airs, was obstinate, but finally backed down and 'graciously' allowed us to stay until morning."[17]

In the morning Sofia went to Leonid's apartment and conferred with Konstantin. They decided that Konstantin had to get out of Kiev as quickly as possible and that Sofia and the children would follow soon. Konstantin would get across the Dnieper River and go into hiding in the village of Slobodka. Sofia returned to the hotel and she and the children began packing. Once done they were able to get a cart, and Kolia was sent with the cart to their new dwelling. It was a small cabin of a few rooms. They had one room in the cabin, and it had a stove for heating the room. It was winter, it was cold, there was already snow on the ground, and the family did not have any warm clothes. Daily conditions were difficult. Konstantin and the children slept on the floor on mats filled with straw. Sofia got the one camp cot.

Throughout all of this, Sofia made sure that Lialia and Kolia went to school. But the school was not close by. Every morning she went with them, walking across a long bridge that connected Slobodka to Kiev, and then they had to get on a train to get to the school. On the way, there were corpses lying on the ground. Sofia often stayed in Kiev while Lialia and Kolia were in school, and then on the way home Sofia would worry that Konstantin might have been arrested while she was out.

Life for the Globachevs was once more a major challenge of how to survive day to day, and that included a great deal of fear and anxiety.

Konstantin was in hiding, real hiding. He had to stay indoors as guards were wandering about looking for enemies.

By early February 1919, the Bolsheviks had defeated Petliura, had taken Kiev, and had expanded their search for enemies to Slobodka. The family had to move even farther away, and again Konstantin would have to move fast, with his family following as soon as possible. At least they had Kostia with them in Slobodka for ten days before he had to flee again.

Konstantin was able to use some kind of fake documentation to get him on a train from Kiev to Nikolaev. This was a port city about 310 miles south of Kiev on the Southern Bug River. From Nikolaev, the general hoped to get to Odessa where the White Movement was still fairly strong. Of the journey he wrote: "The train ride from Kiev to Nikolaev was an absolute nightmare; in addition to the train being overloaded with people, there were uninterrupted inspections and searches of the passengers and all kinds of taunts from the Bolshevik inspectors that drove the passengers to near nervous breakdown. From the Dolinsk Station to Nikolaev, heated trains were crammed full of baggage and people, and the train ride dragged on for more than 24 hours."[18] Globachev spent two days in Nikolaev before he was able to get on a ship that was sailing for Odessa; but he did get on and he made it to Odessa.

Sofia, Lialia and Kolia followed Konstantin within a short time. Their train travel was not any better, and perhaps even worse than Konstantin's. Sofia wrote: "At the railway station, as we were leaving, what was going on was unimaginable. All the trains were overloaded with soldiers and civilians who were trying to save themselves from the Bolsheviks, and people were sitting on all the roofs of the cars. We barely got places in the third class section, thanks to giving the porter a good tip for his efficiency. Above us sat soldiers with their legs dangling in front of our faces. We could not even move around, the air smelled awful, and I got such a headache that I could not even move. Unruly, noisy, belching, cursing Bolshevik soldiers went from car to car looking for someone. We finally arrived at the Odessa cargo station after this awful traveling situation."[19] The Globachevs were reunited.

CHAPTER 11

1919 in Odessa

The end of World War I meant the withdrawal of Germany from Ukraine and the introduction of a temporary occupation by the victorious Allied forces. An Anglo-French conference in December 23, 1917 found agreement that the British would have responsibilities for the area between the Volga and Don Rivers while France would be involved with the area west of the Don—namely, Ukraine. Both allies had to consider whether to offer aid, both supplies and military, to Petliura's nationalist forces or to the White Movement under General Anton Ivanovich Denikin. The allies chose the latter.[1]

At this time Odessa, a major port on the Black Sea, was overcrowded with refugees fleeing from the Bolsheviks, from Petliura's forces, and from all kinds of marauding bands that claimed to be armies of liberation. Globachev's flight was somewhat typical to that of others. Many who had been caught up in the mayhem of Petrograd fled south. As the Revolution took hold in Moscow, many fled south from there, and once Kiev fell to Petliura and then to the Bolsheviks, flight farther south was the only way to safety. The result of this mass of humanity in Odessa was that living accommodations were very hard to come by, prices were high, unemployment was high, and the crime rate was very high. There was also considerable profiteering going on. The French sailors and soldiers were not content being in Odessa, so their discontent was felt by the Russians, and also by the French command that was responsible for the area.

Globachev had gotten to Odessa in January 1919, and was able to get a job with the Russian authority of the city. Globachev was favorably known to A. I. Pilts who had various responsible positions in tsarist times and was now the civilian deputy to General Alexei Nikolaevich Grishin-Almazov, the military commander of the region. Globachev was appointed to be in charge of intelligence operations, but this job did not last long. Odessa's status was precarious. By February 1919 Petliura's forces were still a threat as they began to move against Odessa. The White Volunteer Army, with the aid of the French, who by now had naval vessels in the Odessa ports and a presence of sixty thousand troops, were able to hold off the Petliura forces and, separate from that, to hold off the Bolsheviks who were attacking Odessa and were getting very close.

By March the French command had decided that the White Volunteer Army in Odessa that was under Denikin was no longer one that they could support. A separate Russian authority was established in Odessa that operated directly under French command. This Russian command was under Globachev's boss, a young general, Alexei Nikolaevich Grishin-Almazov.

He was young, about thirty-two years old, courageous and smart, but impetuous. The situation in Odessa was too far gone. Not only was the city crime ridden but it was also infested with Bolshevik agents who agitated and propagandized among the working classes of the city, and among the French sailors and soldiers.

Finally, on April 2, 1919 the French command had decided, and announced, that the French fleet would evacuate Odessa within forty-eight hours. They would take with them whoever was at the pier at that time. There was virtually no time for the Russians to get organized. Some had seen this coming and made plans. A number of Russians, mostly the White army's staff and their families, began leaving for Varna, Bulgaria, mostly by ship. Konstantin had tickets to Varna for Sofia and the children, but Sofia refused to leave, insisting that either the entire family went, meaning Konstantin too, or they all remain together. The ships began loading on April 4. The Globachevs were able to get on the French cargo ship *Kavkaz*. Its destination was Constantinople, about five hundred miles from Odessa, while other ships were headed for Novorossiisk.

Globachev describes the evacuation that he was in: "On April 2, 1919, the French authorities announced that they would evacuate Odessa within 48 hours. One can imagine how hastily and in what disorganization the Russians had to turn about to get loaded onto the ships, of which, it must be mentioned, there were not enough, and of those that were, they were not prepared for such a sudden departure. The embarkation

Figure 11.1. Overloaded evacuation ship.

was disorganized, and there was already gunfire heard in the city. The only people who were able to get on the ships were those who were at the pier on April 4. Many were not able to get out and remained in Odessa. In a short while they paid for that with their lives."[2]

The trip was difficult. The ship was not a large one and it was overcrowded with over two thousand men, women, and children. The conditions on the ship were unpleasant to say the least. With that many people the availability of nutritious food was a problem, as were the sanitary conditions. The ship's crew was overloaded with work and the sailors tended to be rude to the refugees. Globachev recalls that the thirteen days that it took to sail from Odessa to Constantinople, a distance of a little over five hundred miles, was a "nightmare of a trip."[3]

Sofia's description is just as graphic. "The ship was loaded in a hurry, and there was no order in people boarding the ship. General Shvartz, the commander of Odessa's defense, was on board, as was Archbishop Anastasi and his clergy. We sailed away from Odessa in beautiful weather. We were given space in the hold of the ship, slept side by side on planks that were covered with some nondescript, dirty-looking grass. One of my acquaintances and I chose not to lie down on those planks; it was disgusting and awful, and it looked like all kinds of worms and insects could crawl out, so we sat in the dining room of the ship for two days, resting our heads in our arms at the table. By the third night we could not take it anymore, and we threw ourselves exhausted on the planks and slept like the dead. While we were at sea we were fed some kind of broth and beans."[4]

The British were also involved in the evacuation, but in a special way. King George V's mother was the Dowager Queen of England, Alexandra, and she was the Russian Dowager Empress Maria's sister. Thus, the British government ordered the dreadnaught *HMS Marlborough*, which had been patrolling the Mediterranean, to sail into the Black Sea to Crimea. Its purpose was to evacuate as many of the Russian royal family as possible. Maria was told that she should board the *Marlborough* on April 5. Maria refused to board unless and until "all the sick and wounded, the priests and doctors, and any other inhabitants of Yalta and its environs who might be in danger from the Bolsheviks were evacuated with Her [*sic*]."[5] Her demand required more British ships to take on all the evacuees that Maria demanded to be helped. The evacuation was successful. The *Marlborough* was able to get a number of Romanovs and other relatives of the royal family out. The evacuees included the Dowager Empress Maria Fedorovna, Tsar Nicholas's mother; the Grand Dukes Nicholas Nikolaevich and his brother Peter Nikolaevich and their wives; the Grand Duchess Xenia Aleksandrovna, Nicholas's sister; Felix Yusupov, one of Rasputin's murderers, and Yusupov's wife, Irene. The ship took these passengers first to the island of Halki and then to Malta. From there, Maria was transported to England where she stayed a while, but then returned to her native Denmark where she died in 1928.

The ship that the Globachevs were on finally arrived in Constantinople where the refugees disembarked and were put into smaller boats that then sailed to one of the Prince's Islands. These islands were zones under Allied control and they were administered as follows: the French, who executed the evacuation from Odessa, were responsible for Halki (modern name, Heybeliada); the British ran Prinkipo (Buyukada), where the refugees from Crimea were sent; the Italians governed Antigone (Burgazada), where others were sent; and the Americans oversaw Proti (Kinaliada), where still others were sent. The Globachevs disembarked on Halki. This island is about ten miles from Constantinople.

Most of the native population on Halki were Greeks and Turks. Most of the refugees were assigned temporary quarters in a Greek monastery that could accommodate about six hundred people, although those Russians who either had some money or something to trade could get accommodations in a Greek or Turkish home. The Globachevs were initially lodged in the monastery in a large room with other families.

Sheets hung from the ceiling or from overhead rods separated the families from one another. However, within a short time the Globachev family was able to find a room in the home of a Greek widow. The Globachev refugees were Russian, the landlady was Greek, and they spoke to each other in French.

The Globachevs arrived on Halki in late April. Sofia's description of their stay on the island reads almost like the reminiscence of a vacation. The weather was beautiful, most of the people were amicable; they became acquainted with the director, officers, and cadets of the Turkish naval academy that was on the island (and is still there). Once again, communication was not a problem. The Turkish naval personnel and these Russian refugees spoke to one another in German. Since Turkey and Germany were allies during the war and often under German command, many Turkish military personnel learned German. The Russian refugees rode donkeys around the island, and enjoyed Turkish food and entertainment. While the life of being refugees who had lost their homeland, and indeed their privileged lives, must have weighed heavily on these Russians in exile, there were lighter and warmer moments on occasion. It was during Sofia's and her children's stay on Halki that she and her friends made the acquaintance of some Turkish naval officers who were assigned to the naval academy on Halki. These officers led the Russians on tours, drank coffee with them, and they enjoyed each other's company. The Russians and their Turkish hosts communicated easily—in German, in which Sofia was fluent. Sofia recalls one charming incident:

"All the naval officers were cultured individuals from the best Turkish families. They led us on tours of the naval academy, strolled with us, and they were attentive and interested in what was going on in Russia. One time an entire group of us Russians were strolling with them and one of them, who was married to the Sultan's sister, said that he was on the battleship *Goeben* when it shelled Sevastopol. Learning that we were there at the time, he said in jest that if he had only known that we were there, he definitely would have given the order to stop the shelling. Another young naval officer, who was in the company of some Russian young ladies, swore on Allah that knowing the Russians he would never again raise a weapon against them."[6]

While the refugees were on Halki the news started reaching them that the White Army was beating back the Reds—that is, the Bolsheviks. This encouraged many of the refugees to plan to return to the Russian mainland. Globachev left Halki after about two months, sailing from

Constantinople to the port city of Novorossisk, and then continuing to Rostov-on-Don by train. This was the continuation of a rollercoaster year for the Globachevs: separation, reuniting, moving from one place to another, and dealing with personal crises. Konstantin wrote to Sofia as soon as he got to Novorossisk, and he maintained contact with Sofia by mail.

The official way that mail could be sent was through the White Movement's postal system, but it could take a very long time and could even be lost. The other way was to have a colleague, acquaintance, friend, or relative hand carry the letter directly to the recipient. As can be seen in Kostia's letter to Sonia, their friend Dobrovol'skii was to have brought Sonia her husband's letter, but Dobrovol'skii had a change of plans, and so the letter went as it did via the slower postal system. Here is his letter:

Tsaritsyn is finally taken—June 1, 1919, Novorossiisk

Dear Sonia,

I am writing to you from the ship, since we have been ordered to disembark and go directly to the train station to catch the 9 o'clock train, so I probably won't be able to see the city. We left Constantinople only at 4:30 p.m. on Saturday and got to Novorossiisk on Monday at 6 o'clock without any incidents or adventure. The weather was perfect and there was not even the slightest rolling or pitching the entire trip. We were docked from Monday until 5 o'clock Tuesday, and it is just now that we are allowed to leave. Judging by what we hear on the pier, the activities of the Volunteer Army are going perfectly.

Everybody is noticeably animated. Kharkov is taken, as is Ekaterinoslav, and all of Crimea. Advance units are nearing Kursk. The Bolsheviks are pretty well being destroyed. All the commissars in Kharkov were hanged. Dybenko was hanged in Yalta. Tomorrow the ship with the refugees from Crimea is sailing for Yalta.

Now, regarding money: only Don, Kerenki, and best of all Tsarist money is exchanged here. Other money is not used. Bread costs 2.5 rubles a pound, and I don't know about other products because I have not been in the city, and this information I have only from Ekaterinodar. So Sonia, that is all the news I have about myself. I am sending this letter along with letters of the Polianskiis' via Colonel Dobrovol'skii, who is going to Prinkipo with his family in two days and will stop off at Halki on the way.

The ship will not be going to Vladivostok, at least that is what the officers at the pier said, and that everyone would be ordered to go to Ekaterinodar.

I ask you not to be nervous and not to worry; I feel that everything will be all right for you and me. In general, I am happy to be back in Russia. All the stories that you hear from you-know-who on Halki are nonsense. God willing we will see each other in a month.

I send you my kisses and my love. Kiss the children. I am your loving Kostia.

There's been a change. Dobrovol'skii is not going, so I am sending this through the agency.[7]

Kostia's letters to Sonia can use some explanation. His heading that "Tsaritsyn is finally taken" refers to the White Army recapturing the major port city that is known today as Volgograd. Novorossisk was the port of entry to White Russians returning to their homeland. Kostia would try to join the Volunteer Army. His letter is optimistic as he writes of the places that have been won back by the Whites. Some of his information must have come to him through hearsay, and was incorrect. He refers to "Dybenko [who] was hanged in Yalta." The only Dybenko who was in that general area and had some notoriety at the time was the Red leader Paul Efimovich Dybenko. P. E. Dybenko was a Bolshevik leader in the south of Russia around the time and was not hanged, but he was executed in 1938 by the Soviet government during the Great Purge, as a traitor.

The economic situation in the area controlled by the Whites is demonstrated by the different kinds of money that was used. The Don currency was printed by a local government, the Kerenki (named after Kerensky) was the currency that had been established during the Provisional Government's tenure in 1917, and tsarist money was still honored.

Finally, Kostia mentions Vladivostok. The ship, the *Kherson*, that he was to be on had Vladivostok as its original destination. This would have brought people to assist Admiral Alexander Kolchak, the White leader in Siberia. The journey would have been incredibly long—through the Bosporus into the Mediterranean, the Suez Canal, around India, through the Sea of Japan, and finally Vladivostok. The change of plans ordered the passengers who landed in Novorossisk to head for Ekaterinodar.

As soon as Globachev got to Novorossisk he tried to join the Volunteer Army. There was an application process, and for former tsarist generals it was rigorous. A general's application first went to a general who was on the staff of the commander-in-chief of the Volunteer Army, who did a preliminary review, and then it went to a commission that reviewed the application in detail, and finally it was forwarded to the commander-in-chief, General Anton Ivanovich Denikin, who made the final decision to accept or reject the applicant joining the Volunteer Army. The entire process could take weeks before a decision was made.

Globachev's next letter to Sonia was written several weeks later:

24 June [Old Style]
Ekaterinodar

My dearest Sonia!

I arrived at Ekaterinodar 5 days ago, but I didn't write immediately because I was involved in personal bustling about. I went to the general in charge with a list of questions and was told that my matter would be forwarded to a certain commission. It was only today that I met the chairman of the commission, where my matter would be examined, which would take at least a week, after which a report would be made to Denikin and he would decide whether or not to accept me into the Volunteer Army. All generals who come to Ekaterinodar are subjected to this ordeal; but staff officers and senior officers are immediately assigned to combat units or to administrative duties. Former gendarme officers, and especially generals, are treated with prejudice and are not given higher-level responsibilities, especially in government security. I saw Mr. Nikol'skii but based on what was said, it was obvious to me that I would not be serving under him because I could not count on having a more or less decent position given the current political situation. A.I. Pilts is away and will be back in five days, so I haven't seen him, but I have high hopes when I meet with him.

My late arrival played no significant role. Shredel' and Mezentsev are still unemployed. In any event, don't you worry, as soon as I get through the Commission I will be settled, but I don't know where, since the territory is expanding and all the major administrations intend to transfer to the south. I think that I will be employed either as the Chairman of the Requisitions Commission or, maybe, in the civilian administration. In any event, it is better that you did not come, and unpleasant as that is, you must wait (until I have a definite job) and until I write to you to come.

There are no apartments at all. I am staying at Malenovskii's in a really small room in the courtyard of a foul building, and thank God even for that. Living conditions are pretty expensive. The most expensive are textiles, and they are scarce, so they have to be gotten from Turkey. For example, women's white stockings of very poor quality cost 275 rubles. Further, sugar—100 rubles per pound, chocolate—100 rubles per pound, candy—the same, a box of matches—5 rubles, bread—2 rubles, 50 kopeks per pound, beer—6 rubles for a bottle. I eat in the building dining room, two courses—10 rubles. So, food is less expensive than in Turkey but other things are more expensive. When you do leave, stock up on sugar, tea (100 rubles per pound here), linen goods and shoes. One can't get any uniforms here.

I gave your message to E.N. Pilts and E.L. Beletskoi's letter to Colonel Tikhobrazov. The weather here alternates between very hot and pouring rain. The city is not bad. It's big and decent enough; there are several theatres and good movie houses, and a big city park.

I must admit to you that I lost the enthusiasm I had when I came here because this place smells of a Kerensky-type government. In general my mood is not that good now, and who knows, maybe it will improve, but maybe it would have been better to go elsewhere.

All the lower ranked people have already found work in various government duties. Moskvin is in Novocherkask. Podgornitskii is here on duty with the railroad. In any case, don't be lonely and don't worry about me, I will write to you as often as I can, but in the meantime stay in Halki until I send for you, since coming here with living accommodations and not knowing for how long isn't possible. I will send this letter either with General Mustafin or some other way. You probably already got my first letter (the letter from Novorossisk).

Give my regards to Ekaterina Leonidovna and to all our other acquaintances. I embrace you and kiss you and love you.

I kiss the children, your loving Kostia.

Globachev's difficulty in joining the Volunteer Army, as well as that of certain other generals, becomes clear in one of Globachev's phrases that "*this place smells of a Kerensky-type government.*" Commander-in-Chief General Denikin had a number of individuals in his government and on his staff who were former members of the Provisional Government and others who were left-leaning members of the pre-Revolution Duma. This culture was highly suspicious, especially of former gendarme and Okhrana officers. There was, however, the possibility of getting into the Volunteer Army. Kostia was well acquainted with Alexander Ivanovich Pilts, the latter being a highly respected former civilian governor general of Irkutsk. Pilts was now in Denikin's government, and a recommendation from him could be helpful. Kostia wrote:

1 July 1919

Ekaterinodar

My dear Sonia!

My file is still in the hands of the Commission, and I cannot be assigned a duty until Denikin finally decides. I got a job in the main department of military supply, and in all probability I will be the Chairman of the Inspection Commission, so I've been promised. I already go to work and am getting acquainted with the job. A. Pilts arrived just today and was very happy to see me, but he didn't offer me anything, and I did not ask, because if they do have something for me, it wouldn't be suitable for me. It would be better for me to serve in a military capacity and when I am accepted, then maybe I can have some choices of work, and it is a fact that it will happen.

In the next few days all the major administrative offices and the Commander in Chief's staff will be moving to Rostov and Taganrog; I don't know where I will be, so that is why I am not asking you to come yet. Ekaterinodar is awfully overcrowded; all our people live in communal accommodations under terrible conditions. Food rations are less expensive but everything else is terribly expensive; for example, men's shoes—1,600 rubles. I gave mine to have new soles and heels, and it cost 160 rubles. So stock up on shoes and dresses, the prices here are exorbitant.

Nikol'skii gave me a magnificent reference, which is why I was accepted into the supply staff. E.N. Pilts sends her regards and is appreciative that you had her in your thoughts. When you do leave, buy some more chocolate, sweets are very expensive. I suggest that you also buy and bring coffee; there is none at all here.

All the Odessa inhabitants who were on Halki are slowly coming here from Turkey. Gornostaev gave me your greetings, and I got your letters from P.A. Ivanov. Write to me at the following address: Dmitrievskaia, No. 76, Government Staff Office, care of S.V. Savitskii to be transmitted to me, because if you write to me at my apartment, where I am staying (Kotliarovskii, No. 90) and I wind up moving to Rostov, it won't be forwarded to me, but Savitskii will always notify me.

I want to see you all very much and soon, but what to do, since I still am not settled and do not have particular duties. I think something definite will be known in about two weeks, and then I will write to you immediately.

The general situation here is unchanged, but according to newspaper reports, things are very bad in the Caucasus. Give my regards to E.L. Veletskaia and all our acquaintances of whom, I hear, there are fewer, they all left for Vladivostok. Tell Kostia Polianskii that the conscription age is 19. Until we meet, I hug you, kiss you, and love you. Kiss Lialia and Kolia.

Your loving Kostia

By the beginning of July 1919 Globachev's application was still in the commission's hands. This meant that he could not have a position in the Volunteer Army yet, but he could work in an agency that was supportive of the army. The general was able to get a job working in the White Movement's Supply Administration, first in Ekaterinodar, and then in Rostov-on-Don. Rostov was the military and administrative center of the Volunteer Army. So, Globachev was employed, and while he had the experience of administrative responsibility, the job was deadly boring. He was not using the skills that he was trained for. And it was an unpaid position.

Kostia's letter also contains a foreboding of things to come, as he writes "*according to newspaper reports, things are very bad in the Caucasus.*" Still, the general was willing and hopeful of getting a responsible position with the Volunteer Army.

In the two months that Globachev was back on Russian soil he was back and forth between Novorossisk, Ekaterinodar, and Rostov checking on his application, trying to get work, and having to tell Sonia not to join him yet. Then came his August 25 letter to his wife:

Rostov, Romanovskii 122

25 August [Old Style] 1919

My *dear Sonia!*

Things are not going well for me; it's no wonder that I had a foreboding about going to Novorossisk. In the last letter I wrote to you that I had already been appointed to Kiev as the Chairman of the Interdepartmental Requisition Commission, and that I had no doubts about going. Things worked out differently—Denikin turned me down. I went to Taganrog to find out why—it seems that the issue is my former duties in the Corps of Gendarmes and the Security Section. The Chief of Staff promised that he would resubmit, and I await the result. Of course, I won't get to Kiev, but it's important to me to be enrolled in the reserves, since I don't have anything to live on, without pay. If I am turned down again, I will be finished with the Volunteer Army, and I will try to get work in any other place. All these unpleasantries have exhausted me. The boredom is terrible, I do nothing, and I sit in my little room or wander the streets. In general my life is unenviable. Could anyone have thought that I would have been treated this way? Besides that, I am worried about you; only two letters in all this time, via Terehov and Sotiri. What is with you all? I don't know anything and I can't even write to you to let you know where you should come. It's simply awful. I will finally find out in the next few days whether I will serve in the Volunteer Army, but I have to write you without waiting since today is the opportunity to go to Novorossisk.

As soon as I find out something, I will write immediately. Everyone who came from Turkey has been appointed jobs, except generals, and especially those from the Corps of Gendarmes.

Rostov is a nice city, but twice as expensive as Ekaterinodar. I miss you all very much, how good it would be to be united.

Well, let's not lose our good spirit, maybe everything will work out for the best.

I kiss and embrace you all, lovingly Kostia.

Globachev's application to join the Volunteer Army was to no avail. He had applied several times, and he was rejected each time. He finally was able to see General Denikin's chief-of-staff, General Romanovskii, to find out why he was rejected. General Denikin did not want any officers, especially senior ones, who had any past experience, position, or association with tsarist political investigative agencies. This included the Special Corps of Gendarmes and, of course, the Okhrana. Globachev was told that Denikin had nothing personal against him, but Globachev's background was what determined the decision to not accept him. Even though Globachev had support from some respected individuals, such as A. I. Pilts, who had been the governor general of Siberia, it did no good. Globachev's assessment of this matter was that Denikin was accommodating the left wing of his administration, which included former members of the Kadet and Socialist Revolutionary Party. These were some of the people who were responsible for the monarchy's collapse. Globachev certainly thought so.

By September 1919, things had changed. The general was offered a position on General Romanovskii's staff as assistant to the head of counterintelligence. He declined because he was soured by his application experience and because he would not be able to function within the kind of government that Denikin was in charge of.

Sofia and the children were on Halki all the while that the general was on the Russian mainland trying to get into the Volunteer Army. Sofia, Lialia, and Kolia finally sailed to join Kostia who was in Rostov. They probably sailed around September 1919. Rostov was full of former tsarist officers and officials. They were employed in various jobs that they never would have held in the past. Sofia ran into General Balk, the former city prefect of Petrograd. He was training men who were mostly in their sixties how to march carrying rifles. The Whites needed the help of anyone they could get.

Sofia also ran into someone personally closer. She writes, "Walking home along the bank of the River Don, and being lost in thought, I didn't notice a gypsy woman who was walking toward me. She stopped and fixed her eyes on me and said, 'There is a cross behind you of which you are not yet aware.' Three days later I ran into Colonel Skvortsov, formerly a member of the General Staff, who was married to the sister of my brother's wife. I did not know anything of my brother since his arrest by the Bolsheviks in Petrograd. I asked Skvortsov about him, and he said that the Bolsheviks had shot my brother. So, here was that cross that was behind me, of which I did not know at the time."[8]

It was now November 1919 and the general got a job more in keeping with his experience, although it meant moving again. He was appointed the head of naval counterintelligence in Odessa. Naval counterintelligence had been organized anew and the general would be able to select his own staff. It was a difficult situation that he was moving into. Militarily, the Reds were gaining on all fronts and the probability of the Whites winning was worse than problematic, since Odessa was an important target for the Reds. But Globachev did his best. He organized his operation by finding the best people to lead. He was able to put together his staff pretty quickly, but then he ran into the very fundamental problems of getting office space, basic office equipment, such as desks, chairs, and heating fuel. It was winter and the temperature hovered between 2 or 3 degrees constantly.[9] The agencies that were supposed to provide supplies were short of everything, and it became necessary for Globachev and his staff to buy or request what they needed from wherever they could find it.

Odessa was in bad shape. The Whites were holding on, but it was a losing situation. The streets were full of soldiers and officers moving through the city to be reassembled in new units for the move to the front line, which was getting closer and closer to the city. It was probably around the beginning or middle of January that a British commander of a minesweeper offered Globachev to transport Sofia and the children to Constantinople, because the Reds were closing in. Sofia refused the offer because to leave Kostia now might mean that they would never see each other again.

The Volunteer Army's military commander of Southern Russia, which included Odessa and Crimea, was General Nicholas Nikolaevich Shilling, a friend of Konstantin's from academy days. By January 20, 1920, the commander's general staff was developing plans to evacuate Odessa and sail to Sevastopol. On January 23, one of the senior officers, General Vitvinitskii, had ordered all equipment loaded onto one of the evacuation ships, the *Vladimir*. But he did not inform everybody. Globachev discovered what had happened only after arriving at his office and finding it empty of all office equipment and no staff there. On January 24 the British made an official announcement that an evacuation would take place. The evacuation was more than poorly organized.

Figure 11.2. Evacuation of the White Army.

What happened next rivals anything that you might see in a fictional adventure/action film, or read in a fictional dramatic adventure novel. But this was real! By January 25, the height of winter, the evacuation was under way. Some of the overloaded ships were able to get out of the harbor on their own, while others had to be helped by icebreaker tugboats. Globachev and his family were on the *Vladimir*, waiting to cast off. But then General Vitvinitskii, the same who had ordered the initial phase of evacuation two days earlier, told Globachev that the *Vladimir* would not cast off unless the crew was paid. Globachev was asked to go into the city to the bank and get two million Kerensky rubles to pay the ship's crew. There was an automobile at the end of the pier where the *Vladimir* was docked. Globachev took two of his subordinates, who were armed, and the ship's paymaster, and they got into the car. They did not have much time. They had to move quickly because the ship was to cast off at 1 p.m. When they arrived at the bank there was a crowd of people waiting to get in to withdraw whatever money they could. Globachev told his subordinates to wait in the car while he and the paymaster went in to get the needed funds.

The bank director was very helpful because he was supposed to be leaving on the *Vladimir* in a short while, too. But outside there were unruly reservists who joined the crowds and seemed to be instigating a riot. Globachev edged out of the building to signal the driver of the automobile to move around to the side of the bank building. The car was gone. The crowd had pretty much blocked off most of the doors to the bank and the reservists were now yelling threats to anyone in the bank. Telephoning the Volunteer Army's defense headquarters for help was no use—the phone line was dead. There were already armed troops in town and Globachev and the director were sure that it would not be long before the bank would be attacked. The decision was made to give the money to a representative of the reserves, who had posted themselves at the various doors to the bank, and to get out of the area as soon as possible. Everyone around the outside of the bank ran to the money. Globachev, the director, the director's sister, and the paymaster sneaked out of the building through a side door.

Before Globachev and the others had left the building, the director of the bank informed the general of something quite surprising, to say the least. This information "generated a feeling of horror and anger that we wound up in this stupid and useless trap because of General Vitvinitskii's cowardice and loss of composure in sending me to the bank to get the Kerensky money when the money, according to the bank director, had for the most part already been loaded on the *Vladimir* and that was something that Vitvinitskii had to know."[10]

By now the Reds were in town and there was fighting in the streets. There were small arms, rifle, and machine-gun fire all around. Globachev and the others had to run to the pier as bullets whizzed past them, and at street intersections they had to run even harder and faster. There were already bodies lying in the streets. As they got to the pier, all the evacuation ships had already gone except for the *Vladimir*. And it had begun to cast off. The Bolsheviks were already close enough that they were firing on the ship with cannons. Panic was rampant on the ship as the shells were landing closer to the ship. It was winter, it was cold, the general was almost fifty years old, and now he was literally running for his life.

Sofia was on board the *Vladimir* and it was in the morning that she was told that Kostia had left the ship to go into town for money. She and the children became more and more worried and frightened as the morning wore on and the *Vladimir* was the only ship left and cannon fire could be heard closer and closer.

It was time for the ship to cast off the lines and move out. Cannon and rifle fire was getting close. Sofia ran to the captain to try to get him to stop the ship from leaving the pier. It seemed to no avail, so Sofia was going to get off the ship no matter what. She would not leave Kostia, even though the stern of the ship had already moved away from the pier. Just then there was a commotion on the deck and passengers began yelling that Globachev was running to the ship. Lines were thrown to the runners and Globachev had to jump to catch onto a line. He was pulled up, as were the others. They were saved.[11]

Kostia was on board and so was Vitvinitskii—and so were Globachev's two subordinates who had left with the car. The general's daughter, Lydia, recounted how she had never seen her father so angry ever before or ever again. He did not yell at the recipients of his anger. His voice was louder than usual, more animated, but still under control. The Civil War was on and he had no military authority over his subordinates, so he could not punish them, but he did call them cowards and a number of other epithets. Vitvinitskii got the same treatment.

Sofia gives a vivid description of what those final moments in Odessa were like: "There were already a lot of dead bodies lying in the street on the way to the ship. As the ship began to move away from the dock, the Bolsheviks began to fire on the ship. We could hear one cannon shell and then another as they exploded near the ship. The panic on board the ship was awful, and some officers who were unable to get on the ship because there was no more room, shot themselves on the dock. This was hell in reality. An unseasonable frost and stormy weather was rampaging here in the south, and it seemed like all of hell's forces were working to aid the Bolsheviks. Even when we finally arrived in Sevastopol, in the frenzy to get off the ship, two people were crushed to death."[12]

The ship sailed to Sevastopol. It took only about a day and a half, but it was rough. There were passengers on the deck of this overcrowded ship suffering from typhoid, the weather was blisteringly cold, and a storm hit. The ship barely made it into Sevastopol's port, and the situation here was the same as in Odessa. Ships were being loaded and evacuation was imminent. It was only a matter of little time before the Reds would take over the entire southern area of Russia.

There was nothing for Globachev to do, even though the general was offered a job in counterintelligence, which he declined, because it was very clear to him that the efforts of the Volunteer Army were doomed and that Sevastopol would soon fall to the Reds. He and the family decided to head for Constantinople where there was still the semblance of a Russian government in exile. It was early February 1920. Globachev was able to arrange for the family and for those who had been on his staff in Odessa to sail with their families on the British coal tender *Mercedes*.

CHAPTER 12

Loss

The ship sailed south toward Constantinople. It was a long voyage, lasting twelve days. The ship stopped a number of times to load or unload coal at one port or another. With all that had happened, the Revolution, the Civil War, Globachev moving from one job to another in Kiev, Novorossisk, and Odessa, the Globachevs did not know that they would never see their homeland again. Konstantin was fifty years old, Sofia was forty-five, Lydia was nineteen, and Nicholas was seventeen.

For the Globachevs, and for many others, their world had ended. They were lucky to get away alive, but life would be different. It would be more difficult socially because they no longer had status and privilege. And life would certainly be harder economically. Again, they were lucky to be alive considering the fate of others with whom Globachev had had close professional relations.

The Bolsheviks had executed a significant number of the tsarist officials with whom the general had worked or to whom he had reported. Three of the five ministers of the interior that Globachev had reported to in the last two years of the monarchy had been shot—Maklakov, A. N. Khvostov, and Protopopov. Vissarionov, who had been critical of Globachev's performance when the general was the chief of the Warsaw Okhrana, was shot, as was Beletskii, who was Khvostov's deputy; both of them had conspired to murder Rasputin back in 1916. Old Sturmer probably would have been shot, but he died of uremia while incarcerated in the dank Peter and Paul Fortress in late 1917.

On July 17, 1918, the Tsar and his whole family were shot in the basement of what the Bolsheviks called "the House of Special Purpose" in Ekaterinburg, a town just east of the Ural Mountains, about 1,100 miles east of Moscow. Several members of the royal family's staff were also executed—the family physician, Dr. Eugene Botkin, Alexandra's maid Anna Demidova, and several others. They were not the only ones executed. Of the royal family's closest relatives, the Tsar's younger brother Michael was shot in June 1918 in Perm, a town in Siberia where he had been sent under arrest. Alexandra's sister, Elizabeth, was arrested by the Bolsheviks and was sent to Siberia. In July 1918 she was thrown down a well and the executioners tossed grenades down after her. In addition, there were probably ten more Romanovs who were executed at various times and in various places.

The Globachevs certainly understood and felt the horror of the deaths of people they knew, even if these individuals were not personal acquaintances or friends of theirs. But the indescribable sorrow of loss hit home much harder.

Sofia never saw or heard anything of her two sisters again. She saw her two remaining brothers once more in Constantinople, and then never more. She would only hear later about their deaths. Kostia would never see or hear anything of his mother. He never saw his brothers again, and only later did he have some correspondence with his stepbrother Leonid Axenov, who had immigrated to Germany.

By April 1920, the White Army was in desperate straits, having sustained heavy losses across all fronts. Tsarytsin, Taganrog, Novocherkassk, Rostov-on-Don, Odessa, and Novorossisk had fallen to the Reds. The only hope was a change in leadership. Denikin turned over command of the White Army to General Baron Peter Nikolaevich Wrangel, a member of the Russian nobility who had a highly respected military career as a brave and capable commander during World War I. He was a capable organizer and leader; however, his limited number of military successes against the Reds in 1920 could not be sustained. In addition to the Red Army's superiority in numbers, they also had a strong underground in the White Army's rear.

The most widely known evacuation of the White Army is Wrangel's evacuation of Crimea on November 16, 1920 (Old Style). Except for some pockets of White resistance in 1921, especially in Central Asia and farther east, the Civil War was over. The estimates of the number of persons who evacuated through Crimea at this time vary between 140,000 and 200,000.[1] There were, however, prior escapes and flights from Russia by Whites and others who were against the Bolsheviks, and by those who simply feared what was happening. Some of the destinations were Finland, Poland, Germany, the Baltic states that had declared their independence, and, in the east, to Harbin in China. There were, therefore, many more Russians leaving and fleeing than just the number cited for the Crimea evacuation. The evacuation from Crimea had only one place to go, and that was south toward Constantinople.

CHAPTER 13

Constantinople

The population of Constantinople in 1920 was estimated at somewhere between 800,000 and 1,200,000 inhabitants. These numbers come from approximations made by the Ottomans and may have included the Prince's Islands, refugees, and the occupation forces of Great Britain, France, Italy, and Greece that had been in Constantinople since the end of 1919.[1] While estimates of the exact number of Russian refugees vary, the Russian population in Constantinople by the end of 1920 could have been as high as almost 20 percent of the total population of Constantinople. The Russian influence on the city was such that one Russian woman said that "wherever we are, we bring much of ourselves. . . . we adorn the strangers' way of life with ours, and it often seems that we did not come to them, they came to us."[2] Sofia Globacheva was even more expressive: "With the arrival of the White Army, Constantinople came alive and filled up with military uniforms of all kinds, making a strange picture of the city. Constantinople was conquered by the Russians, who had inundated every street in the city. Life was in a feverish full swing."[3]

The military White Russian refugees were mostly officers. There was also clergy, and among civilians there were former government officials, businessmen, former restaurateurs, performing artists, the spouses and children of all these people, and certainly there were not a few individuals of suspicious backgrounds. These included people who had been part of revolutionary groups, former officials of the Provisional Government, and individuals who were simply involved in shady enterprises.

Churches were established. A number of high prelates of the Orthodox Church, such as Archbishop Anastasi, had been part of the evacuation and were now in Constantinople. Restaurants and cabarets that had Russian menus popped up. One popular spot was an entertainment garden established on the outskirts of the city. It offered a new music—jazz. The owner was Fedor Fedorovich Tomas, whose real name was Frederick Bruce Thomas. He was born in Coahoma County, Mississippi in 1872, the son of former slaves. The story of his life is just beginning to become known, but he did venture to Russia before the Revolution where he opened a variety theatre called Maxims. Following the Revolution, he fled to the south of Russia, and, as with other refugees, he evacuated Russia in 1919 and wound up in Constantinople.[4] Over the next several years he opened what became a popular entertainment "garden" in Constantinople that attracted many people, especially when he introduced American jazz. He did, however, fall on hard times, lost his business, and died in a debtor's prison in 1928.

Shops that carried goods, including expensive items like jewelry, appeared all over the city. A lot of this was what the Russian refugees were able to take out of Russia. Individuals of the arts community got organized. A ballet troupe was created and performances were held in the city. The humorist writer Nadezhda Teffi spent some time in Constantinople, and among performers there were a number who were very well known to the refugees. Alexander Vertinskii had made a career for himself in the last few years before the Revolution. He wrote his own songs, which were often melancholy, but had beautiful lyrics. He always performed dressed as Harlequin. His songs of lament over lost loves, nostalgia for past times, and the sadness of life connected with the Russian refugees. Iuri Morfessi was an opera singer and Nadezhda Plevitskaia was quite a popular singer of Russian folk and Gypsy songs. Serge Jaroff, who had been a young Don Cossack officer in the White Army during the Civil War, organized the Don Army Chorus in 1920 in Constantinople. The chorus sang Russian church music as well as folk music. In 1921 the chorus moved to the Greek island of Lemnos, and from there to Bulgaria and then into Europe and the United States, where it became a favorite entertainment for American and international Russophiles.

In addition to the non-Russian occupation forces there were some non-Russians who were in Russia when the Civil War broke out. One such person was the Romanian violinist Jean Gulesko, who had been quite popular in Petrograd. He made his way south to Constantinople. He was a favorite of the Russians.[5]

While there were a number of entertainment venues and people to distract the refugees from their condition, not everyone was lucky enough to have a job that paid, nor did they have adequate living accommodations.

"Constantinople presented a strange picture in these days—it was absolutely overrun by Russians who inundated the city's streets," Globachev writes. "Most of the refugees were homeless; they wandered about looking for work, they sold those few belongings that they were able to get out of their homeland at markets and in the streets, and they slept at the entrances to the mosques or in bathhouses.

"On Pera, near the Russian embassy, huge crowds of Russians would gather to sell their belongings and to sell Russian money, which was worth nothing at the time.

"The embassy courtyard and all the offices of the embassy were overcrowded with Russian refugees. Some were there for passports, others for aid, but there were many who had no business there, but were just drawn to be on Russian territory. Within this mass of people there were also those who could just as easily have stayed with the Reds—there was no threat to them because their ideologies were closer to that of the Bolsheviks, so it was surprising that they left Crimea. This latter element of society stole from the embassy, spread false rumors that any day now the embassy would be seized by the Bolsheviks and, disturbing the public with this danger, they proposed that they could protect the embassy with the help of some secret organization."[6]

Figure 13.1. Main entrance to the Russian Embassy in Constantinople.

The Globachevs were initially settled on the island of Prinkipo. However, within a few weeks of being on Prinkipo, Globachev was able to get employment in the Russian Embassy in Constantinople. Sofia and the children, however, stayed for a few more months on Prinkipo.

The Russian Embassy, which was still part of the old regime, in those early days did not have a professional who could handle security and intelligence matters. The embassy needed someone who had the kind of professional experience that Globachev could claim, and the general's reputation was one of competence, and he was well respected. It helped further that the head of the White Russian army in Constantinople was General Alexander Sergeevich Lukomskii. He and Globachev had known each other since their days together as young officers at the General Staff Academy. Globachev had the highest regard for Lukomskii, considering him capable and a man of honor with a strong sense of duty. Globachev's official title was head of passport control. But this position was more than bureaucratic passport processing. A major part of it was intelligence and counterintelligence work.[7] There were always individuals with fake identities and forged passports, and Globachev had to know how to deal with all this, especially because of the Bolsheviks who were active in Constantinople. "I was a member of General Lukomskii's office and was in charge of passports; that is, granting visas, control of transportation to Crimea, and information coming out of the Middle East regarding Bolshevik propaganda and activities. My job required me to give General Lukomskii daily reports."[8] Bolshevik activities included agents who sought to merge in with the refugees to disrupt morale and the White Army organization itself.

All of this made Globachev's job even more challenging. Many Russians missed their homeland and had relatives in Russia, so they wanted to return even though it was now a Communist state. For Globachev this was the emotionally difficult part of the job. Then, there were also those who saw the White Army as a lost cause and were willing to go over to the Bolshevik side. This is where his past experience of dealing with intelligence matters was important. Some of these people had already gone over to the other side and were transmitting information and, in some cases money, from the White Army funds to their Bolshevik contacts. Globachev had to stay on top of this.

The commander in chief of the White Army tried everything to strengthen the army through discipline and training. He also saw the need for intelligence information. Wrangel came to the conclusion himself that confirmed Globachev's lament that experienced tsarist security and intelligence officers were cast aside. Wrangel was quite clear. "Our badly organized police and counter-intelligence systems are a great help to the Bolshevist [*sic*] agitators in their subversive work behind the lines. Each of these two systems works independently of the other; the officials are both underpaid and unsuitable."[9]

On May 3, 1920, Wrangel appointed Globachev, very unexpectedly for Globachev, to become director of the police in Crimea. This would put the general on Wrangel's staff and he would be in charge of all political and criminal investigations. Globachev declined for several reasons. He saw that Crimea was lost, and many of the people in the police functions there had been within the Denikin fold. Globachev's superior, Lukomskii, contacted Wrangel and told him that he needed Globachev to stay where he was because of the importance of his position in Constantinople. The matter was closed.

On the relatively few occasions that Globachev had some time away from the job, he and his family, once they were able to join him in Constantinople, would enjoy the city and get together with friends. The Globachevs and the Nikol'skii family were close. Vladimir Pavlovich Nikol'skii was a major general, and before the Revolution he was the chief of staff of the Special Corps of Gendarmes, so he and Globachev

Figure 13.2. Globachev in uniform with Sofia and friends in Constantinople, 1921.

were well acquainted. The wives were friends, and both couples had a son and daughter who were about the same age. Lydia Globacheva and Xenia Nikol'skaia were fast friends as were Nicholas Globachev and Nicholas Nikol'skii. The Globachevs had also made friends with Turkish officials and officers, some British officials, and the Globachev children with Turkish youths and cadets. Life for Globachev's family was actually relatively pleasant in Constantinople, but pleasant meant that Globachev was employed and that he and his family had living quarters that, although small, were livable.

But there was more serious work for Sofia and others. From their arrival in the Bosporus area in 1919, through 1920, there was a constant flow of refugees coming from Russia. "The Bosporus became a sorrowful and shocking sight for us as the Russian warships and passenger ships came one after the other and dropped anchor."[10] The Allies did not allow the Russian refugees to leave the ships until they were processed and their documents were checked. The passage from Crimea to the Bosporus was lengthy and food was a problem, namely the lack of food. Sofia told Konstantin that she would volunteer to take bread and buns to the ships to help feed the refugees as best she could. She volunteered her daughter Lydia and had

Figure 13.3. Lydia and Sofia, circa 1922.

some of her friends help. Sofia was also able to get an orderly to help. She got a motor launch and bags of bread and buns. The launch sailed from ship to ship and the volunteers either put bags of bread onto hooks that then pulled the food up or, in some instances where this was not possible, Sofia and her volunteers threw loaves of bread up to the refugees on deck who would catch them. Sofia and her friends were not the only help. There were charitable organizations, the American Red Cross, private individuals, Russians, Greeks, Turks, and others who provided foodstuffs, mostly bread products, to the Russian refugees.

Sofia and some of her lady friends were also de facto ambassadors of good will. There was Madame Catherine Veletskaia, the mother of Sofia's good friend and the Empress's lady in waiting Lili Dehn, and General Nikol'skii's wife, whom Sofia had been a friend with for years. As these women socialized with one another, they became friends also with a number of Turkish officers and their wives. In addition to having good social relations with the Turks, the latter came to know the plight of many of the refugees and were able to offer more help, as they could.

Sofia was involved in various projects to help Russian refugees as they continued to come to, or through, Constantinople. There was also

Figure 13.4. Konstantin and Sofia in Constantinople, circa 1922.

a social life that Sofia describes in her memoir, and it was one that she participated in actively. The Globachevs made new friends in Constantinople that they would keep for the rest of their lives. It is not clear whether Sofia hoped that the family might return and settle in Warsaw, a place that she loved so well. As late as October 1922 Sofia had been in correspondence with an attorney in Warsaw to find out the status of the property that she owned in Poland. The attorney had gone to the location to assess the situation, but it came to naught. The new government in Poland had annexed the property and distributed it.

The three years that the family spent in Constantinople was a reprieve from the anxieties that Sofia had especially felt that the general's position in the Corps of Gendarmes and the Okhrana in Russia might lead to his assassination, as it did to some of his predecessors. The general was pleased to be doing the kind of work that he had been trained for and where he had absolute faith in his superior, General Lukomskii, a far cry from the prerevolution leadership in Petrograd. The Globachev children, Lydia and Nicholas, who were nineteen and seventeen years old, respectively, in 1920, recalled their years in Constantinople as a great adventure. They had some good Russian émigré friends such as Xenia and Kolia Nikol'skii, the children of Major General Vladimir Nikol'skii. These young folks went places together and became friends with many of the local native population. Even in Lydia's and Nicholas's much later years in the United States they remembered that time as a lot of fun.

Globachev wrote his memoirs while living in Constantinople. It is not known exactly when he began writing his memoirs, but he did finish them in December 1922, some months before he and his family left for the United States. His original manuscript was probably handwritten and then typed, and it is only the typed document that still exists. The type is clear with occasional penned in corrections, but the paper is almost one hundred years old and, while in fairly good shape, it has acquired a sepia shade, especially along the edges of the pages.

There were several reasons for putting his pen to paper, as the introduction to his published memoir explains: "He was one of the first representatives of the political police who began to describe the events of those years, while 'the trail was still hot,' and he finished them in one year (1922) with the possibility of having them published. Evidently, he was also pushed to this by the prevailing conditions that he found himself in; those conversations and arguments among the emigrants who blamed each other for what happened in February 1917. It is possible that not the least role in this was the recent publication of A.A. Blok's 'The Last Days of the Old Regime,' that was reprinted by G.V. Gessen in an edition of 'The Archive of the Russian Revolution.' Blok had participated in the work of the Extraordinary Investigative Commission of the Provisional Government, and investigated the activities of former ministers and other responsible persons; thus Blok had access to archival documents of the last days of the Russian Empire and he attended the interrogation of ministers and heads of the political police. In his book, Blok repeatedly cites Globachev's reports to the Minister of the Interior and the Department of Police, in which Globachev reports on the mood in the capital and the necessity to take firm action against the growing revolutionary movement."[11]

Globachev was certainly quite busy in Constantinople, but he made time to write his memoirs, and in putting them together he had time to recollect and reflect on all that happened and what he had experienced. His recollection of people, the sequence of events, and the economic, political, and social conditions are all interesting in themselves as he presents them, but his reflections on the whys and wherefores of what happened allows us to understand his position on the truth of the Russian Revolution.

Globachev's memoirs were written in two major sections. The first one consists of ten chapters that dealt with the period of his tenure as chief of the Petrograd Okhrana, from his appointment in January 1915 to the Revolution in late February 1917. He completed this section of his memoirs in January 1922. The second section of his memoirs consists of eleven chapters that span the time from his arrest in March 1917, through his incarceration, his release in October 1917, his flight south, the various jobs he had between 1918 and 1920, and his evacuation and life in Constantinople. He completed this section of his memoirs in December 1922. This second section, especially the part dealing with the evacuation from Russia and the government in exile in Constantinople, was written almost as events there were occurring. It was written almost in "real time."

His recollections include the various highly placed officials under whom he worked during the last two years of the Russian monarchy, and his evaluation of their qualifications, competence, and character, and how some of them contributed to the problem. He deals with the February Revolution, his arrest and incarceration under the Provisional Government, and how that government was simply unable to put things in order. His life and flight after the Bolsheviks took power presents a truly incredible story of escape and survival, and finally the last years during which he was still wearing a Russian uniform end in Constantinople. But just as important is his assessment of why and how it all came about. He writes, "Over a two year period I was witness to the preparation of the riots against the sovereign power, unstoppable by anyone, bringing Russia to unprecedented shock and destruction."[12]

Globachev's position is that the responsibility for the development of turmoil in the capital that led to the revolution rests on the intelligentsia. He was not the only one who had this view of the fundamental cause of the downfall of the Tsar and government.[13] The term "intelligentsia" as used by Globachev and others at that time did not refer to just educated and cultured people. It had the political connotation of people who were certainly educated, but who were political activists also. This political activism took the form of harsh criticism of the government that sometimes bordered on calls for resistance and revolution.

Globachev's criticism centers on two individuals especially: Alexander Kerensky and Alexander Guchkov. The former was an attorney by training and a member of the Socialist Revolutionary Party. He was a representative member of the State Duma. Guchkov was a well-to-do businessman, also a member of the Progressive Bloc in the Duma. Both men were highly critical of the government and were vocal about this in the Duma and in public. Globachev's narrative about Guchkov is the more critical. He faults Guchkov with having created a committee, the Central War Industry Committee, which was supposed to help with getting supplies and military equipment to the front, but which Globachev claims was a cover for Guchkov and others in his party to incite an antigovernment mood within the population. According to Globachev, by 1916 Guchkov began to plan for a palace coup to remove the Tsar.

Thus, the general's overall assessment of the February Revolution was a combination of ineffective leaders in Petrograd and a State Duma that was destructive in its members' motivations and actions. As for the Bolshevik Revolution eight months later, Globachev attributes its success partly to the poor organization of the Provisional Government, and he gives grudging credit to the Bolsheviks for being more organized and having a greater sense of purpose.

Globachev was a modest man by nature, and a hard worker who took his job seriously. He was not a self-promoter as were some of his colleagues. Globachev preferred not to indulge in discussions and debates about what went wrong and who was to blame. Verbal personal attacks were not part of his persona, nor did he like to hear such things from others. He had lived through the events leading up to the Revolution, he had lived through it, and he had lived through the Civil War. As a highly placed official, he had firsthand knowledge of all that had happened, so he decided to put his knowledge of past events on paper, and that was that. The general's only other writing about the Revolution would be a lengthy letter to the *New York Times* several years later. The reader will see it.

CHAPTER 14

Farewell to Constantinople

Not only had the White Army lost the Civil War, but the days were also numbered for the government in exile in Constantinople. Even looking back when the fighting was still going on between the Reds and the Whites in 1920, three of the Baltic countries that had been part of the Russian Empire but were now independent had given diplomatic recognition to the Soviet Union. Over the next few years, while the Allied forces were giving aid to the White refugees, there were already negotiations between the Allied countries and the Soviet Union.

The commander in chief of the White Army in exile was General Baron Peter Nikolaevich Wrangel. His headquarters and living accommodations were on the yacht *Lukul*, which was anchored off the coast of Constantinople. On October 15, 1921 an Italian passenger ship, the *Adria*, sailing from the Soviet port of Batumi in Georgia, had headed for the Bosporus. Within proximity of the *Lukul* the *Adria* suddenly changed course and rammed the *Lukul* amidships. Several Russian sailors were killed. The *Adria* backed out and left the scene, offering no rescue support to the *Lukul*'s personnel. Wrangel and his family and staff were ashore at the time. The *Lukul* sank with a large amount of the White Army's funds.[1] Many Russians considered this event not as an accident but as an assassination attempt by the Soviets.

Wrangel moved into the Russian Embassy, but shortly thereafter, in 1922, he moved to Serbia where King Alexander was generally welcoming to the Russians. Bulgaria was also willing to offer support. Wrangel was able to operate with a greater sense of security and support from Serbia, and he continued to be the leader, organizing support for the White refugees and keeping the army together. He left General Lukomskii, in whom he had great faith, and others in charge in Constantinople.

Turkey recognized the Soviet Union as the legitimate government of Russia in July 1923. Official recognition of the White Army in exile withered. It was the end.

In July 1923 Globachev's position with the Russian Embassy in Constantinople was abolished, as were many other positions at the embassy. "In 1922 and 1923, 1,771 Russians went from Constantinople to France; 2,011 went from Constantinople to the United States."[2] Between the time that Globachev finished writing his memoirs and the middle of 1923, he did have to spend some time, in addition to his job at the embassy, in acquiring visas for himself and for his family. He knew that the Russian government in exile was coming to an end. Globachev's position at the Russian Embassy allowed him to become acquainted with senior staff members of the embassies of various European countries. This helped him and his family to consider several countries to which they might immigrate. They were able to get visas to Bulgaria, Serbia, France, the United States, and Spain. With Spanish visas they could have also gone to the Balearic Islands or to the Canary Islands. They could even go to Bizerte where there were many Russian refugees already. They decided to go to the United States, basing their decision on the belief that they could survive the best in the States. Globachev and his family left Constantinople in 1923 on the British ship *Constantinople*, arriving at Ellis Island on August 1, 1923.

The general was fifty-three years old, Sofia was forty-eight, and Lydia was twenty-two. Their son Nicholas had left sometime earlier to study voice in Italy. He had an operatic quality bass-baritone voice. He was twenty years old. He joined them later in 1923 in New York, where he continued his lessons and performed in several concerts. For the next several years Sofia, Konstantin, and their children rented rooms in a boarding house on St. Nicholas Avenue on the Upper West Side in Manhattan. They did this because they were somewhere between certain and hopeful that communism would be overthrown in Russia and that they would be returning home. For this reason Konstantin did not seek to make a career in the United States. As a matter of fact, he had several temporary jobs, even one mowing lawns in a cemetery. He enjoyed this because it was peaceful and quiet. He and Sofia even kept a suitcase filled with tsarist paper money and stock certificates under their bed. As time went on it became clear that things would not change in

Russia and that they would never return. Sofia and Konstantin became United States citizens in August 1929.

The Globachevs had many friends in New York, almost all of them Russian émigrés just like them. But in all this time, from 1923 through 1929, the general kept in contact with former tsarist officers and officials, many of whom were in Paris. He also kept abreast of news of Russia in the American press, and in the two Russian language newspapers in New York. *Rossia* was conservative, whereas *Novoe Russkoe Slovo* was left of center. The latter newspaper had a much bigger circulation than *Rossia* and a bigger staff. Globachev did not like the editorial articles in *Novoye Slovo*, as most people called it, but it did provide more news than *Rossia*.

In October 1924 a three-article series was printed in the *New York Times*. The author was none other than Michael Stepanovich Komissarov. The articles dealt with his claims of having had close ties with the imperial family and some of the confidantes of the family, such as Anna Vyrubova. It is not clear how his contact with the *New York Times* came about, but it seems to have been with help from Herman Bernstein, who was a journalist, poet, and author, with some diplomatic experience. He was a scholar and expert on Russia. He also had occasional journalistic ties with the *New York Times*.

Komissarov produced three articles. The first was titled:

"NEW LIGHT CAST ON KITCHENER MYSTERY

Former Head of Russian Secret Police
Tells of How Tipsy Czar Let Slip News of
British General's Voyage—Bragging Palace Officer
Told Friend, Who Gave Facts to German Spy."
Sunday, October 12, 1924

The second article was:

"RASPUTIN AS REVEALED BY HIS SHADOW

Russian Secret Police Chief Tells Intimate Story
of the Peasant Who Gained a Sinister Influence Over
the Czarina—How His Murder Was Planned."
Sunday, October 19, 1924

The third article was:

"ROYAL WOMEN FOUGHT OVER RUSSIAN PEACE

Czar's Police Chief Tells How Dowager Empress Halted Czarina's Deal With Germany." Sunday, October 26, 1924

The historical data are voluminous and clear. Komissarov's articles were fraudulent. Komissarov certainly wrote the articles, but they were replete with absolute lies. The publication of these articles can be criticized as not worthy of accurate journalism; however, there are other ways of viewing how this could have happened. Almost all, but not absolutely all, of the individuals who knew Komissarov in any official capacities were dead. The two ministers that he was associated with, Khvostov and Beletskii, had been executed by the Bolsheviks. So had others who might have interacted with him when he was head of a Gendarme Administration in Perm, such as Maklakov and Vissarionov, and the royal family was dead. So, who was there to corroborate or refute his statements? Herman Bernstein accepted Komissarov as a major source of information, however. "The General knew the Czar [*sic*] and the imperial family intimately and was charged with the responsibility of guarding them and the various distinguished foreign personages who visited Russia," Bernstein wrote in his introduction to the articles.[3] It is peculiar that Bernstein's assessment is not more accurate. Komissarov never had any contact with the imperial family. Indeed, the security of the palace was the responsibility of General Spiridovich. Bernstein's role in publishing these articles is perplexing, as is the newspaper's.

Globachev was not going to allow Komissarov's fraudulence to pass. The general responded to what Komissarov had written with five typed pages addressed to the *New York Times*. Here, then, in his own words, is Globachev's letter to the editor, which was published in the *New York Times* on Sunday, December 14, 1924.

In the New York Times of Oct. 12, 19 and 26 there were published articles by General Komissarov, in which he told various libelous stories about the Russian imperial family. The aim of said article was to discredit the Imperial regime. He equally asserted that the death of Lord Kitchener was due to the indiscretion of the late Emperor Nicholas II, who had divulged the information regarding

Lord Kitchener's proposed journey to Russia to General Voeykoff, the Palace steward. I feel it is my duty to state that all of what General Komissarov has written is utterly untrue.

First of all, General Komissarov has never held the office of Chief of the Petrograd Secret Police (alias the Department of Public Peace and Order, the so-called Okhranka).

Beginning from February 1, 1915, up to March 13, 1917, I was Chief of said police.

As regards General Komissarov, he was not living nor holding any office in Petrograd from the year 1907 up to October, 1915, for he was at that time holding the office of Chief of the Gendarmerie in Perm on the Ural. Later, in January, 1916 he was actually appointed Governor of the City of Rostov on the Don, and held no office whatsoever in Petrograd. Six months later Komissarov had been dismissed from the Russian Government service by a ukase [decree] of the Emperor for indulging in liquors and participating in public scandals. He was deprived of the right to wear the uniform and was allowed no pension.

On the other hand, contrary to General Komissarov's utterance, I maintain that no orders were ever given directly by the Emperor either to the Chief of the Secret Police or to any general or officer connected with the secret police. Under the Russian laws such orders could be given only to the Secretary of the Interior, who in turn was authorized to institute investigation, which were carried out by the Chief of the Petrograd Secret Police. Equally, the latter had no right to report directly to the Emperor the results of his investigation, but he had to report to the Secretary of the Interior, who submitted same to the Emperor.

I can state with confidence that in the particular case of Lord Kitchener's death there has been made no investigation whatsoever, as this case has been generally ascribed to nothing but a fatal accident of war.

I can also assert that the late Emperor Nicholas II had never indulged in liquors, so that neither Rasputin nor anyone else had any reason to prevent him of so doing. He was positively incapable of divulging any secret, for he was of a distrustful and secretive nature.

General Komissarov took no part in the search for Rasputin's body. Having held no office at that time he obviously could not have any agents. The search for Rasputin's (body) was made by me, together with the Chief of the Detective Service, Mr. Kirpichnikoff, and it was found by a member of the staff of the river police.

Contrary to his statement, Komissarov could not have ever given orders to the commander of Petrograd, General Dratchevsky, for Komissarov never held an office in Petrograd at the time when General Dratchevsky was commander of said city.

All and any information regarding the intrigues of the court: the hostility between the Dowager Empress and the Empress Alexandra Feodorovna (Czarina); the proposed wedding of the Grand Duke Mikhail Alexandrovich; the attempt on the life of Czarevitch Alexis; the alleged endeavors of the Czarina Alexandra Feodorovna to conclude a separate peace treaty with Germany; the order given by her to Mr. Protopopoff to get, to that end, in touch with German agents in Sweden; the admittance to the Empress of German spies under the pretext of war nurses; the Secret Council held by the Emperor before taking personal command of the Russian armies, etc. . . . all this gossip was never reported, nor could it be to Komissarov in his official capacity. It should be remembered that Komissarov was never Chief of the Petrograd Secret Police and that he was, in wartime, only for three months attached to the Secretary of the Interior's staff (from October, 1915, up to January, 1916).

All the stories that General Komissarov told were unmistakably proved false by a most careful investigation which was conducted after the revolution by order of the Provisional Government of Russia by District Attorney Roudneff.

Said investigation, the impartiality of which has never been questioned, has beyond doubt established the fact that neither the late Emperor Nicholas II, nor the Empress Alexandra Feodorovna (Czarina) ever dreamed of a separate peace treaty with Germany, nor did anything to this effect. Even upon his abdication, the Emperor Nicholas II issued his last order to the Russian armies, urging them to fight the Germans to a final victory.

[The following paragraphs were part of Globachev's letter to the Times, *but were not printed by the* Times*].*

How far General Komissarov's statements can be relied upon will be seen from the following:

At the time of the Provisional Government of Russia General Komissarov was incarcerated. He was placed in the same prison where some of the Bolshevik leaders were also detained. Komissarov entered into friendly relations with some of them and, as a matter of fact, the Bolsheviks after their release from prison requested the Secretary of the Interior, a socialist by the name Maliantovich, to parole Gen. Komissarov. On the very day of his subsequent release from prison, the Bolsheviks took him away in their automobile.

At the time when General Wrangell (sic) was commanding the Russian White Forces, Gen. Komissarov proceeded to Germany, having no official capacity. In Germany, styling himself as Representative of General Wrangell he deceived the Bavarian Monarchists by telling them that General Wrangell seeks to establish a joint front with the Germans with the aim of restoring the monarchist regime both in Germany and in Russia. He extorted from them under false pretense about 100,000 German marks and left, accompanied by the Bavarians, ostensibly for the Crimea. However, instead of that he remained in Budapest under the pretext of a new order, received from General Wrangell. The Bavarian Monarchists, having arrived in Sevastopol, were not received by General Wrangell, since the latter naturally had given Komissarov no authority whatsoever.

At the time when I was holding office of the Chief of the Russian Passport Division in Constantinople, both the Allied Intelligences and I had been informed that the arrests of the Russian generals and officers, belonging to the White Army, by the Bulgarian Government of Stamboulinsky, had been made upon the advice and at the instigation of General Komissarov, who was acting in the interests of the Soviets. This took place in 1922.

I also wish to call the attention of your readers that the Russian "Right Cause" Weekly, published in New York by the Association on "Unity in Russia" in its issue No. 88 of the 5th of April 1924 publicly announced that General Komissarov, who then recently arrived in the United States, was a famous provocateur and should be avoided by all the Russian immigrants.

This statement has never been refuted by Komissarov.

I am strictly inclined to think that the libelous statements of General Komissarov against his late Sovereign must be attributed

> *to his present close relations to the Soviets, whose agents are of course, in duty bound to conduct venomous propaganda against the Imperial Government of Russia, which has always been the sincere friend of the United States of America.*

There is no evidence that Komissarov ever refuted, or tried to refute, the information in General Globachev's letter to the *Times*.

In the ensuing years, Globachev continued to be employed in various jobs, but he stayed in touch with several of his former colleagues, and with the activities of a Russian organization in Paris, the Russian All-Military Union. These contacts would lead to one more adventure for the general.

CHAPTER 15

The General's Last Assignment

After the February and October Revolutions of 1917, and the Civil War between the Reds and Whites of 1918–21, those who were part of, or loyal to, the old regime, and who lived to flee, evacuated Russia as political refugees and scattered all over the world, often forming Russian enclaves, or "colonies," as some of these Russians referred to their communities. Paris was one such place with a large community of Russians where they not only had their own stores, restaurants, nightclubs, and churches but also their political organizations. One such organization was the Russian All-Military Union (Russkii Obshche-Voenskii Soiuz), often referred to by its initials, ROVS. It was established by General Wrangel in 1924 in Serbia. Several years later the organization moved to France with Paris as its headquarters. When General Wrangel died in 1928, the rumors spread within the Russian émigré world that Soviet agents had poisoned him. Such a possibility has to be considered, because ROVS was active not only in anti-Soviet propaganda, but in various other counterrevolutionary efforts in the hopes of bringing down the Soviet regime. ROVS had a sizeable membership. Various sources number the total membership of ROVS (including members of the organization living in other countries) as anywhere from 40,000 to 100,000 in the late 1920s to the early 1930s.[1] There were probably several thousand members in Paris alone and most, if not all, were former tsarist officers. Many of these officers were of high rank and still had some connections in Soviet Russia, former colleagues, friends, and relatives, and all these could be sources of information useful to ROVS and supportive of the organization's activities. Consequently, ROVS was a threat to the Soviet government.

It should also be noted that not every Russian in Paris was a former tsarist officer or official. There was a sizeable enough number of people who had to emigrate from Russia after the Revolution and Civil War who had been in the active opposition to the tsarist government and had to leave because of their vulnerability to being executed by the Bolsheviks. So, in the mid to late 1920s and into the 1930s these included Kerensky, Pavel Miliukov, Georgii Lvov, Pavel Pereverzev, and the two warlords during the Civil War, Nestor Makhno and Petliura. And there were Soviet agents in France.

With Wrangel's passing a new leader was selected. It was the ex-tsarist cavalry commander, General Alexander Pavlovich Kutepov. On January 26, 1930, he disappeared in Paris. It was generally concluded that he had been abducted and done away with by Soviet agents. His replacement was another tsarist officer, Lieutenant General Evgenii Karlovich Miller. He had held various staff positions in the Tsar's army during World War I and was the commander of the northern White Army headquartered in Archangelsk during the Civil War.

In an attempt to thwart the infiltration of Soviet agents and others who might harm it, the ROVS organization decided that a unit had to be set up to deal specifically with intelligence and security issues. As chief of the Secret Political Section, Miller chose General Abram Mikhailovich Dragomirov, who was a member of Miller's "inner circle." Dragomirov's entire military experience had been primarily as a senior cavalry line officer, and he had only a very limited background and experience in the area of security and intelligence when he was put in charge of establishing intelligence and counterintelligence operations in Denikin's White Army.[2]

Several senior members of ROVS knew Globachev from previous years and especially from his time in Constantinople where he had been in charge of "passport control"—meaning intelligence—and, over the past few years, Globachev and various ROVS leaders had been in correspondence. This communication was often ROVS seeking Globachev's advice on various intelligence issues, but also about various people who wanted to join ROVS.

In 1930 Dragomirov had been in touch with Globachev, and with General Miller's concurrence he contacted Globachev and offered Globachev the job as his assistant, which really meant that Globachev would be in charge of the section that was responsible for the collection of intelligence information and reporting it to the ROVS leadership. This, of course, involved Globachev establishing contact with, and using, informants, keeping track of individuals who wanted to join ROVS, and maintaining a working relationship with the Paris police.

Globachev's daughter later speculated on why her father was selected for this work, since there were other former gendarme officers still around who were quite capable and competent. In her view, Martynov was somewhat of an intriguer and had been quite outspoken about some of the tsarist leaders, especially about his animosity toward Dzhunkovskii, which was no secret. Indeed, Martynov himself admitted to having had past personal difficulties. During the Civil War, Martynov had applied for a position with the White Movement, was not accepted, and was told, "Your very name is odious."[3] Spiridovich was very capable, too, but he tended to have an abrasive personality, and there were still people who were troubled by his possible involvement in the assassination of Russia's prime minister, Peter Stolypin, in 1911. Indeed, even during the tsarist regime, Minister of the Interior Maklakov referred to Spiridovich as Stolypin's murderer.[4] There was Colonel Pavel Zavarzin, who had been the chief of the Warsaw Okhrana, and later of the Moscow Okhrana. Of Zavarzin, Globachev's daughter only knew that he was a pleasant, gregarious man, and a great storyteller.

On August 18, 1930, Dragomirov sent Globachev a formal job offer letter. Based on the wording in the letter, they had been exploring Globachev joining ROVS. The letter is interesting in the way that Dragomirov words the offer in patriotic terms, but also how he describes Paris of 1930. His letter follows:

18 August 1930

b, Rue de Renard
Paris, 4 me

Most Respected Konstantin Ivanovich

Before anything else, allow me to offer my sincerest thanks for your willingness to join General Miller and me and to share the burden of the task that fate has assigned to us. I believe deeply that your rich experience will allow you to do everything in your power to bring success to our cause.

To show that we are doing everything that we can to help you to come to Paris, enclosed is a check made out to you for

$350. This sum should cover two tickets, second class to Paris and other expenses. Regrettably, because of our current funds I am not able to cover the cost of moving your entire family that consists of five people, as you had written. It may be possible that you could find a less expensive way to travel, for example "Tourist Cabin," or as a last resort to travel third class, in which case you could cover three travelers.

Regarding your work in Paris, you will receive 2,000 francs per month, on which sum two people can live, but they would have to watch each centime. Your budgetary wellness will be improved if members of your family can get jobs. In the final analysis, most of our compatriots were able to find reasonable jobs, and many especially those who knew English actually got good salaries of 2,500–3,000 francs, and some got even more, but they often had to start at lower wages.

Getting apartments is a tough issue, and getting one in Paris it is by chance that one can find an acceptable apartment. But still, the problem is considerably lightened in the suburbs that are near to the belt of the old fortifications, and with the abundance of the transit lines, connection with the city center does not pose any problem, and sometimes one can get into the city center from the suburbs faster than from the outskirts of the city if one took the underground, trolley, or bus.

During your first several days in Paris you will need to find a hotel. It is best to stay on the Right Bank in the area of the large boulevards (Madeline, des Italiens, Haussmann, Montmartre, etc.), from where you can [find] convenient transportation to any part of the city. There are small side streets in this area that have many small hotels where you can get very acceptable rooms with two and sometimes three beds for 25 francs (without meals). Also, if a boarding house is not full, one can be tight-fisted and get accommodations for 10–12 francs per person.

This is only for the first 2–3 days while you are looking for a less expensive place, or where you want to settle in.

If you do not have any acquaintances in Paris who could help you to find a place in a hotel on your arrival, then I am fully prepared to offer you my help, even though I myself fumble about Paris, and even up to now I find it hard to endure this bustling and nerve-racking city life.

Please do let me know that you received the check and what your thoughts are about when you will probably arrive.

I sincerely wish you a successful relocation and in finding acceptable living accommodations.

With great respect,

Dragomirov[5]

So, in the latter part of 1930, Globachev and Sofia sailed to France. Their son Nicholas and their daughter Lydia, who had recently married George Marinich, a former officer in the 9th Kazan Dragoon Regiment during World War I, had to pay their own way. They sailed just a little later.

They were now in Paris and Globachev began his work as deputy director of intelligence for ROVS, and his work was really cut out for him This paramilitary organization of tsarist officers functioned to help White Russian émigrés in general, and to gather intelligence on other Russian émigrés who may have been in the employ of the Soviets and whose purpose was to infiltrate and disrupt ROVS. There were also "fakers" who wanted to join ROVS. These were individuals who claimed to have been of noble birth, in more senior positions in tsarist times than they really were, or who claimed unproven heroic deeds during the war. After all, there were few to no documents to disprove such claims. Globachev had encountered such situations when he worked in Constantinople; so, over the several years that Globachev had maintained contact with former colleagues and émigré organizations, and with ROVS personnel, he was quite familiar with ROVS and with the kind of tasks he would have to take on.

As for the other gendarme officers already mentioned, Martynov had immigrated to the United States in 1923 and was living in New York in the 1930s. For several years he held jobs managing security in banks and corporations. Following his wife's death in 1948 he moved to Los Angeles and died there of natural causes in 1951. Komissarov spent some years as a secret agent of the Soviet Union. He was uncovered in Paris and left for the United States where he allegedly continued to be a Soviet agent. He settled in Chicago and was killed in a trolley car accident in 1933. Spiridovich was living in Paris in the 1930s, writing, lecturing, and participating in various Russian groups. There is no information that he was associated with ROVS. He subsequently immigrated to the United States and lived in New York, where he died in 1952. Little is known of Colonel Paul Zavarzin who had been an Okhrana chief in Warsaw and Moscow. He had immigrated to Paris where he died in 1932.

It is estimated that the Russian population in France in the early 1930s "probably did not much exceed 120,000" and "the capital and its surrounding districts certainly harboured more one-time subjects of Nicholas II than did any other region in France."[6] Further, some data show that in 1930, there were over forty-three thousand Russians living in the twenty Parisian arrondissements with an additional ninety-five hundred in the suburbs. Globachev's job would be to keep track of all, or as many as possible, of these Russians. Once in Paris, Globachev threw himself into his work.

Life in Paris was not at all bad for Globachev and his family. The family's move to Paris in 1930 allowed it to escape the Great Depression that had hit the United States in October 1929. Globachev was now employed by ROVS, and his son-in-law was able to get work there also as a maintenance worker in the building that ROVS occupied, and as an occasional chauffer for ROVS personnel. The family was able to get a decent apartment at 8 rue du Commandant Leandri in the XVth Arrondisement. They even purchased two Whippet puppies, and named them Volga and Ural. Evenings were often spent at restaurants with acquaintances, and the weekends were spent sightseeing in Paris, visiting friends who lived in the suburbs, and going to the horse races.

There were also the Sunday services at the Cathedral of St. Alexander Nevskii on the Rue Daru. The Orthodox church had a fairly sizable congregation, just about all Russian, and almost all of them refugees from the Revolution and Civil War—former officers, government officials, and other members of the former "establishment." Many of the parishioners found meaning in their faith, but for many the church was a place to meet former comrades and acquaintances and have some sense of a common past. The end of the service, which was in the traditional Church Slavonic, was followed by tea, pirozhki, and other familiar and favorite foods at the several Russian restaurants in the neighborhood of the church. Conversations often focused on current events, especially those happening in Russia, reflections on days gone by, who was to blame for what, and what some of the émigrés were doing these days.

As in other parts of Europe and elsewhere this was a familiar scene. These Russian émigrés were not people who had willingly left

Figure 15.1. St. Alexander Nevsky Cathedral in Paris.

their homeland to seek a new life of promise in a better place. They had been forced to flee. Had the Revolution not happened, they would still be enjoying a good life in Russia. Now they were here, and many of them longed for what was in their past. So, they clung to their past by staying Russian. Some of them got along more easily because they were fluent in French. However, there were those who spoke broken French and never had to improve their linguistic ability because all their friends and acquaintances outside of whatever work they had were Russian.

While the Globachevs were far from the United States, some of what was going on back in the United States resonated especially for Globachev. Franklin Roosevelt's election in November 1932 did not sit well with the general. He thought that FDR was liberal to the point of being a socialist and, worse still, a year later, in November 1933, the United States gave formal diplomatic recognition to the Soviet Union. This certainly troubled him, but his work went on.

As Globachev had experienced throughout his career, intelligence work was challenging, and now he had a new challenge. There was no established system of procedures, protocols, or record keeping at ROVS, because this was a brand new function that ROVS created. An office assistant position was created who would work under Globachev. An important part of the general's job was to establish contact with people and develop relationships with them as sources of information and to collaborate with ROVS. It was also important to establish a mechanism of who should get intelligence reports in terms of who had the need to know.

While Globachev initiated intelligence and surveillance operations against Soviet agents, operatives of OGPU (the acronym for the Soviet secret police from 1922 to 1934), and suspicious "white Russians," there were other problems that affected ROVS operations. One was that ROVS was running out of money, and another was personality conflicts among the ROVS leadership. There were ex-tsarist officers who held grudges against one another over some disagreement or slight during World War I or during the Civil War following the Revolution. This did not make things easy for Globachev, even though he was not involved in such squabbles.

Among the top echelon of leaders in ROVS were Miller, Dragomirov, General Fedor Fedorovich Abramov, General Pavel Alexeevich Kusonskii, Major-General Nikolai Vladimirovich Skoblin, and General Pavel Nikolaevich Shatilov.

Detailed information about ROVS can be found in Shatilov's memoirs, which are in the Bakhmeteff Archives of Columbia University. Shatilov had been a cavalry commander in the tsar's army, and was Wrangel's chief of staff during the Civil War. His reputation as Wrangel's immediate subordinate was one of a capable officer, but prone to get involved in intrigues. He had antagonized some White general officers and now they were senior members of ROVS. From Shatilov we learn that beginning in the summer of 1930, Miller began to have weekly meetings with his senior staff. Shatilov states that from the outset "all these people . . . immediately demonstrated ill will toward me."[7] This was not entirely just Shatilov's perception. His relationship with Dragomirov was not good. Miller noticed that there seemed to be animosity between the two, and when he asked Shatilov about it, the latter did not know why Dragomirov harbored ill will toward him. Miller then confronted Dragomirov, who admitted to the problem and said that it went back to the Civil War, during which time Shatilov was responsible for keeping Dragomirov from getting an official position in Wrangel's government. Shatilov's antagonism apparently did not extend to Globachev, even though Globachev had been hired by Dragomirov.

Much of Globachev's intelligence work involved keeping track of those Russian émigrés who either showed some suspicious side or wanted to join ROVS. In either case, ROVS needed to be watchful for Soviet operatives infiltrating the organization. A number of émigrés, wanting to join ROVS, claimed past positions in the tsarist government or military and, since most records were either lost or still in Soviet Russia and therefore not available to ROVS, verifying the loyalty and reliability of many émigré applicants was a difficult chore. There were also the émigrés who were trying to locate a relative or friend with whom they had lost contact as a result of the Revolution and Civil War.

In 1932, a Russian émigré, Pavel Timofeevich Gorgulov, shook the world. He had arrived in Paris and had become known as someone who was preaching anticommunist rhetoric and a return of Russia to its glorious past. He did not seem to draw much attention, and when holding meetings he did not draw much of a crowd. It seemed that his presence in Paris was that of an eccentric, so that Globachev "did not seem concerned and failed to warn the French police. A short while later Gorgulov assassinated the French President Paul Doumer."[8]

A recent historian writing about the White Russian Army in exile clearly sees Globachev as failing to recognize Gorgulov as dangerous, and, thus, not thwarting this major catastrophe.[9] Shatilov's view of this is different. Shatilov states that it is hard to blame Globachev since he never had any corroborating information about Gorgulov, and often when there was corroborating information from informants, it was unreliable. Shatilov also pointed out that Globachev's operation consisted of just him and one office-staff worker. There was also the issue of the relationship between ROVS and the French prefecture in terms of cooperation in general and information sharing. Part of it may have been a personality problem. The head of the prefecture had confided in Shatilov that Dragomirov's relationship with the prefecture was not what it should be, and that the prefecture preferred that its point of contact be Shatilov. Globachev agreed with this.[10]

As early as 1932, Globachev had been given information by an agent, who had gotten it from an OGPU informer, that a certain general who was very close to Miller was in the pay of the Bolsheviks. The informer had not named the general, but said that if he mentioned the name of the general, everyone would be thoroughly shocked. Globachev told Miller what he had learned and Miller became very upset and replied to the effect that he refused to believe such a thing about one of his colleagues, especially if it was one in Miller's inner circle of trusted subordinates. Thus, Globachev was unable to get Miller's support in attempting to locate the traitor.

In 1933 Abramov recommended that Globachev's operation should be discontinued and intelligence work should be transferred to other personnel. Miller disagreed and stated that transferring Globachev's duties to another, who did not have Globachev's experience, was not the best decision.

By 1934, however, the financial condition of ROVS forced the organization to reduce its expenses and, therefore, its staff. By the early summer of 1934, the Secret Political Section was disbanded. General Dragomirov, who was its head, left for Yugoslavia and Globachev was given notice. During their last meeting Globachev asked Miller how the work of security and intelligence gathering would continue. Miller answered that he would be taking on those functions himself.[11] Thus, pursuing the lead of the probability of a traitor in Miller's inner circle came to an end.

CHAPTER 16

Toward the End

The entire Globachev family returned to the United States in mid-1934 on a popular French passenger ship, the *Ile de France*. Globachev would have to start anew in seeking employment back in the United States. He was able to use other skills that he possessed. As mentioned, even in his youth Globachev was quite an accomplished self-taught artist. During his years of service in the Tsar's government, he devoted the few leisure moments he had to oil painting. He particularly enjoyed painting landscapes and portraits. So, it was a fortunate happenstance that he was able to get a job as a commercial artist upon his return to the United States in mid-1934.

Sergei Sergeevich Krushinskii, a former tsarist officer himself, was the owner and operator of a small company that produced batik art on scarves and clothes. Krushinskii, as other Russians who became somewhat successful in this new land, gave employment preferences to his compatriots. There were other companies, especially in the New York area, where Russian émigrés could find work. Prince Matchabelli Perfumery was owned by the prince, who was Georgian. He was sympathetic and supportive of the refugees. The Lion Match Company had been started by Professor Boris Bakhmeteff. Russians were welcome there. And Charles Scribner's Sons, a publishing house, had Prince Igor Kropotkin as a senior manager. Lydia found work at Matchabelli's perfumery and her brother Nicholas at Scribner's.

By 1934 the Globachev family had already increased. Their daughter Lydia had given birth to her first son, Oleg, in Paris just several months before their return to the United States. With the increased family size the choice of living in a boarding house and simply occupying rooms, as they had in the mid and late 1920s, was no longer practical, and it was quite clear that they would not be returning to their homeland.

At this time there were probably over six thousand Russian émigrés in New York City.[1] The Globachevs rented an apartment on the Upper West Side of Manhattan in New York City. This section of the city was a Russian enclave. Not only were there a number of Russian families living within a twenty-block area, but there were also two Russian delicatessens that carried a full range of foods that Russians bought for *zakuski* (appetizers). As Russian Orthodox Easter approached, these stores also made sure that *kulich* and *paskha* were available (although many Russians preferred to make their own rather than to buy the premade ones). There was also a Russian pharmacist and an eastern European butcher who spoke Russian. There were a number of Russian émigré physicians, and many of the émigrés used their services. The neighborhood Russian Orthodox Church of the Holy Father was hardly a church in the usual sense. It was a large room in the unfinished basement of an apartment building. The iconostasis could not reach the ceiling, since the building's water and heating pipes were in the way. The congregation was small, but faithfully attended services, and the priest was Alexander Krassnaumov, a former tsarist officer. There was another Russian church, but just a little farther away, on 121st Street and Madison Avenue. There the priest's last name was Kurdumov. He was also a former tsarist officer.

A local public library, on 145th Street, between Broadway and Amsterdam Avenue, had a decent Russian collection and on Saturday mornings there were lessons offered to the preteen and teenage first-generation Russian Americans in how to read and write in Russian. There was also religious instruction. The instructors were mostly Russian tsarist émigrés. There were still the two Russian newspapers, *Novoye Russkoye Slovo* (New Russian Word), still thought by Globachev to be a little too left wing, and the more right-wing *Rossia* (Russia), whose publisher and editor was a member of the Kropotkin Russian nobility. Both newspapers were read in the Globachev family.

The little Russian colony in and around New York consisted mostly of ex-officers, tsarist government officials, and some individuals who had been successful merchants, academics, and businessmen in Russia. They all saw themselves as members of the intelligentsia. This term, "intelligentsia," had changed in its meaning. In prerevolutionary times it referred to liberal activist individuals and groups that, in general, were highly critical of the government. Now, to the émigrés it was a reference to Russian educated and cultured people, such as most of the émigrés were. Most of them indeed were well educated, came from good families, and were bilingual or even trilingual. Within the Globachev family, Konstantin spoke French, and Sofia was fluent in French, German, and Polish. Their daughter and son, Lydia and Nicholas, were fluent in French and German. Lydia's husband, George Marinich, was fluent in Ukrainian and Serbian. They were all fluent and literate in their native Russian, but with the exception of Lydia, they spoke English badly, because just as in Paris their social world was Russian. Very Russian. There were major social functions in the city for these émigrés. One of them was the annual "Russia Ball" that was sponsored by the publisher of the newspaper *Rossia.* It was usually held in some large auditorium that had a stage. There was entertainment—traditional Russian dancers and singers of Russian songs and Russian operatic arias. The food was Russian fare. There was another major function that was similar in content to the Russia Ball but had a more select population. A social group called "The Garrison" organized it. The members were all former tsarist officers and their wives and children. Many of the children, especially those of the younger tsarist officers, were born outside of Russia in a European country such as France, but the majority were born in the United States. They were first-generation Russian Americans.

Konstantin Ivanovich and his son-in-law occasionally attended the "Garrison" socials. At one such gathering a gentleman came up to Globachev. He recognized the Keksholm regimental medallion that the general always wore on his lapel, although he did not recognize Globachev right away. He introduced himself, saying that he had been a member of the Keksholm Regiment, and then asked the general if he had been in the regiment. Konstantin Ivanovich said that yes he had been in the regiment and when he gave his name, the gentleman extended his hand and bowed to his Excellency General Konstantin Ivanovich.

In addition to these formal balls that kept the Russian community together, the major Russian holiday was Orthodox Easter. Families would fast during Lent; some would live on bread, water, and vegetables, while others abstained from meat products only. Several days before the Easter service at the local Russian Orthodox churches the families would prepare to celebrate Christ's resurrection. The Globachev family made ready for the celebration, as so many other Russian families did, that would follow the midnight service at their church. The table in the dining room was laid out with Russian dishes. There were the various smoked and pickled fish, kielbasas, salad Olivier, vinaigrette, pickles, olives, and mushrooms, and these were the starters—*zakuski* in Russian. The main course would be either a ham or a leg of lamb with all the associated vegetables. Vodka and wine were on the table. There were two very traditional desserts. Both had to be prepared carefully. Konstantin was in charge of that project.

Paskha was a cheese mold, similar in taste to creamy cheesecake, but without crust. It took a few hours to mix the ingredients, but then it had to stand in the refrigerator for several days. *Kulich* was a sweet bread that had raisins and citron in it. The dough had to be kneaded carefully and then had to be baked carefully so as not to be under- or overdone. Konstantin was the one who mixed the ingredients and saw to it that it all went well.

The family would attend the midnight service at church. It was a long service that began at about 11:00 p.m. At about 11:45 a procession would march out of the church and parade around the church three times. The doors to the church were shut. At the stroke of midnight the priest leading the procession of acolytes, the choir, and many parishioners would knock on the closed doors and proclaim "Christ is Risen." The doors of the church would be opened and the procession would enter with the priest greeting everyone with "Christ is Risen." Parishioners responded with "Truly He is Risen."

Returning home from church the Globachev family would celebrate Easter, as did many other Russian families, by indulging in the feast that had been planned and waiting for them in the dining room. The celebration would go on until three or four in the morning. Such was a major part of Russian émigré culture in the United States.

Globachev enjoyed his employment as a commercial artist. There were other Russians working for Krushinskii and this made things comfortable. The general also enjoyed painting. In the evenings at home, he continued his landscape and portrait painting, except now he worked exclusively in watercolor and pastels. He liked chess and working on picture puzzles. About once a week he and his son-in-law would get together with acquaintances and play bridge. Most of the acquaintances were former tsarist officers, just as he was. Globachev was a good bridge player. He had always enjoyed smoking. His favorite brand in the States was Chesterfield, and just as he had done in Russia, he always used a cigarette holder, as did some of his bridge playing acquaintances. Sometimes the room where they played became smoke filled. He also enjoyed going to the movies, and he would try to do this at least once a week. He was content with his life in the United States.

Globachev was at peace within himself. He tended not to get into conversations with his acquaintances about how things could have been in Russia before the Revolution. He had done his best back then, and he had written his memoirs analyzing how things happened, why they happened, and how things could have been different. And he was clear on his role in trying to have had at least a part in trying to save Russia.

Everyone in the Globachev household was employed except Globachev's wife. The family decided that she should stay home and care for the household. They all pooled their money to take care of the household expenses and each took an allowance for personal expenses and entertainment, including Sofia Nikolaevna, and by the end of 1936 there were two grandsons whom she took care of and, as they grew, she taught them to read and write Russian.

Globachev continued to maintain contact with the ROVS operation in Paris, advising and consulting with General Miller and his assistant, General Kusonskii, on various matters pertaining to the organization's activities, but ROVS was a thorn in the Soviet's side, and it is possible that Globachev's continuing contact with ROVS was an irritation to the Soviets. What follows comes from Globachev's daughter Lydia, who recounted this incident: her father was working as a commercial artist, as mentioned above. During a coffee break at work in the early spring of 1935, the office boy at the studio went for coffee. As Globachev recounted his workday when he got home, this young Hispanic man was an ardent communist, who often and openly expressed his views. On this particular day he brought coffee for everyone, and passed the cups around. As soon as Globachev finished his coffee he doubled up with severe cramps and literally rolled on the floor in pain. His coworkers rushed to him and began to assist and comfort him as best they could. In the confusion and concern for the agonized general, nobody noticed the young man. He disappeared that day from work and was not seen again either at his apartment or neighborhood, nor could anyone locate him.

When Globachev was brought home his condition had worsened. The doctor who was summoned was unable to determine the cause of the illness. As a long shot the doctor administered a powerful dose of castor oil, causing violent nausea and respiratory reaction, but it saved Globachev's life. His convalescence took over two months, and during most of that time he was too weak to leave his bed. He did recover and return to work. He was sixty-five years old and his close brush with death did not diminish his vitality or his mental alertness. He continued to correspond with Paris, and it was only after the Soviet abduction of General Miller in 1937 that contact between the general and ROVS began to peter out. However, even in one of Globachev's last letters to Kusonskii, Globachev voiced his disappointment that Miller had never told Globachev that Miller had been told by an agent that Nikolai Skoblin, a general in Miller's "inner circle," was a Soviet plant in ROVS. And Skoblin's wife, Nadezhda Plevitskaia, was a Soviet agent also. Globachev speculated that had he known, perhaps Miller's abduction could have been prevented.[2]

One of the last references to Globachev's work for ROVS comes from Kussonskii. He states that "fairness requires me to say that Globachev's intelligence documents, which I still use, are without a doubt valuable, insofar as he was able to operate under his given conditions and budget."[3]

While communication with ROVS ebbed as a result of Paris becoming occupied by the Germans in 1940, Globachev maintained an interest in what was happening in Europe. He had maps that he studied and tried to keep abreast of news, as he was able to get it from various sources. When Germany invaded the Soviet Union (although Globachev referred to the invasion of "Russia"), he kept even greater track of what was going on. He and some of his acquaintances who were former tsarist officers or government officials had some similar views on Germany's invasion of Russia. There was some agreement that if Germany came into Russia as liberators rather than as conquerors, there might be a Russian uprising and the Bolsheviks (they were still called that by the émigrés) could be kicked out. Beyond that there was little talk of how things might work out if that were to occur. Globachev's dislike of Roosevelt made him doubt how the United States government would eventually respond to Germany's invasion of the Soviet Union. Sofia did not agree with Konstantin about the president. She had a mind of her own, but she also had the sense of not wanting political family squabbles. At one of the presidential elections Sofia told Lydia not to tell "Papa" that she had voted for President Roosevelt.

Early in 1941 Globachev's daughter and her husband purchased a two-room bungalow in New Jersey, about sixty miles southwest of New York City. They wanted to have a dacha, as all good Russians should have. The location was also close to a Russian community that was about six miles away from their dacha, and some of the Globachevs' dearest friends lived close by, especially the Zarrins—he was a former colonel in the tsarist Hussars—and the Basarevichs who had been a successful business family in Russia. Sofia was delighted with the dacha. Konstantin groused a bit about a needless purchase, but he soon came about and enjoyed the trips from New York. Gentleman and former officer that he was, he could never be totally informal or casual in his attire. Even when he did some minor gardening work at the dacha or played with his grandsons, he always wore a dress shirt and tie.

On December 1, 1941, just six days prior to the Japanese attack on Pearl Harbor, the general woke up at about five in the morning complaining of a severe headache. He went to the dining room and sat down at the table. He complained to his wife that he just was not feeling well. Finishing that statement, he collapsed. His son-in-law and Lydia were awakened and they carried him back into his bedroom. For a few moments they thought that he had simply fainted. Then they realized that he was gone. He was seventy-one years old. He was lying on his bed and for the next several hours Sonia sat next to her Kostia

Figure 16.1. The last portrait photo of the general, circa 1940..

and wept quietly. His funeral was held in the Russian cathedral in the Bronx, and Archbishop Vitalii conducted the service. Globachev's coffin was draped with the Russian national flag. Many of the Globachevs' friends and acquaintances attended the service. The church was full. Several friends stood at each corner of the coffin as a guard of honor. There were no hyacinths at his funeral. He was buried in the Russian Orthodox section of the Rutherford, New Jersey cemetery.

Sofia Nikolaevna outlived him by nine years. For the first year after becoming widowed Sofia wore black every day, and when she went out of doors she wore a black hat with a black veil covering her face. Konstantin's death was a severe shock to her. They had been married for forty-three years and had been true partners. They experienced the importance of their social position prior to 1917 and the hell of living through the Revolution, the escape from Petrograd, and the Civil War. They also lived through Kostia's bout of having been poisoned. Now, he had been in good health for the previous several years. In her remaining years, Sofia Nikolaevna continued to be a member of the Russian Orthodox Church, but she explored other denominations of Christianity and she formed some new personal acquaintances, especially with a woman whose last name was Tarasenko, who was an evangelical Baptist. Sofia Nikolaevna also studied Christian Science and would go to their local reading room in New York City for discussions. She was obviously looking for some kind of meaning and answers.

Within several months of Pearl Harbor, Globachev's widow got training to become an air raid warden of the local block in Manhattan. She had her armband and Civil Defense helmet. This gave her some purpose, although her primary interest and care was for her grandsons.

World War II ended in 1945. Sofia was somehow able to locate the address of Kostia's stepbrother, Leonid Axenov. He was living in Germany with his wife and daughter Ronia. Sofia maintained an active correspondence with the Axenovs and regularly sent CARE packages to them. Leonid died in March 1950. Sofia continued to correspond with Leonid's wife and daughter Ronia, as did Lydia.

Sofia had a good number of acquaintances, mostly Russian émigrés like herself, but also others. Within a block of where Sofia lived with her family there lived a German couple, the Hibers. They had left Germany because of Hitler and settled in New York. How Sofia met them is not known, but their close and cordial relationship with Sofia lasted to the end of Sofia's life.

Figure 16.2. Sofia Nikolaevna Globacheva in 1947.

The Hibers were an educated and cultured couple. They were of Sofia's generation, and they were close to fluent in English, but they were quite content to converse with Sofia in German, a language in which she was perfectly fluent. They would get together fairly often in the Hibers' apartment, and they would chat on all kinds of subjects—international politics, religion, literature, and whatever else—while they had tea.

But Sofia's closest and dearest friends were Nadejda Sergeevna Zarrin and Anna Ivanovna Basarevich. It was always a feast when the families got together. The host family would prepare a four-course meal, *zakuski*, soup, the main dish, and dessert. All the items were Russian.

After eating, Sofia and her dear friends would chat about all sorts of things. Sometimes current events, and sometimes they would talk about their youth and respective institutes that they had attended as girls. They would recount who their closest friends were during those years, and which teachers they liked, and which they did not like, and why. The conversations would sometimes also include what happened to some of these classmates in later years.

Sofia was diagnosed with uterine cancer in early September 1950. She died on November 3, 1950, at the age of seventy-five. Her funeral was at the Russian Church of the Holy Father in New York City. Father Alexander Krassnaumov presided. She is buried next to her husband in the small Russian Orthodox section of a cemetery in New Jersey. Their son Nicholas died in 1972 at the age of sixty-nine. He had spent most of his adult life employed by the publishing company, Charles Scribner's and Sons, where he was in charge of the stockroom. His rich bass singing voice allowed him to perform in local concerts in the New York area.

Their daughter Lydia carried on the correspondence almost to her very end with Ronia, Leonid Axenov's daughter, who lived in Germany. Lydia died in 1997 at the age of ninety-six. Most of her working life in the United States was spent as a supervisor in various perfumeries, such as Prince Matchabelli[4] and Schiaparelli. Throughout her career in these perfumeries she tended to hire Russian émigré women. She never forgot her heritage, even though she had lived in Russia for only nineteen of her ninety-six years.

CHAPTER 17

Conclusion

Konstantin Ivanovich Globachev was just a few months or so short of his forty-fifth birthday when he took over as chief of the Okhrana in Petrograd. He had been a member of the Special Corps of Gendarmes for ten years and had already had several important postings—Bialystok, Lodz, and Warsaw, three cities that were notorious for terrorist activities. Then there was Nizhni Novgorod, the industrial city on the Volga that was famous for its international Fair that attracted masses of merchants not only from all of Russia, but from Europe too. In 1913 the Tsar, his family, and his entire retinue came through the city in celebration of the three hundredth anniversary of the House of Romanov. This alone required extra security measures and having the latest and most accurate intelligence information. It was at this time that Globachev made a very favorable impression on the assistant minister of the interior, General Dzhunkovskii. From Nizhni Novgorod, Globachev's next posting was to the southern city of Sevastopol on the Black Sea that would soon be in the throes of being bombarded by a German warship during the early stages of World War I, and that is when Globachev was the head of the Gendarme Administration there. Each of these postings had its own unique challenges—terrorism, the Tsar's travels, and the start of the war.

Globachev's career and advancement were quite swift once he joined the Special Corps of Gendarmes. In a little more than eleven years he rose from his transfer from the Keksholm Regiment as a captain to be the head of the Russian capital's Okhrana. His track record was impressive, although there were some bumps along the way. Despite the poor evaluation that he received when he was head of the Warsaw Okhrana, he was not dismissed, as were so many other Okhrana and Corps of Gendarme chiefs. He had the strong backing of the governor general of Poland and of the governor's deputy. He was, however, transferred to another position, this time Nizhni Novgorod, where his performance was challenged. The result was that Lieutenant Colonel Martynov, who performed the investigation of Globachev, was reprimanded severely by the minister of the interior and by the director of police for having, in effect, fabricated a case against Globachev.

Globachev's experience in Petrograd over his last two years of tsarist service, which years were also the last two of the Russian monarchy, was very different. His position as the head of a security bureau in the capital put him in closer and more frequent contact with government leaders whose positions and responsibilities were national in scope. He was also very aware of the political intrigues that were practiced by senior government officials. Herein was Globachev's challenge. How would his intelligence information be received and acted upon by individuals that history has shown were often incompetent, uninterested in intelligence information, antagonistic to security and intelligence agencies, and often preoccupied solely with personal power and self-interest.

And Globachev's organization had to provide protection for Rasputin and maintain surveillance over him. As history has shown, to run afoul of the *starets*, or even not to be in his good graces, usually meant the end of a career, or at least dismissal from one's current position and a transfer to elsewhere, as was demonstrated by the dismissals of Dzhunkovskii, A. N. Khvostov, Shcherbatov, Beletskii, Komissarov, and A. A. Khvostov. But, in addition to Rasputin's influence in most of these changes, there were also the "reassignments" of the Petrograd city prefect, director of the Department of Police, and the commander of the Petrograd Military District. This administrative turmoil did nothing to make matters in the capital safer. The turmoil, in fact, extended throughout Russia.

Throughout it all Globachev was the only senior official who lasted the entire two years preceding the Revolution as head of the Security Bureau in Petrograd. The poet and intellectual Alexander Blok was employed in May 1917 by the Extraordinary Commission of the Provisional Government to take stenographic notes of parts of the commission's interrogations of senior tsarist officials who were under investigation for unlawful acts during their time in office. Blok wound up having a lot of information. In 1921 his notes and transcriptions were published and titled *The Last Days of Imperial Power* (*Poslednie Dni Imperatorskoi Vlastsi*).

There are some frequent references to the Okhrana and to Globachev in Blok's book. One of the most telling is Blok's argument that the only agency that might have been able to stem the oncoming upheaval was the Department of Police, and in particular that "the reports of the Okhrana in 1916 give the best characterization of the public mood; they are filled with alarm, but their voice could not be heard by the dying regime."[1]

Blok had access to tsarist political police records, such as survived much of the destruction of Okhrana and Department of Police buildings and records during the February Revolution, at the time of the investigations of the Extraordinary Commission of the Provisional Government. Such records have become available to researchers since the Russian government archives became open to researchers.

Globachev's record as chief of the Petrograd Okhrana is clear. He was effective in neutralizing, through arrests, the revolutionary groups in and around Petrograd. The police reports show the record of Globachev's organization's arrests and seizure of illegal presses, pamphlets, and other revolutionary documents. But, dealing with corruption, the Duma, and the quality of his superiors and some colleagues was another matter, and some of this was out of his control. The machinations of Khvostov, Beletskii, and Komissarov as they circumvented Globachev's surveillance and security over Rasputin made Globachev's officially specified job more difficult, since the minister who had responsibility over that function was violating it at the same time. The last minister, Protopopov, fawned over Rasputin, was delusional, and used astrology to validate his activities. This was definitely not an easy minister to work for.

The Duma was a particularly difficult matter. As elected representatives, Duma members had immunity. They could criticize the government with impunity, and often the attacks on the government were seditious. The general points out that the authorities would not authorize arrests of the opposition leaders, even though it was clear that there could be evidence that their activities were unlawful, because the authorities feared the potential indignation of society supporting the immunity of Duma representatives. Globachev lamented that there were no laws or procedures by which the government could deal with such behavior.[2]

The Okhrana's relationship to the military establishment was well defined. The abolition of agents within the military was an act initiated by the very individual who was responsible for political police matters, General Dzhunkovskii. Dzhunkovskii felt that having agents in the army was immoral. After Dzhunkovskii's dismissal by Nicholas II, Globachev and an assistant minister of the interior tried to reverse this decision, but they were overruled by the army and the generals rejected the Okhrana's request to reintroduce agents into the military. After all, the army generals were agreeing with Dzhunkovskii's decision.

Similarly, as the February Revolution drew closer and Globachev repeatedly warned of the unreliability of the Petrograd troops, the last two commanders of the Petrograd Military District, Generals Nikolai Tumanov and Sergey Khabalov, flatly rejected Globachev's arguments with varied excuses. The argument of a gendarme officer like Globachev must have come across to the Military District commanders as an attack on the army's honor, a concept and tradition that was quite ingrained in the Russian military.[3]

Globachev's reputation as chief of the capital's Okhrana was that of an honorable and capable officer; his record of effective investigations, arrests, and neutralizing underground illegal revolutionary groups is detailed in Blok's book. The various reports that the Okhrana sent to the Department of Police and to the minister of the interior are documented proof of the Petrograd Okhrana's effectiveness. There were very few who had doubts about him.

Globachev even received a compliment from an archenemy of the tsarist government. Leon Trotsky, a leader in the Social Democrat Party (subsequently a Bolshevik), was in no way a friend to anyone or anything having to do with tsarism. He mentions Globachev one time only in his *History of the Russian Revolution*. Trotsky refers to the general as the "venerable General Globachev" (маститый Генерал Глобачев).[4]

At least one foreign diplomat, and an important one at that, also mentions Globachev. Maurice Paleologue was the last French ambassador to the Russian court. He was quite a prolific writer, having written a multivolume memoir of his posting in Petrograd at the same time that Globachev was head of the Okhrana. As conditions in Russia went from bad to worse with the war going badly and discontent in the population growing more and more, Paleologue writes about Globachev in a positive but cautious manner. "What is the Okhrana contemplating now? What plot is it weaving? I am told that its present Chief, General Globatchev [*sic*] is not altogether deaf to reason. But in times of crisis, the spirit of an institution will always prevail against the personality of its chief."[5]

There was one individual who recognized Globachev's finer points, but set forth his doubts about the Petrograd Okhrana chief. Major General Alexander Ivanovich Spiridovich was a colleague of Globachev's and had worked with him in the past. Spiridovich was a few years younger than Globachev. In early 1917 Globachev was not yet forty-seven years old and Spiridovich was about forty-four. Between 1912 and 1916 the latter had been head of palace security, and in 1916 he was appointed city prefect of Yalta. He had scholarly interests, and after the Revolution he emigrated and spent time lecturing and writing in Paris. He subsequently moved to the United States. A number of his writings were published, almost all in Russian, and they dealt with World War I, the Revolution, and life during the tsarist regime. Globachev is mentioned several times in Spiridovich's writing.

Spiridovich's assessment of Globachev is one that damns with faint praise. Spiridovich found Globachev to be "clever, industrious, efficient, dependable, and profoundly decent. He was a typically good gendarme officer, with a profound sense of duty and love for the Tsar and motherland. But he was soft and could not press his supervisors too much. He was good for peacetime, but soft for the coming troubled times. He did not have any of [Alexander] Gerasimov's mettle, who together with Durnovo and Stolypin, suppressed the first Russian Revolution."[6] What is peculiar about this evaluation is that Spiridovich, a student of history, presents a faulty comparison and a rather superficial criticism. Spiridovich knew that the individuals that he mentions were strong and decisive individuals indeed. But he also knew, or at least knew of, the current leadership to whom Globachev was subordinate. Protopopov and Vasiliev were certainly more in contrast rather than in comparison to Stolypin, Gerasimov, and Durnovo. Spiridovich continues that Globachev constantly spoke of the inevitability of a revolution, yet he missed its start. Notwithstanding Spiridovich's respect for the chief of the Petrograd Okhrana, he considered that Globachev was not able to take the proper measures. "He was a realist who understood well the unfolding events, but he did not know how to deal with them."[7] Spiridovich does not say what missing the start of the Revolution means, nor what the proper measures should have been, nor what actions the Okhrana should have taken. It was an easy criticism for Spiridovich to make without giving much detail.

But then Spiridovich pivots his assessment somewhat, stating that Globachev was very concerned about the seriousness of the evolving political situation, and that the Okhrana, under Globachev, was even better informed of what was going on than the Department of Police. But Globachev was powerless because of his superiors in the Ministry of the Interior, who were preoccupied with their own self-interests.[8] It is possible that Spiridovich misunderstood Globachev's modest personality for weakness.

Some historians have criticized Globachev for his alleged weakness, and therefore his lack of effectiveness as head of the Petrograd Okhrana. The criticisms are often mostly based on Spiridovich's statement. More comprehensive data, such as Globachev's reports, Blok's assessment, Paleologue's observation, and Trotsky's mention of Globachev, present a different perception and they come from different perspectives. The Okhrana chief's record is clear, based on his reports, his testimony, and the comments about him as expressed by his superiors, colleagues, and foes alike, and thus cannot be dismissed.

Globachev understood the causes of the Revolution as he foresaw the Revolution's inevitability during his two years as head of the Petrograd Okhrana. There certainly were many factors that came into play. The army's defeats in the war caused social anxiety, and as the war continued to go badly for Russia, there was war weariness. There was the profiteering and other machinations of corrupt individuals, such as the leaders of the Central War Industries Committee, which stymied military effectiveness at the front. Rasputin's influence at court and the damage he did to the reputation of the Tsar and Tsaritsa have to be included. The activities of the various revolutionary groups, the SRs (Socialist Revolutionaries) and SDs (Social Democrats), were a constant source of danger. However, the record shows that their efforts were often defeated by the authorities—namely, the Okhrana, the Department of Police, and other Corps of Gendarme units. The incompetence and self-interests of the highest government officials must also be included, and these the Okhrana often could not contain because some of the individuals involved were the superiors of the Okhrana and of the other police agencies.

The major culprits, however, that Globachev clearly accuses were the various progressive and left-wing factions within the Duma. It was here that Globachev admits to the lack of an effective policy on the government's part. The Duma's vitriolic attacks on the royal family and on the government, in general, fomented social discontent. And the more that problems increased, the more the opposition groups fanned the flames of a discontented Petrograd society. The Duma was a platform from which representatives could speak freely and with immunity.

While Globachev understood the role that demonstrators and striking workers played in the collapse of the regime, he noted precisely the foundation of it all: "Naturally, in this state of affairs where the revolutionary and insurgent mood was growing, workers' groups and their periphery were mainly responsible, but the leaders of the intelligentsia slipped by and continued to be involved in their criminal affairs."[9] He continues, "Russian hands created the February Revolution in Russia. We already know whose hands these were, and who it was that needed a revolution. It was needed by a small group of people of the Kadet Party and progressives, who affiliated themselves with it and who for the last two years had shouted about the need for a Russian government that could be trusted by the people, and that government would be selected by themselves."[10]

Finally, for the lay reader and for the historian, Konstantin and Sofia Globachev's lives present a vivid picture of a senior government official and his wife during a multiyear crisis and how they endured it and survived. But there is more of a lesson to be considered in the official responsibilities that were the general's, and the environment within which he worked.

There was a frequent turnover of ministers, not only in the Ministry of the Interior, within which Globachev worked, but also in the ministries of foreign affairs, justice, war, and others, including the office of prime minister. This turnover and the lack of competence and the corruption of some of the appointees created major problems of coordination, cooperation, communication, and the effective administration of the government. In a number of cases, Rasputin's influence was obvious in the selection of candidates for high office even though the candidates were clearly unqualified for the office.

Globachev was an important source of intelligence at a time when the government needed accurate and factual information on those elements in society that were a danger to the government. The record of the rejection and dismissal of Globachev's accurate intelligence reports is history that cannot be dismissed. The governmental environment at the time and the authorities' lack of attention to Globachev's ceaseless efforts to warn them of the impending crisis are a metaphor for current times.

Appendix A

Globachev's Service Record and Biographical Outline

The following is a direct translation of the first page of Globachev's Service Record of July 1, 1914. It is organized into sections just as in the original Russian document. This first page was a standard one that identified the individual—name, date of birth, religion, and so forth. Subsequent pages include data from the Service Record in normal typed font. Information that is not from the official record is typed in italics. This record has entries only up to 1914, and from that point on information about Globachev's life comes from other sources, such as his resume, memoirs, official documents, and letters. Events that are not part of his service record and those that occur after 1914 are shown in italics. All dates up to 1923 are in Old Style (Julian Calendar).

Service Record
Colonel Globachev

I Rank, name, patronymic, and last name	Colonel Konstantin Ivanovich Globachev
II Service Post	Chief of Sevastopol Gendarme Administration
III Decorations and medals	St. Vladimir's medals, 3rd and 4th degree, Austrian Order of Franz Joseph, silver medal on Alexandrian ribbon in memory of the reign of Emperor Alexander III, silver medal in memory of the 50th jubilee of His Imperial Majesty Austrian Franz Joseph, the August 1st honorary commander of the regiment, bronze medal in honor of the 100th anniversary of the War of 1812 for the fatherland, and a gift of high honor of a gold watch in celebration of the 300th anniversary of the House of Romanov.
IV Date of Birth	April 24, 1870
V Family title and place of birth VI Religion	Hereditary nobility, Ekaterinoslav Province Orthodox
VII Education	Polotsk Cadet Academy, completed full course in the 1st Pavlovsk Academy first class, and completed the class at the Nikolaevsk Academy of the General Staff, second class
VIII Service allowances	Salary . . . . 1,200 rubles Board and lodging . . . . 2,100 rubles Hired servant . . . . 192 rubles Additional funds based on location

SIGNED 1914 Colonel Globachev

Globachev Biographical Outline

April 24, 1870	Born into a family of hereditary nobility in Ekaterinoslav. Educated at the Polotsk Cadet Academy.
1875	*Sofia Nikolaevna Popova born in Warsaw.*
1888	Completed the Pavlovsk Military Academy and began his military career as a junior lieutenant in the Keksholm Life-Guards Infantry Regiment that was stationed in Warsaw.
1894	Enrolled at the Nikolaevskii General Staff Academy in St. Petersburg
1896	Returns to regiment following completion at Nikolaevskii General Staff Academy
1897	Temporary assignment to St. Petersburg to be part of the greeting of the Austrian Emperor Franz Joseph, who was the honorary commander of the Keksholm Regiment. Globachev received a commendation medal.
January 1898	*Marries Sofia Nikolaevna Popova.*
May 1, 1899	Appointed staff officer of the regimental court.
September 25, 1900	Appointed head of the regimental training command. Shortly thereafter promoted to Captain.
February 1903	Applied to transfer to the Special Corps of Gendarmes.
September 23, 1903	Transferred to the Special Corps of Gendarmes with the rank of Captain.
September 30, 1903	Appointed Adjutant to the Petrokovsk Province Gendarme Administration.
May 29, 1904	Transferred to Grodno Province Gendarme Administration headquartered in Bialystok, and appointed head of the Okhrana.

September 5, 1905	Appointed head of the Lodz and Lassk region's Gendarme Administration.
April 2, 1906	Promoted to the rank of Lieutenant Colonel.
April 22, 1907	Awarded the St. Vladimir Cross, fourth degree, for meritorious service.
December 29, 1909	Appointed head of the Warsaw Okhrana.
April 18, 1910	Promoted to the rank of Colonel.
November 20, 1912	Assigned as head of the Nizhni Novgorod Provincial Gendarme Administration.
April 14, 1913	Awarded the St. Vladimir Cross, third degree, for meritorious service.
February 1, 1914	Appointed head of the Sevastopol Gendarme Administration.
March 1, 1915	*Appointed head of the Petrograd Okhrana.*
January 1916	*Promoted to the rank of Major General.*
March 1917–November 1917	*Under arrest.*
Early 1918	*Worked in the anti-Bolshevik underground.*
Summer 1918	*Flight from Petrograd to Kiev.*
1919	*Various jobs within the White Movement; Rostov, Odessa.*
1920–1923	*Evacuation to Constantinople. Appointed head of passport control and intelligence at the Russian Embassy in Constantinople.*
1923–1930	*Immigrated with family to the United States. Worked in several menial jobs in New York.*
1930–1934	*Moved to Paris, France, on invitation to be employed by ROVS to be in charge of counterintelligence.*

1934–1941	*Returned to New York and worked as a commercial artist specializing in batik.*
December 1, 1941	*Konstantin Ivanovich Globachev died in New York at the age of seventy-one.*
November 3, 1950	*Sofia Nikolaevna Globacheva died at age seventy-five in New York.*

Appendix B

How the Okhrana Was Run

Before going into the structure and responsibilities of the Petrograd Okhrana, it may be beneficial to see how the Okhrana fits into the Russian Empire's governmental structure. This should be helpful in understanding how Globachev functioned in terms of his responsibilities, authority, and interaction with his superiors.

The Okhrana was a bureau within the Ministry of the Interior. By 1915, when Globachev assumed his assignment as head of the Petrograd Okhrana, the Ministry of the Interior was one of the more powerful ministries in the empire.

The Ministry of the Interior's responsibilities and authority were vast. The minister of the interior was appointed by the Tsar and reported directly to him, and the minister in turn had subordinate administrators who reported directly to him. Some of the departments within the ministry were the Department of General Affairs, which dealt with personnel issues and the election of marshals of the nobility; the Department of Peasant Affairs; the Department of Posts and Telegraphs; and others.[1] An important position in the ministry was that of the assistant minister of the interior for political affairs. His primary job was the nation's security. There were two major governmental agencies under his command, the Special Corps of Gendarmes and the Department of Police, and Globachev was to operate within this world.

The Special Corps of Gendarmes had been a unit within the Ministry of War since 1836. It was a military unit whose responsibilities were the investigation of criminal activities and political disturbances. In 1880 the Corps of Gendarmes was transferred to the Ministry of the Interior, and two of its added responsibilities were the security of the empire's railway system, which was the major transportation network in Russia, and passport control at borders. Even as the Corps of Gendarmes was now a part of the Interior Ministry it kept its military status, although to some it has also been referred to as a paramilitary organization. In 1914 Dzhunkovskii introduced a set of regulations that specified the requirements that applicants had to meet to enter the Special Corps of Gendarmes. An applicant had to have three years of military service in a regiment as a commissioned officer and preferably be a person of noble birth. The applicant had to pass an entrance examination, could not have any serious debts, and had to have high recommendations from a regimental commander. An applicant could not be a Jew, a Pole, a Catholic, married to a Catholic, or be of Jewish background, even if converted.[2] Applicants who were accepted into the Corps of Gendarmes kept their military rank. If in their career there they deserved merit, the medals they were awarded were the same as those who were in the army would get. Gendarmes had their own blue uniforms by which they could be recognized, and as career gendarmists' organizational positions increased their promotions within military ranks increased. Globachev is a typical example. From 1890 to 1903 he was an officer in the Keksholm Regiment, and upon his transfer to the Special Corps he entered it as a staff captain, the same rank as he had in the regiment.

Recruits went through approximately a year of training in St. Petersburg. This training included the organization of various security agencies, the study of civil and criminal law, methods of investigation, and the history and organization of revolutionary groups. Upon successful completion of the course, and passing of the final examination, the recruit was ready for an assignment. In September 1903 Globachev was assigned as adjutant to the Petrokovsk Province Gendarme Administration, and within several months he was transferred and appointed head of the Bialystok Okhrana.

The other major agency under the assistant minister was the Department of Police. Its head was the director of the Department of Police who reported directly to the assistant minister of the interior. The director was almost always a civilian with prior legal experience or some other governmental background. The responsibilities of the department were to oversee the activities of the various Corps of Gendarmes and Okhrana operations, establish procedures and guidelines for these offices, and evaluate the performance of the offices and their staff. The department also coordinated the compiling of reports with local police where suspicious or criminal political activities occurred.

There were security bureaus (Okhrana offices) that were subordinate to the Department of Police. The official name of the organization to which Globachev was appointed was the "Bureau for Public Security, Safety, and Order in Petrograd."

The Petrograd Okhrana was the largest of the three major security bureaus. As mentioned, the other two were in Moscow and Warsaw. Petrograd was the capital and the largest city in the Russian Empire. Based on the only official census for the Russian Empire, which was conducted in 1897, the population of St. Petersburg (as it was known then) was between 1,264,900 and 1,267,023. By 1916, one estimate had Petrograd's population at 2.4 million.

The Petrograd Okhrana was formally subordinate to the city prefect (*gradonachal'nik*) of Petrograd. The Tsar, usually at the minister of the interior's recommendation, appointed the city prefect and the prefect reported to the minister. The prefect was responsible for the city police, postal system, maintaining communication with the various consulates in the city, and ensuring that commerce within the city functioned effectively.

The Petrograd Okhrana was subordinated to the city prefect because the Petrograd Okhrana's responsibility was to provide security, investigations of illegal political organizations, and intelligence on any possible unlawful politically oriented demonstrations, strikes, or other such events that were within the city and its immediate environs, although the security of the palace at Tsarskoe Selo, where the royal family lived, was not under the Petrograd Okhrana's authority. Palace security was under the direction of the palace commandant. The Petrograd Okhrana actually reported to the Department of Police and, even more precisely, if we read Globachev's reports and note his references in his memoirs and the testimony he gave to the Provisional Government's investigative committee, as chief of the Petrograd Okhrana he really reported directly to the minister of the interior. Globachev's written reports and personal meetings tended to be with the minister. It should be noted, though, that intelligence information collected by the Okhrana in searches or as part of its normal intelligence gathering operations was documented and sent to the minister of the interior, the assistant minister, the director of the Department of Police, the city prefect, the commander of the

Petrograd Military District, and the palace commandant. Thus, all the major offices requiring information on security within the capital and its surroundings were always kept apprised.[3]

Globachev's work was cut out for him, but he was well prepared for the task by his prior experience as the head of several Gendarme Administrations and as chief of the Warsaw Okhrana agency where he was responsible for the entire region.

The Petrograd Security Bureau consisted of six hundred employed personnel, and this did not include paid and unpaid informants, about whom, even in the later investigations of the Provisional Government, accurate numbers could not be established. But there were many informants.

The chief of the Okhrana in most cities was a gendarme commissioned officer, originally from an army regiment, who transferred to the Special Corps of Gendarmes where he received special training and then was assigned to a gendarme office. These new gendarme officers kept their military rank. The career path of such individuals could lead to a promotion as head of a provincial gendarme headquarters and eventually to be the chief of one of the major Okhrana bureaus. The minimum rank of an Okhrana chief was colonel.

The Petrograd Okhrana was divided into a number of organizational units, all under the authority and direction of the chief of the Okhrana: the Security Division, consisting of the Secret Service Unit and the External Surveillance Unit, the Central Agency, the Okhrana Command, and the Registration Department.

The Secret Service Unit was the main source of intelligence information. Secret agents provided the Okhrana office with information about the activities of unlawful underground organizations, rumors of impending demonstrations, strikes, plans of revolutionary organizations, and so forth. The secret agents were often collaborators who belonged to various organizations and they provided their gendarme handlers with intelligence information. These collaborators were paid for their services in amounts of anywhere from five rubles a month to over five hundred rubles, depending on the importance of the collaborator's involvement in a revolutionary organization.

The External Surveillance Unit had the duty of maintaining surveillance over individuals or groups from a distance. It consisted of approximately one hundred civilian "detectives" (*filiors*) and several officers and staff workers to support the work of these detectives. The

Okhrana hired men for this work who had prior military service, preferably former noncommissioned officers. They had to be literate, mature, and of high moral standards. These men would either perform their duties as plainclothes men or in simple disguise, such as cab drivers, building janitors, doormen, or railway porters. The job of these agents was strictly external. They did not join organizations or establish any relationships with individuals that they were assigned to watch. Their job was surveillance. The supervisors of these men were in almost all cases gendarme officers. Poles and Jews were generally "excluded from any kind of employment in the External Service."

The Central Agency was a special group of the Okhrana. It employed about seventy-five agents. This unit was made up of specially selected and experienced agents. It was the responsibility of these agents to undertake top-secret assignments that could take them outside of Petrograd or to any other part of the empire, as might be necessary. The agents had the full support of the bureau's resources, everything from facial disguises, costumes, and equipment with which they could pass themselves off as merchants, newspaper vendors, and so forth. This part of the Okhrana employed both male and female agents.[4] This group of agents was under the supervision of a special officer who was particularly experienced in this type of clandestine work and who was responsible directly to the chief of the Okhrana Bureau.

The Okhrana Command had three hundred persons and was headquartered in its own building at 26 Morskoi Street. One of its functions was as a training center where classes were held on various policies, procedures, and relevant laws on security. The Command was also responsible for the security of the Tsar, the imperial family, and highly placed officials when they were in the capital.

The Registration Department was responsible for keeping track of suspicious persons entering the city. The department had files on all such persons and kept track of them through agents and a system of informants who were doormen, concierges, servants, cabbies, porters, janitors, and so forth. The department was manned by approximately thirty supervisory personnel who worked with local police in keeping suspicious persons under surveillance. The whereabouts and comings and goings of suspicious persons were tracked in detail: when they arrived in the city, where they stayed, who they saw, when and where they met.[5]

The Okhrana did not have a law enforcement unit. Consequently, when there were major searches and arrests that were warranted, the chief of the Okhrana had to use city police troops or members of the Petrograd gendarme mounted garrison. Consequently, Globachev had to maintain close communication and coordination between his organization and the city prefect and the Corps of Gendarmes.[6]

As head of one of the three major Okhrana offices, Globachev's salary and living conditions were comfortable. According to his daughter's recollection, Globachev's base salary was somewhere between six hundred and seven hundred rubles per month. A more detailed accounting comes from Globachev's colleague, Colonel Alexander Martynov, head of the Moscow Okhrana. In 1914 Martynov's income was 450 rubles per month salary, and 4,000 rubles annually as "bonuses" from the funds of the Moscow City Prefecture, and 1,000 rubles from the Department of Police. The Okhrana chiefs' salaries were over 10,000 rubles a year. In the early 1900s, "in material terms the chiefs of the three bureaus were in exceptionally good shape."[7]

Globachev was also provided with an allowance for travel expenses and to purchase and maintain his uniforms. He had a chauffeured automobile assigned for his use, a sled carriage and horse for winter use, and apartments in the Okhrana headquarters. These headquarters and the Globachevs' living accommodations were in the Oldenburg Palace on the Mytninskii Embankment of the Neva River. The inside of the building had many large rooms that were decorated with plaster sculpted ceilings, mirrors, and chandeliers. Globachev's sizeable office was decorated in oak.[8]

Globachev's challenge as the head of the security bureau was to manage such a large and complex operation in the capital during a two-year period of war, to communicate with senior government officials of questionable competence and morality, with the frequent turnover of his superiors, a contentious Duma, the many domestic problems that involvement in a war produces, and governmental instability as a result of the presence and influence of Rasputin.

Globachev's problem right from the start was that the Okhrana had scant intelligence information on the mood of the Russian military, especially the Petrograd garrison, and the work of activists in secondary schools and universities, since Dzhunkovskii had prohibited the use of secret agents as informants in the army and the navy and in educational institutions. While the chief of the Okhrana disagreed with this policy, he obeyed it. However, "After Dzhunkovskii's dismissal the new Assistant Minister who understood the harm of the aforementioned directive brought up the matter of its repeal, but as it turned out it was too late.

The commission that was set up to deal with this was defeated by a majority vote from the army. The commission consisted of: the chairman, Lieutenant General Leontiev, who was at that time the Quartermaster General of army headquarters and two of his subordinates who were officers on the general staff; Major General N. M. Potapov and Colonel Machul'skii (both of whom got prominent positions with the Bolsheviks after the October Revolution). The Vice Director of the Department of Police, E. K. Smirnov, and I represented the Ministry of the Interior. Our two votes to repeal the directive could do nothing against the three votes from the army that were for the continuance in force of the directive, thus this matter was completely defeated."[9] The result of this meeting was predictable: "Most of the military commanders, one might almost say deliberately, closed their eyes whenever it was a question of revolutionary intrigues among their units. These officers simply refused to admit, either to themselves or to anyone else, the barest possibility of there being anything like indiscipline or political ferment among the men under their command."[10] This matter would come up again and more often in Globachev's reports as turmoil increased.

The other continuing vexing dilemma was the State Duma. This was the "lower house" of a system that approximated a parliamentary one. It was a legislative body with very limited actual authority. It could be dissolved by the Tsar, but that did not stop the speeches and actions in the Duma that were highly critical in their attacks on the autocracy. And that incited political groups, both legal and unlawful ones: "Every foreign and domestic misfortune was almost always explained as being caused by treachery or treason and blamed on the Tsar, his Court, and his ministers. The State Duma set the tone for all this and took advantage of the government at this difficult time to revolutionize the people. It was not a representative organization that had an obligation to lift patriotic feelings and to unite everybody in support of the Tsar and government. On the contrary, it was the center of opposition that took advantage of the country's stressful moment to incite revolution among all classes against the existing order."[11] Many newspapers in the capital and other cities in the empire supported Duma positions and were just as critical of the government.

Globachev's assessment of the situation was that the Okhrana was very effective in neutralizing the various revolutionary organizations, but he lamented that the political security force was well trained and equipped "for combat with the revolutionary movement but was utterly powerless to combat the growing public revolutionary mood of the activist . . . intelligentsia, which required other means of a general political nature."[12] There was always the communication and coordination of the Okhrana with other agencies. All official reports by the Okhrana that were not specific to a particular office went to the minister of the interior, with copies to the Department of Police, the city prefect, and to the Ministry of Justice. Globachev also had to follow directives from above as to what groups should be left alone. Okhrana agents were not to maintain surveillance over various monarchical and right-wing organizations.[13] Globachev's frustration over this matter comes through clearly in his memoir.

The workload of the Okhrana officers and civilian staff was very time consuming. Staying ahead of the plans and actions of revolutionary groups and their conspiracies, maintaining intelligence on individuals coming into the capital at a time of war, and the Duma's inciting the public was not something that could be handled within normal working hours. A number of senior security officers noted the long hours of work in their memoirs. The clerical staff of the Okhrana and of the gendarme administrative offices worked regular hours, but the heads of the various units and departments within the security agencies worked until as late as three or five in the morning. There were massive reports to be written, and incoming reports to be read and processed. These higher officials also had to meet with secret agents at times, and this required establishing the time and location of such meetings. Safe houses were used, and the Okhrana officials, who had gendarme rank, would wear civilian clothes to such secret meetings. Dzhunkovskii commented on this, as did Martynov.[14] Sofia Nikolaevna, Globachev's wife, also affirmed the hard work and long hours that were part of the daily life of the Okhrana.[15]

Appendix C

Ministerial Leapfrog

The first use of the term "ministerial leapfrog" is attributed to Vladimir Mitrofanovich Purishkevich, a member of the Fourth Duma (and one of Rasputin's assassins), in a speech in the Duma. The phrase was a criticism of the frequent turnover in the Ministry of the Interior. The phrase could also apply to the several assistant ministers and directors of the Department of Police, some of whom lasted in their posts for only a few months. The chart below shows that during Globachev's tenure as chief of the Petrograd Okhrana, there were six ministers of the interior, six assistant ministers, and five directors of police.

Minister of the Interior	Assistant Minister	Director of Department of Police
Maklakov December 16, 1912– June 5, 1915	Dzhunkovskii	Brune de St. Hyppolite
Shcherbatov June 5, 1915– September 26, 1915	Mollov	Brune de St. Hyppolite Mollov Kafafov
A. N. Khvostov September 26, 1915– March 3, 1916	Beletskii	Mollov Kafafov Klimovich
Sturmer March 3, 1916– July 7, 1916	Stepanov	Klimovich
A. A. Khvostov July 7, 1916– September 16, 1916	Kurlov	Klimovich
Protopopov September 16, 1916– February 28, 1917	Kukol-Ianopol'skii	Vasiliev

From Globachev's testimony of June 26, 1917, in *Pravda*, 421, where he names all of these individuals.

Directors of the Department of Police

V. A. Brune de Saint-Hyppolite	February 3, 1914–September 4, 1915
R. G. Mollov	September 6, 1915–November 23, 1915
K. D. Kafafov	November 23, 1915–February 14, 1916
E. K. Klimovich	February 14, 1916–September 15, 1916
A. T. Vasiliev	September 28, 1916–February 28, 1917

From *Tsarskie Zhandarmy*, www.Hrono.ru./Ukazatel' Zh.

Appendix D

Annotated List of Names

NOTE: There were several sources for the people identified below. The noted and highly respected Professor Zinaida Ivanovna Peregudova of the State Archives of the Russian Federation provided very detailed glossaries in her works on Globachev's Russian language memoirs and on Alexander Blok's book, which she edited. Jonathan Smele's *Historical Dictionary of the Russian Civil Wars, 1916–1922*, was thorough and useful. Russian Google was also used since it had much more pertinent information than that of U.S. Wikipedia and other U.S. sites. There are a number of names mentioned by the Globachevs for which there is little information. These is sometimes a subordinate of Globachev's, an acquaintance, or just a mention of someone in passing about whom there was no further information.

The one-paragraph biographical entries that follow are, of course, not at all comprehensive, but they do provide readers with a bit more information on the individuals mentioned in the book without having these biographical entries embedded in the text and, therefore, being a distraction to the continuity of the narrative.

Abramov, Fedor Fedorovich (1870–1963). He was a line tsarist officer in World War I and an active senior officer (lieutenant general) during the Civil War. In 1930 he became deputy chairman of ROVS in Paris. In 1948 he immigrated to the United States. He was killed in a car accident in 1963 and is buried in a Russian Orthodox cemetery in New Jersey.

Alekseev, Mikhail Vasilievich (1857–1918). Infantry general. At the beginning of World War I, he was the commander of the Southwestern Front. From 1915 to 1917 he was chief of staff of the High Command. Following the Revolution he was one of the organizers of the White Movement. He died in September 1918 of heart failure.

Anastasii (birth name: Alexander Alexeevich Gribanovskii) (1873–1965). Ordained into monastic orders in 1898. In 1901 he was promoted to archimandrite and then to bishop of the Moscow Episcopate. In 1916 he was elevated to archbishop. In Constantinople in 1920 he was head of the Russian Orthodox community. He was chosen to be Metropolitan in 1935 and in 1936 he was elected by the Synod of the Russian Orthodox Church Outside of Russia to be its head. From 1950 he resided in the United States.

Axenov, Leonid (?). Step-brother of Globachev. Spent his life in the medical profession specializing in ophthalmology. During the Russian Civil War he immigrated to Germany where he spent much of his professional time providing medical services to Russian refugees. He died in the late 1940s in Germany.

Balk, Alexander Pavlovich (1866–1957). Graduated from the Cadet Academy and the Pavlovsk Military Institute. He had initial postings in infantry regiments. He was appointed assistant to the Warsaw chief of police and subsequently became police chief in Moscow, and was promoted to major general. In November 1916 he was appointed, and became, the last city prefect of Petrograd from November until February 17, 1917. He was arrested and detained by the Provisional Government, but was later released. He and his family fled south to join the Whites. After the Russian Civil War he immigrated to Serbia and then to Brazil, where he died in São Paulo in 1957.

Beletskii, Stepan Petrovich (1872–1918). Director of the Department of Police from 1909 to 1912. From September 1915 to February 1916 he was the assistant minister of the Interior. He was arrested in March 1917 by the Provisional Government, and following the Bolshevik Revolution of October 1917 he remained incarcerated by the Bolsheviks. He attempted escape but was caught and executed by the Bolsheviks in the fall of 1918 along with several other former tsarist officials.

Blok, Alexander Alexandrovich (1880–1921). A poet who was invited in 1917 to edit the various reports of the Extraordinary Commission of the Provisional Government. The result was his publication entitled *The Last Days of the Old Regime*, which included a number of Globachev's reports and testimony.

Chebykin, Alexander Nesterovich (1857–1920). He began his military career in 1879 as a junior officer in the Finnish Life Guards Regiment. As he rose through the ranks he became a member of the Tsar's retinue, and in 1894 he was on the staff of the minister of war. His career continued and he held positions of command in regiments and brigades. By 1916 he held the rank of lieutenant general and was appointed commander of the reserve troops in Petrograd. He was deputy under General Khabalov and in January-February 1917 he was responsible for the reserve forces in Petrograd. He was retired from service in early 1917 due to illness, and that same year he died.

Denikin, Anton Ivanovich (1872–1947). Lieutenant general as of 1916. He took over command of the Volunteer White Army in 1918 and replaced Admiral Kolchak as supreme commander in 1919. After the failed campaign to take Moscow from the Red Army, he relinquished command to Baron General P. N. Wrangel. He immigrated to France where he lived from 1926 to 1945. He then moved to the United States. He died in Michigan in 1947 while visiting some Russian friends.

Dragomirov, Abram Mikhailovich (1868–1955). Graduated from the Corps of Pages, the Academy of the General Staff, and in 1896 from the Officers' Cavalry School. He rose through the ranks of line officers and during World War I was a cavalry corps commander. During the Civil War he held major commands in the Volunteer Army and was evacuated to Constantinople where he was a close advisor to General Wrangel. With the dispersal of Russians from Constantinople, he emigrated to Serbia and then to Paris. He became one of the senior leaders in ROVS. He died in one of the suburbs of Paris in 1955 at the age of eighty-seven.

Durnovo, Petr Nikolaevich (1845–1915). Minister of the interior in 1905–6. He suppressed revolutionary groups, but because of the turmoil he was dismissed and later appointed to the State Council where he served until his death.

Dzhunkovskii, Vladimir Fedorovich (1865–1938). General and governor of Moscow, 1905–13. He was appointed assistant minister of the Interior in January 1913. He was dismissed by Nicholas II in August 1915 for submitting a negative report on Rasputin. From 1915 to 1917 he was a division commander in World War I. He remained in Russia after the Revolution. He was arrested by the Soviet regime, released, and may have worked for the Soviet government for a while. He was arrested again and shot in 1938.

Gerasimov, Alexander Vasilievich (1861–1944). He attended a military school and upon completion he began as an infantry junior lieutenant. In 1889 he transferred to the Special Corps of Gendarmes. From 1889 on he served as deputy head and head of various gendarme and security bureau administrations. From 1905 to 1909 he was the head of the St. Petersburg Okhrana. He was successful in thwarting a number of assassination attempts on government officials by revolutionaries. He resigned in 1914 and was promoted to lieutenant general. He was arrested by the Provisional Government and later released. He immigrated to Berlin where he died in 1944.

Gorgulov, Pavel Timofeevich (1895–1932). Lieutenant in the army during World War I. Joined the Volunteer Army during General Wrangel's tenure. He immigrated to France where he practiced medicine illegally. He claimed to be the leader of the Russian Nationalist Fascist Party. He assassinated French president Paul Doumer in May 1932. He was tried, convicted, and guillotined in Paris in September 1932.

Grishin-Almazov, Alexei Nikolaevich (1880–1919). Artillery officer who rose in rank during World War I commanding various Siberian army units. He joined the White Army in 1918 and commanded the defense of Odessa. In May 1919, while on his way to join Admiral Kolchak in Siberia, a Soviet destroyer attacked his ship in the Caspian Sea. Rather than be captured, Grishin committed suicide.

Guchkov, Alexander Ivanovich (1862–1936). One of the founders of the Octobrist Party. He was chairman of the Third Duma in 1910 and was chairman of the Central War Industries Committee during World War I. He supported the idea of a palace coup to depose Nicholas II. He was minister of war and navy in the Provisional Government. He was active in anti-Bolshevik movements between 1917 and 1921. He immigrated to Paris.

Guseva, Khionia Kuzminievna (1880– ?). A peasant woman from Simbirsk. She was originally an admirer of Rasputin, but later grew to hate him. In 1914 she attacked him and stabbed a knife into his stomach. She was confined to a clinic for the insane and in 1917 Kerensky ordered her released.

Karinski, Nicholas Sergeevich (1873–1948). Graduated with a law degree from the University of Moscow around 1898. Spent the years before the Revolution in various judicial positions. Became a senior prosecutor in the Petrograd Judicial Court of the Provisional Government. On July 23, 1917, he ordered the arrests and incarceration of A. V. Lunacharskii and Leon Trotsky. After the Revolution, he eventually immigrated to the United States and died in Sussex, New Jersey.

Kerensky, Alexander Fedorovich (1882–1970). A lawyer by training and a political activist, he was elected to the Duma in 1912. In March 1917, he was appointed minister of justice in the Provisional Government. He also held the positions of war minister and prime minister. As a result of the Bolshevik Revolution in October 1917, Kerensky left Russia and lived in France and Berlin. In 1940 he emigrated to the United States where he wrote and lectured and was associated with the Hoover Institution of Stanford University as a scholar in residence. He died in New York.

Khabalov, Sergei Semionovich (1858–1924). A graduate of the General Staff Academy. Much of his career was spent teaching in military academies. He held the rank of lieutenant general and in late 1916 he was appointed military commander of the Petrograd District and its troops. He was arrested at the outset of the February Revolution, but released in October. He moved to the south of Russia in 1919. The following year he immigrated to Greece, where he died in 1924.

Khvostov, Alexander Alekseevich (1857–1922). Minister of justice from 1915 to 1916. Appointed minister of the interior on July 7, 1916. He was dismissed from that position on September 16, 1916. His tenure as minister of the interior lasted less than three months.

Khvostov, Alexei Nikolaevich (1872–1918). Born to nobility. Between 1904 and 1912 he was vice governor of Minsk, then of Tula. In 1906 he became vice governor and then governor of Nizhny Novgorod. Appointed minister of the interior on September 1915. He was dismissed on March 3, 1916. He was arrested by the Provisional Government during the February 1917 Revolution and continued to be incarcerated during the Bolshevik Revolution. He was executed in 1918 along several other former tsarist officials.

Klimovich, Evgenii Konstantinovich (1871–1930). A career gendarme officer. His education was typical as that of many of his contemporaries who served in the gendarmes. He attended the Polotsk Corps of Cadets and then the Pavlovsk Military Institute. Upon graduation he was assigned to an infantry regiment. In 1898 he transferred to the Special Corps of Gendarmes and over the next years held a number of positions in various Gendarme Administrations and in the offices of several city prefects. He rose in rank to major general, and shortly after being assigned as director of the Department of Police in 1916 he was promoted to lieutenant general. During the Revolution the Provisional Government detained him for a while. With the Bolshevik takeover he fled south and joined the White Movement. During the Civil War he was in charge of counterintelligence under General Wrangel. With the end of the Civil War he moved to Serbia where he died in 1930.

Komissarov, Mikhail Stepanovich (1870–1933). A gendarme officer who was personally tasked by Minister A. N. Khvostov and S. P. Beletskii to establish a friendly relationship and surveillance over Rasputin. This surveillance would be outside of the official functions of the Okhrana. After the Revolution, Komissarov pretended to work for the White Movement for his own personal gain. Once the Bolsheviks won, he joined with them to be a secret agent who was to join the White émigré community in Europe to spread misinformation and to discredit White efforts to combat Bolshevism. Upon being uncovered he immigrated to the United States around 1929. He was killed in Chicago in 1933 when a trolley car ran him over.

Kornilov, Lavr Georgievich (1870–1918). A general in World War I. In the first month of the February Revolution he was made commander of the Petrograd Milo District. He continued to be active during the months of the Provisional Government. Following the Bolshevik Revolution he joined General Alekseev in establishing the White Army. He was killed during the White Army's attack on Ekaterinodar.

Kukol'-Ianopol'skii, Stepan Alexandrovich (1859–?). Member of the State Council. Served a short while as assistant minister of the interior in 1916.

Kurlov, Pavel Grigorievich (1860–1923). Assistant minister of the interior from 1909 to 1911. After Stolypin's assassination he was dismissed. He was appointed to that position again just before the Revolution. He was arrested by the Provisional Government but released when the Bolsheviks came to power. He emigrated in 1918.

Kusonskii, Pavel Alexeevich (1880–1941). He was a tsarist officer who attained the rank of lieutenant general in 1922, during the latter part of the Russian Civil War. He was active in the White Movement and after the defeat of the Whites he immigrated to France and became one of the leaders of ROVS in Paris. He was arrested by the Gestapo in June 1941 and beaten to death by the Gestapo in August of that year.

Kutepov, Alexander Pavlovich (1882–1930). He was a tsarist officer who became one of the most able generals of the White Movement in the south of Russia. After the Whites' defeat he moved to Bulgaria and then to Paris where he became the head of ROVS. Soviet agents abducted him in 1930 and he either died of a heart attack or was killed by his abductors.

Lenin (Ulianov), Vladimir Ilyich (1870–1924). Marxist revolutionary. In 1893 he became a major figure in the Marxist Russian Social Democratic Labor Party (RSDLP). In 1903 he led the Bolshevik faction of the party in an ideological conflict with the Menshevik faction. After the February Revolution he campaigned to oust the Provisional Government, and in October 1917 he led the overthrow that established Bolshevik rule and the creation of the Soviet Union.

Lukomskii, Alexander Sergeevich (1868–1939). A lieutenant general during World War I and chief of staff of the High Command. Following the Revolution he was one of several organizers of the White Movement.

He and General Wrangel worked closely together during the Civil War. After the White defeat he evacuated to Constantinople where Wrangel appointed him head of the White Army in Constantinople. He probably left there around 1923 when the Whites' funds had been depleted and several European countries recognized the Soviet regime. He immigrated to Paris where he was an aide to Grand Duke Nicholas Nikolaevich. Following the latter's death in 1929, Lukomskii was active in ROVS. He died in Paris in 1939.

Lvov, Georgii Evgenievich (1861–1925). A member of the Kadet Party in the First State Duma. After the February Revolution he became prime minister of the Provisional Government. He resigned in favor of Alexander Kerensky in July 1917. He was arrested by the Bolsheviks following the October Revolution, escaped, and immigrated to Paris.

Makhno, Nestor Ivanovich (1888–1934). An anarchist. He began a partisan war against the German occupying forces in Ukraine and against Skoropadskii's government in 1918. He also fought against the Volunteer Army, the Bolsheviks, and Petliura. After the defeat of the Volunteer Army, Makhno's forces were threatened by the Soviet forces. He fled to Paris in 1921, where he died at age forty-five.

Maklakov, Nikolai Alexeevich (1871–1918). Minister of the interior from 1913 to 1915. He was dismissed from this position, but was appointed to the Finance Committee of the State Council. Following the Bolshevik Revolution he was arrested and shot.

Manasevich-Manuilov, Ivan Fedorovich (1869–1918). Began governmental work as an agent in Rome maintaining surveillance over Russian revolutionaries there. His next assignment in 1902 was to represent Interior Minister V. K. Pleve in Paris. In 1914 he met and became Rasputin's close associate. In October 1917 he attempted to flee to Finland. He was identified by Red border guards, captured, and shot immediately.

Martynov, Alexander Pavlovich (1875–1951). He attended the Moscow Corps of Cadets followed by attendance at the Alexandrovsk Military Institute. After several years in the grenadier unit of an infantry regiment he transferred to the Special Corps of Gendarmes in 1899. For the next twelve years he held positions in various Gendarme Administrations. In

1912 he was assigned to the Moscow Okhrana as its head. He held the rank of lieutenant colonel, and in 1915 he was promoted to the rank of colonel. He was the last head of the Moscow Okhrana, serving in this capacity from 1912 to 1917. He fled south with his family at the outbreak of the Bolshevik Revolution. Around 1920 he evacuated to Constantinople where he started a private detective bureau. In 1923 he immigrated to the United States. He died in Los Angeles in 1951.

Matchabelli, Prince Georges (1885–1935) A member of the Georgian nobility. He left Russia after the Revolution and immigrated to the United States. He and his wife began a perfumery that was popular for its scents and for the crown-shaped bottles that the perfumes came in. Matchabelli hired many White Russian émigrés to work for his company.

Miliukov, Pavel Nikolaevich (1859–1943). A historian who was politically active. He was a Kadet representative in the Third and Fourth State Dumas in St. Petersburg. He became foreign minister in the Provisional Government. He resigned in May 1917. He immigrated to France in 1918.

Miller, Evgenii Karlovich (1867–1939). Cavalry general. During World War I he was chief of staff of the Fifth Army. During the early part of the Civil War, Admiral Kolchak appointed him supreme commander of the Northern Province. Following defeats by the Red Army, he fled to France. From 1930 to 1937 he was the head of ROVS. Soviet agents kidnapped him in 1937 in Paris and smuggled him to Moscow where he was interrogated and possibly tortured. He was executed in May 1939.

Mollov, Ruschu Georgievich (1867–1925). Director of the Department of Police, 1915–16. During the Civil War he argued for continued support from France and the formation of a Russian government that was not dependent on the White Army.

Nikol'skii, Vladimir Pavlovich (1873–1960). Major general. Initially an officer in the Grenadier Artillery Brigade from 1903 to 1913. He also taught military subjects at the Moscow Military Academy. From 1913 to 1917 was chief of staff of the Special Corps of Gendarmes. Following the Civil War he held a senior position in the Russian Embassy in Constantinople. Around 1923 he immigrated to Bulgaria.

Obolenskii, Alexander Nikolaevich (1872–1924). A member of a princely family. He attended the prestigious Corps of Pages and upon graduating was assigned to a guards regiment as a junior lieutenant. By 1906 he was a battalion commander for a short while, and in 1907 he was attached to the Ministry of the Interior and served as a vice governor and then as a provincial governor. In 1914 he was appointed city prefect of Petrograd and in 1916 he was removed from office due to friction between him and Minister Protopopov and was assigned a brigade command. During the Civil War he served in the White Army. He immigrated to Paris where he died in 1924.

Papadjanov, Mikhail Ivanovich (1869–1929). He was born in Armenia to a noble family of Yerevan Province. He spent the first thirty years of his life active in Armenian politics. In 1912 he was elected to the State Duma, and joined the left-wing Kadet faction in the Fourth Duma. In 1917 he became a member of the Provisional Government with responsibility for the registration, detention, and release of former tsarist officials. He was subsequently appointed commissar of the Transcaucasian Committee of the Provisional Government. He continued to work on behalf of Armenian interests up to his death in 1929.

Pereverzev, Pavel Nikolaevich (1871–1944). Prior to the Revolution he worked as a defense attorney. He was a member of the Socialist Revolutionary Party. In 1917 the Provisional Government appointed him prosecutor of the Petrograd Judicial Court, and in April he was appointed minister of justice. In July 1917, he published information that alleged Lenin's connection to the German General Staff. This highly controversial publication created a furor and forced Pereverzev's dismissal. Following the Bolshevik Revolution in October 1917, Pereverzev immigrated to Paris where he died in 1944.

Petliura, Simon Vasilievich (1879–1926). Leader of the Ukrainian Social Democratic Workers' Party. Overthrew the government of Skoropadskii in 1918. The Soviet government tried to have Petliura handed over. He left Ukraine and after living in several countries, he settled in Paris in 1924. He was assassinated in 1926 by a Ukrainian anarchist.

Plevitskaia, Nadezhda Vasilievna (1879–1940). Plevitskaia was born in Kursk in 1879. By the time she was in her twenties, she was a renowned singer primarily of Russian and Gypsy folk songs. By 1909 her fame had spread and she performed in Moscow and St. Petersburg theaters. Nicholas II heard her and referred to her as the "Kursk Nightingale." After the 1917 Revolution Plevitskaia was in the south and continued to entertain within the White Russian culture. She evacuated as the Whites lost ground and spent some time in Constantinople. In 1921 she married the popular young general Nicholas Skoblin. By 1930 they were in Paris and she and her husband became Soviet agents. Skoblin fled without her after the abduction of General Miller in 1937. She was arrested by French authorities and sentenced to twenty years' imprisonment for being involved in the abduction. She died in prison in 1940.

Potapov, Nikolai Mikhailovich (1871–1946). He graduated from the Moscow Cadet Corps and then from the Mikhailovskii Artillery School. In 1907 he graduated from the Nikolaevskii Academy of the General Staff. During part of World War I he was the Russian military advisor to Montenegro. Around 1915 he was on the General Staff in Petrograd. Following the 1917 Revolution he joined the Bolsheviks and spent years in the employ of the Soviet Union in charge of various disinformation and propaganda projects. He retired in 1938 and died in Moscow in 1946.

Protopopov, Alexander Dmitriovich (1866–1918). Member of the hereditary nobility and initially a member of the Duma. Appointed minister of the interior on September 18, 1916. The Provisional Government arrested him, and when the Bolsheviks took power he was shot by the Cheka.

Purishkevich, Vladimir Mitrofanovich (1870–1920). Member of the Duma and one of several conspirators to kill Rasputin. The Provisional Government arrested him for counterrevolutionary activities. In 1917 he was given amnesty by the Petrograd Soviet. He moved to the south of Russia, where he died of typhus.

Rasputin (Novykh), Gregory Efimovich (1864–1916). A peasant from Tobolsk who became known to the royal family as a healer and a holy man. The tsarevich's hemophilia gave Rasputin access and influence with the Empress. Several monarchist conspirators wanted to save Russia from Rasputin. He was murdered on December 30 (Old Style, December 17), 1916.

Romanov, Prince Dmitrii Pavlovich (1891–1942). A first cousin of Tsar Nicholas II. He attended cavalry school, at the end of which he was assigned as an officer in the Life Guards Horse Regiment. He participated in the 1912 equestrian events in the Olympic Games in Stockholm and won some prizes. During World War I he fought on Russia's eastern front and was awarded a medal for valor. By 1916 he had become involved with others who saw Rasputin as a threat to both the royal family and to Russia. He became one of the conspirators in the assassination of Rasputin. Nicholas II exiled him to the Persian front. After the Revolution he immigrated to France where he spent most of the rest of his life. He may have died of tuberculosis.

Shatilov, Pavel Nikolaevich (1881–1962). He was a cavalry commander of a division during World War I. In 1915 he was awarded the Cross of Saint George for valor. He was promoted to general in 1917. During the Civil War he was chief of staff under General Wrangel. He immigrated to France and was one of the leaders of the Russian All-Military Union (ROVS) in the 1930s. He continued to live in France until his death in 1962.

Shcherbatov, Prince Nikolai Borisovich (1868–1943). He was born into a family of landowners. He was educated in the Corps of Pages and served a short while in a dragoon regiment. He was a deputy in the First State Duma. In 1913 he was appointed head of the government horse breeding agency. In 1915 he was appointed minister of the interior and served from June 15 to September 21, 1915. He immigrated to Germany after the Revolution, and died there in 1943.

Skoblin, Nikolai Vladimirovich (1885–1937). During World War I he rose in rank from a junior officer to colonel. He joined the Volunteer Army and between 1918 and 1920 he commanded battalions, brigades, and a division. He immigrated to Paris where he and his wife Nadejda Plevitskaia enlisted into Soviet service as Soviet agents around 1930. Skoblin joined ROVS and was involved in the planned abduction of General Miller in 1937. Skoblin apparently fled to Spain when ROVS discovered that he was a Soviet agent, and, according to rumors, Soviet secret police agents murdered him.

Skoropadskii, Pavel Petrovich (1873–1945). Born into Ukrainian nobility. Graduated from the Corps of Pages in St. Petersburg and entered the Russian army as an officer. Promoted to lieutenant general in 1916. Spent his career prior to 1917 as a cavalry commander. After the February Revolution he was active in Ukraine and was proclaimed leader of a major local military council. He was chosen hetman of Ukraine with the support of the German occupying forces. In November 1918 he was removed from power by Petliura. He emigrated from Ukraine to Germany and died during World War II in an Allied bombing raid on Regensburg, where he lived.

Spiridovich, Alexander Ivanovich (1873–1952). A gendarme officer who achieved the rank of major general. He was head of the Kiev Security Bureau (Okhrana) at the time of Stolypin's assassination. He was named in the investigation into the responsibility for inadequate security that led to Stolypin's death; however, Spiridovich's role in the incident was dropped by order of Nicholas II. Spiridovich was appointed head of palace security. In 1916 he was appointed city prefect of Yalta. After the Revolution he immigrated to France and then to the United States. He and his wife subsequently moved to New York where he died in 1952.

Stavrovskii, V. D. (?). An investigator in the Provisional Government's Petrograd Judicial Court. He was appointed to handle Globachev's case in mid-1917 while Globachev was detained at Furshtatskaia Street.

Stolypin, Petr Arkadievich (1862–1911). Held several provincial governorships: Grodno from 1902 to 1903 and Saratov in 1906. He suppressed a peasant uprising in Saratov in 1906 and won the Tsar's favor. He was appointed minister of the interior and at the same time chairman of the Council of Ministers (prime minister). A former agent of the Kiev Okhrana assassinated him in 1911.

Sturmer, Boris Vladimirovich (1848–1917). Began his career in the Ministry of Justice in 1876. In 1892 he transferred to the Ministry of the Interior. In January 1916 he was appointed chairman of the Council of Ministers (prime minister), and in March 1916 he also took on the position of minister of the interior. He held the latter office from March 3, 1916 to July 7, 1916. He left office because of suspicion of being pro-German because of his German name. He was arrested in 1917 by the Provisional Government and died of uremia in the Peter and Paul Fortress in September 1917.

Sukhomlinov, Vladimir Alexandrovich (1848–1926). A cavalry general who rose to the rank of army chief of staff in 1908 and in 1909 was appointed minister of war. He was dismissed in 1915 for abuse of power and for protecting friends from espionage charges. He spent some time under arrest and was released in 1918. He immigrated to Finland and then to Germany.

Tomas, Feodor Feodorovich (1872–1928). His real name was Frederick Bruce Thomas. He was born in 1872 in Mississippi, the son of freed Black slaves. He traveled to Russia in his late twenties and was able to establish an entertainment salon in Moscow. After the Revolution he fled to Constantinople where he opened an entertainment salon again. A changing political and economic culture in Turkey caused his decline. He died in poverty in 1928.

Trotsky, Lev Davidovich (1879–1940). Active Marxist revolutionary. Initially siding with the Mensheviks, he joined the Bolsheviks in July 1917. After the October Revolution he was commissar of foreign affairs, commissar of war, and then head of the Red Army during the Civil War against the Whites. On Stalin's orders he was banished from Russia in 1929. He was murdered in Mexico on Stalin's orders.

Tumanov, Nikolai Evseevich (1844–1917). Engineer general. Most of his career was as an engineering officer. During the Russo-Japanese War he was inspector of engineering of the Russian 1st Army in Manchuria. His next assignment was as head of army engineers of the Warsaw Military District. In September 1915, with the rank of general, he was appointed head of the Petrograd Military District. In July 1916 he was transferred and appointed commander of military supplies for the Russian western front. Following the February Revolution, he retired to his home in Pskov Province and died there in the latter part of 1917.

Uritskii, Moisei Solomonovich (1873–1918). Prior to 1917 he was a member of the Menshevik faction. Between 1905 and 1914 Uritsky was active in revolutionary programs. He was arrested twice and served internal exile in Siberia. In 1914 he emigrated to France. He returned to Russia immediately upon the collapse of the Russian monarchy and joined the Bolshevik Party. Following the October Revolution he became head of the Petrograd Cheka in March 1918, and in April he was appointed

Peoples' Commissar of Internal Affairs for the Northern Region. He was assassinated in August of that year.

Vasiliev, Alexei Tikhonovich (1869–1919). The last director of the Department of Police from September 1916 to February 1917. Formerly employed in the St. Petersburg District Court. In 1913 he joined the staff of the Department of Police. After the Revolution he immigrated to France, where he died.

Vertinskii, Alexander Nikolaevich (1889–1957). He was born out of wedlock and spent his early years in various jobs, mostly writing short stories and articles for periodicals. He participated in World War I as a medical assistant caring for the wounded. In 1916 he began his career as a singer specializing in songs whose lyrics were melancholy and of love lost. After the Revolution he spent some time performing in Constantinople and Europe, always in costume as Pierrot. He returned to the Soviet Union in 1943, where he lived the rest of his life.

Vissarionov, Sergei Evlampievich (1867–1918). Trained in law. Served prosecutorial positions from 1889 to 1908. In 1908 he was on the staff of the minister of the interior and by 1910 he was vice-director of the Department of Police. General Dzhunkovskii dismissed him in 1913. He was shot by the Bolsheviks in 1918.

Vitkovskii, Vladimir Konstantinovich (1885–1978). A member of the St. Petersburg provincial nobility. A graduate of the Pavlovsk Military Academy, he was assigned to the Keksholm Life Guards Regiment. He was a battalion commander during World War I and was awarded the Cross of St. George for valor in 1916. He was a brigade commander in the White Army, and participated in the 1920 evacuation from Crimea. He emigrated to Bulgaria in 1921 and then moved to Paris in 1924. At the end of World War II he moved to the United States where he became the North American head of ROVS. He died in San Francisco in 1978.

Vyrubova, Anna Alexandrovna (1884–1964). She was a lady-in-waiting and a close friend to the Empress. She was also a great admirer and supporter of Rasputin. During the tenure of the Provisional Government she was held under arrest and questioned. In 1920 she was able to escape to Finland where she spent the rest of her life.

Wrangel, General Baron Peter Nikolaevich (1878–1928). The descendant of Baltic Germans, his early education including college was in mining engineering. He entered the military and served in the Russo-Japanese War. Subsequently he graduated from the General Staff Academy and rose in the ranks in various cavalry units. During World War I he distinguished himself in battles and was promoted to major general. When the Bolshevik Revolution began he joined the White Army and in April 1920 became its commander in chief. He organized the massive evacuation of White forces and in 1922 he moved to Bulgaria and was the head of all Russian refugees. He died in 1928 in Brussels and there was some suspicion that he was poisoned by a Soviet agent.

Yusupov, Felix, Feliksovich (1887–1967). Born into a very wealthy princely noble family. His high social status continued with his marriage to Irene Alexandrovna who was a niece of Nicholas II. He was one of the several conspirators who plotted Rasputin's death. In late 1916 Rasputin was murdered in Yusupov's palatial home in Petrograd. Yusupov was exiled to his country home. After the Revolution he and his wife fled south, and in April 1919 they were evacuated from Crimea along with a number of Romanov relatives. They immigrated to Paris where they opened a fashion shop named "Irfe," which consisted of the first two letters of their first names. Irina outlived him by three years.

Zavarzin, Pavel Pavlovich (1868–1932). Born in Kherson Province into a noble family. Attended an infantry academy and entered the infantry as a junior lieutenant. Served in the infantry from 1888 until 1898, at which time he transferred into the Special Corps of Gendarmes. Over the years he held various positions in gendarme offices. In 1906 he was appointed chief of the Warsaw Okhrana, and in 1909 he was transferred to head the Moscow Okhrana. In 1917 he was assigned to the Department of Police. The Provisional Government arrested him in 1917. He was subsequently released, and emigrated to Paris where he died in 1932.

Appendix E

Glossary of Terms

Bolshevik. The derivation of the word is from the Russian *bol'shinstvo*, meaning "majority." The Bolsheviks were a faction within the Marxist Russian Social Democratic Workers' Party, the RSDWP (in some sources the party is named the Russian Social Democratic Labor Party, the RSDLP). The Bolsheviks won a series of issues at the Second Party Congress in 1903; hence they became the majority. The opposition became known as the Mensheviks, from the Russian word *men'shinstvo*, meaning minority.

CARE Packages. The letters represent "Cooperative for American Remittances to Europe." This was a program begun in 1945 to help people in Europe by sending food and other necessary items to people in need who lived in war-ravaged Europe following World War II.

Cheka. This is the acronym for the **All-Russian Extraordinary Commission.** The full name is much longer, but this was the "secret police" that was established by the new Soviet government in December 1917. The Cheka was given great responsibility for ferreting out counterrevolutionaries, illegal presses, sabotage, profiteering, speculation, and any other opposition to the government. The Cheka had the power of arrest, interrogation, and execution.

City prefect (Gradonachal'nik). In tsarist times a military officer with the rank of general or admiral held this position. The position's authority was similar to that of a provincial governor, but the city within the province was independent of a governor's responsibility. A city and its specified surrounding area were the responsibility of the city prefect. The city prefect was appointed by the Tsar.

Dacha. This word does not describe a primary residence. Rather it more accurately can be considered as a get-away or vacation home for people whose primary residence is in the city. It also was a symbol of affluence in tsarist times.

Department of Police. This department reported directly to the minister of the interior. With few exceptions the directors of the Department of Police were civilian men trained in law and with experience in judicial areas. The functions of the department were to coordinate and supervise the operations of the Gendarme Administrations and Okhrana Bureaus.

Extraordinary Commission of Inquiry for the Investigation of Illegal Acts by Ministers and Other Responsible Persons of the Tsarist Regime. As the name states, this commission was established in August 1917 to investigate possible illegal acts of the tsarist regime. The commission was established by the Provisional Government. This commission should not be confused with the Soviet Cheka.

Gatchina. A town approximately thirty miles south of Petrograd that was the site of one of the royal family's palace and parkland/hunting grounds.

Gradonachal'nik. The literal translation of this title is "leader of the city." For a detailed description, see **city prefect.**

Hetman. A military, financial, and political administrative leader of a state. During the Russian Civil War, the title was associated with Pavlo (Paul) Skoropadskii who was given the title of hetman of the Ukrainian State.

Kresty. This was the popular name for the prison in Petrograd. It was known officially as the Vyborg Prison, because it was on the Vyborg side of the Neva River in Petrograd.

Menshevik. The derivation of the word is from the Russian, *men'shinstvo*, meaning minority. Mensheviks were a faction within the Marxist Russian Social Democratic Workers' Party, the RSDWP (in some sources the party is named the Russian Social Democratic Labor Party, the RSDLP).

The leader of this faction, Julius Martov, lost in a disagreement over membership to Lenin at the Second Party Congress in 1903, hence this faction became known as the minority.

Okhrana. This word is a noun that means "security." It was not used in tsarist times as a designation for the security bureau. Modern English authors use it to designate the agency. The official title of the agency in Petrograd was Bureau for Public Security, Safety, and Order in Petrograd. There were three major offices of the governmental agency, in Petrograd, Moscow, and Warsaw. The majority of the chiefs of the Okhrana offices were military men who came from the Special Corps of Gendarmes. The major function of this agency was to combat left-wing revolutionary activity and political terrorism. This included maintaining surveillance over suspicious persons, the use of secret agents, authority to have people arrested, and other counterrevolutionary efforts.

Pale of Settlement. This was an area of over 450,000 square miles within which Jews were required to live by law. The Pale was established by Catherine the Great in 1791. The area stretched from Crimea in the south almost to Riga in the north. It stretched from the provinces of Chernigov and Ekaterinoslav in the east to what is now Belarus in the west. Even within the pale there were cities where Jews were prohibited from living, such as Kiev and Sevastopol. Following the February Revolution, the Provisional Government abolished the Pale.

Petrograd. The original name of the capital, from its founding in 1704 until 1914, was St. Petersburg. With the start of World War I, having the capital's name with a German suffix, "burg," was unacceptable. The name of the capital was Russified to Petrograd. In the Soviet period the name of the city was changed to Leningrad, and following the collapse of the Soviet Union the name was changed back to St. Petersburg.

Progressive Bloc. This was a coalition of several parties in the Fourth Duma that was organized to seek reforms from the Tsar. Among the parties involved were the Kadets and the Octobrists, as well as individual representatives in the Duma.

Provisional Government. Following the turmoil of the February Revolution and the abdication of Nicholas II, senior leaders of the Duma formed a temporary government whose function was to establish order until free elections could be held to form a Russian Constituent Assembly, thereby forming a stable republic. The Provisional Government existed from the beginning of March 1917 until the end of October 1917 when the Bolsheviks overthrew it.

ROVS. Abbreviation for Russkii Obshchevoinskii Soyuz. This organization's title has been translated into English in slightly different ways (Russian All-Military Association, Russian General Military Association, and Russian Para-Military Association). ROVS was established in the late 1920s under the leadership of Grand Duke Nikolai Nikolaevich. Its function was to support White Russian refugees, to maintain information on Soviet infiltrators into the organization, and to promote counter-Soviet activities. The headquarters of ROVS was in Paris. ROVS activities continued there up to World War II.

Social Democrats (SDs). The full name was the Russian Social-Democratic Workers' Party, which was the predecessor of the Communist Party of the Soviet Union. By 1903 there were two opposing factions within the party, the Bolsheviks and the Mensheviks.

Socialist Revolutionaries (SRs). The full name was the Russian Socialist Revolutionary Party. The ideology of the party was that a true revolution would require the uprising of peasants, workers, and the liberal to radical thinking intelligentsia. In the early 1900s the party employed terrorism as a means of destabilizing the government. At the beginning of World War I the party split between those members who opposed the war and those who supported it. A number of SRs held leadership positions in the Provisional Government.

Soviet of Workers' and Soldiers' Deputies. This was a council during the period from March through October 1917 that was a rival and in a power struggle with the Provisional Government. Most of the members of the Soviet were socialists, Mensheviks, and Socialist Revolutionaries.

Spala. Nicholas II's hunting lodge in central Poland. It is between thirty and forty miles from Lodz. In addition to the Tsar's lodge there were also guest accommodations for government officials on vacation and foreign visitors.

Special Corps of Gendarmes. This organization is often identified also as the Separate Corps of Gendarmes in historical literature. This was the political police of the Russian Empire. It was organizationally under the Ministry of the Interior, and its commander was the assistant minister of the interior for political matters. The Special Corps of Gendarmes had several functions: investigating political crimes, maintaining the security of borders and railroads, and cooperating with other police and investigative agencies. Most of its personnel entered this service from the army.

State Duma. This was the "lower house" of a system that approximated a parliamentary one. The Duma was a legislative body whose actual authority was very limited. The Tsar could dissolve the Duma if the Duma's recommendations and attempts at influence were perceived as a threat to the autocracy. Between 1905 and 1917 there were four Dumas; the first two were dissolved by Nicholas II, and the Third Duma was reorganized to be subservient to the Tsar. It lasted its five-year term. The Fourth Duma was dissolved by the Provisional Government.

Tsarskoe Selo. The translation of this is "Tsar's Village." This was the summer and preferred year-round residence of Nicholas II and his family that was about fifteen miles from Petrograd. It was a compound of several palaces. The royal family lived in the Alexander Palace. The compound is most famous today for the Catherine Palace.

Volunteer Army. This was the Russian counterrevolutionary army that was established late in 1917 to combat the Bolsheviks. It was composed mostly of tsarist officers.

White Army. See "Volunteer Army."

White Movement. A generalized term describing the efforts of former senior tsarist officers to create an army and a government to counter the advances of Bolshevik power. This included fundraising, enlisting various Cossack units and Russian frontline units in the south, attempting to attract Czech units, and organizing a government.

Winter Palace. The official residence of the royal family in the capital. Today it is the Hermitage Museum.

Notes

Preface

1. Iain Lauchlan, Russian Hide-and-Seek: The Tsarist Secret Police in St. Petersburg, 1906–1914 (Helsinki: Studia Historica 67, 2002), 365.

Chapter 1

1. The Russian Orthodox Church had two forms of clergy—the "white" secular clergy and the "black" monastic clergy. A member of the white clergy had to be married or widowed, and could move up only to the rank of archpriest.

2. Roman Globachev to V. Marinich (email), October 17, 2017.

3. Roman Globachev to V. Marinich (emails), July 14, 2011 and August 9, 2011.

4. There were basically two types of nobility in Russia, landed nobility and service nobility. The Globachevs' award was the latter.

5. Comment by Lydia Marinich.

6. Since the late 1700s eastern Poland had been part of the Russian Empire.

7. John Bushnell, "The Tsarist Officer Corps, 1881–1914: Customs, Duties, Inefficiency," *American Historical Review* 86, no. 2 (1981): 771–772.

8. In 1894 the name of the regiment was changed from the Keksholm Grenadier Regiment of the Austrian Emperor to the Keksholm Life Guard Regiment of the Austrian Emperor. In July 26, 1914 (Old Style), the name of the regiment was changed to Keksholm Life Guard Regiment. Reference to the Austrian emperor was removed, since Russia was now at war with Germany and Austria.

9. "Korsakov, Semeon Nikolaevich," ru.m.wikipedia.org.

10. Comments by Sofia Globacheva and Lydia Marinich, and data from Russian Wikipedia.

11. Globachev's acceptance document into the Corps of Gendarmes, February 26, 1903. Document 361.

12. A. P. Martynov, *Moia Sluzhba v Otdel'nom Korpuse Zhandarmov* (Stanford, Calif.: Stanford University Press, 1972), 28.

13. Globachev's Service Record (Posluzhnoi Spisok), July 1, 1914. GARF, fond 110. Ol17, d356. L42100.

14. Sofia Globacheva, *The Truth of the Russian Revolution: The Memoirs of the Tsar's Chief of Security and His Wife*, trans. Vladimir G. Marinich (Albany: State University of New York Press, 2017), 11. Globachev's personal resume, author's family collection.

15. Globacheva, *Truth of the Russian Revolution*, 11.

16. Globacheva, *Truth of the Russian Revolution*, 13.

17. Globacheva, *Truth of the Russian Revolution*, 15.

18. Globachev's Service Record (Posluzhnoi Spisok), GARF, fond 110. Ol17, d356. L42100.

19. Globacheva, *Truth of the Russian Revolution*, 16.

Chapter 2

1. Globacheva, *Pravda*, 234 (English translation, 19).

2. Z. I. Peregudova, "Okhrana: Memoirs of Security Bureau Leaders," *Novoe Literaturnoe Obozrenie*, vol. 1 (2004) (hrono.ru).

3. Z. I. Peregudova, ed., *Pravda o Russkoi Revolutsii* (Moscow: Rosspen, 2009), 26.

4. Peregudova, *Pravda*, 27.

5. A. Iu. Dunaeva, *Reformy politsii v Rossii Nachala XX Veka i Vladimir Fedorovich Dzhunkovskii* [Police reforms in Russia at the beginning of the XX century and Vladimir Fedorovich Dzhunkovskii] (Moscow: MVD Russia, 2012), 163.

6. Peregudova, *Pravda*, 27.

7. Memorandum from S. Beletskii to V. A. Tolmachev. GARF f. 102.00, June 11, 1912.

8. Memorandum from S. Beletskii to D. K. Gershel'man. GARF, f.102, November 22, 1912.

9. Peregudova, *Pravda*, 28.

10. Peregudova, *Pravda*, 28.

11. V. F. Dzhunkovskii, *Vospominania*, vol. 2 (Moscow, 1997), 218.

12. Dzhunkovskii, *Vospominania*, 16.

13. Occasional comments of Lydia Marinich.

14. Peregudova, *Pravda*, 235.

15. Memo Beletskii to Martynov, November 28, 1913. GARF f.102.00.

16. Memo Beletskii to Martynov, November 28, 1913. GARF f.102.00.

17. Dzhunkovskii memo to Martynov, December 6, 1913. GARF f. 102.00.

18. Martynov, *Moia Sluzhba*, 215.

19. www.australiarussia.com. Vladimir Kroupnik, "The Gallipoli Battle—a Russian Connection," undated.

20. Dunaeva, *Reformy politsii*, 162.

Chapter 3

1. Globacheva in Peregudova, *Pravda*, 238 (English translation, 30).

2. Globacheva, *Pravda*, 239 (English translation, 32).

3. Cited in Jonathan W. Daly, *The Watchful State: Security Police and Opposition in Russia, 1906–1917* (DeKalb: Northern Illinois University Press, 2004), 172.

4. Richard G. Robbins Jr., *Overtaken by the Night* (Pittsburgh: University of Pittsburgh Press, 2017), 206.

5. Globachev, *Pravda*, 51 (English translation, 1–2).

6. Globachev, *Pravda*, 91 (English translation, 73).

7. The term "leapfrog" was used by Bernard Pares in *The Fall of the Russian Monarchy: A Study of the Evidence* (New York: Alfred A. Knopf, 1939), 376, and by Douglas Smith in *Rasputin: Faith, Power, and the Twilight of the Romanovs* (New York: Farrar, Straus and Giroux, 2016), 548.

8. Vladimir Alexandrov, *The Black Russian* (London: Head of Zeus, 2013), 129.

9. Globachev, *Pravda*, 59 (English translation, 41).

10. Robbins, *Overtaken by the Night*, 206.

11. A very detailed and thorough account of Dzunkovskii's reforms can be found in Daly's *Watchful State*, 136–158.

12. Testimony of V. F. Dzhunkovskii in *Padenie Tsarskogo Rezhima* (Moscow: State Publication, 1926), vol. 5, 70.

13. Peregudova, *Pravda*, 95.

Chapter 4

1. Smith, *Rasputin*, 15.

2. Smith, *Rasputin*, 335–336.

3. Smith, *Rasputin*.

4. Globachev's testimony to the Extraordinary Investigative Commission of the Provisional Government, published in *Voprosy Istorii, Moscow*, vol. 7 (2002), 106.

5. Peregudova. *Pravda*, 80, and Globachev's testimony to the Extraordinary Commission of the Provisional Government on August 6, 1917, in Globachev, *Pravda*, 412.

6. Peregudova. *Pravda*, 83.

7. Boris Kolokolov, *Zhandarm s Tsarem v Golove* (Moscow: Molodaia Gvardia, 2009), 388.

8. Martynov, *Moia Sluzhba*, 232.

9. Martynov, *Moia Sluzhba*, 317.

10. Kolokolov, *Zhandarm s Tsarem v Golove*, 502.

11. Comment by Lydia Marinich.

12. Peregudova, *Pravda*, 94.

13. Daly, *Watchful State*, 172.

14. Peregudova, *Pravda*, 96.

15. Globacheva, *Pravda*, 240 (English translation, 33).

Chapter 5

1. Andrei Maylunas and Sergei Mironenko, *A Lifelong Passion: Nicholas and Alexandra, Their Own Story* (New York: Doubleday, 1997), 434.

2. Smith, *Rasputin*, 452.

3. Peregudova, *Pravda*, 98.

4. A. I. Spiridovich, *Velikaia Voina i Fevral'skaia Revolutsia, 1914–1917*, vol. 1 (New York: All Slavic Publishing House, 1960), 220.

5. Peregudova, *Pravda*, 97.

6. D. A. Baksht, "Stat' Ten'iu Rasputina: Zhandarmskaia Kar'era Mihaila Komissarova." Politicheskaia Istoria Rossii: Proshloe i Sovremennost' ["Standing in Rasputin's shadow: Michael Komissarov's career in the gendarmes." The political history of Russia: Past and contemporary] (St. Petersburg, 2015), 93.

7. Lauchlan, *Russian Hide-and-Seek*, 297.

8. Globachev, *Pravda*, 98 (English translation), 81.

9. Spiridovich, *Velikaia Voina*, 271.

10. I. V. Gessen, ed., *Arkhiv Russkoi Revolutsii* [Archive of the Russian Revolution], vol. 7 (Berlin, 1923), 54.

11. Gessen, *Arkhiv*, 54

12. Lydia Marinich, comment.

13. Smith, *Rasputin*, 240, 241.

14. Lerma's full name is not given in Beletskii's memoir. It is possible that this was Dora Efimovna Lerma, born in 1892 and a professionally trained opera singer.

15. Gessen, *Arkhiv*, 66–67.

16. Gessen, *Arkhiv*, 65.

17. Peregudova, *Pravda*, 99.

18. Smith, *Rasputin*, 505.

19. Letter of Nicholas to Alexandra, January 4, 1916, from Stavka.

Chapter 6

1. Globachev, *Pravda*, 100 (English translation, 87, 88).
2. Globachev, *Pravda*, 103 (English translation, 88).
3. Globachev, *Pravda*, 329–357.
4. Globachev, *Pravda*, 64 (English translation, 45).
5. Globachev, *Pravda*, 105, 106.
6. Globachev, *Pravda*, 106 (English translation, 89).
7. Globachev, *Pravda*, 107, 108 (English translation, 89).
8. Globacheva, *Pravda*, 241 (English translation, 34).
9. Lauchlan, *Russian Hide-and-Seek*, 365.
10. Alexander A. Blok, *Poslednie Dni Imperatorskoi Vlasti* (Moscow: Progres Pleiada, 2012), 16.
11. Globachev, *Pravda*, 31, 32 (English translation, 116).
12. Peregudova, *Pravda*, 31, 32 (English translation, 116).
13. Globachev, *Pravda*, 110 (English translation, 95).
14. Smith, *Rasputin*, 566.
15. Globachev, *Pravda*, 111 (English translation, 95).
16. Globacheva, *Pravda*, 241 (English translation, 34–35).
17. Peregudova, *Pravda*, 31 (English translation, 115).
18. Smith, *Rasputin*, 558.
19. Gibel' Tsarskogo Petrograda in www.Statehistory.ru.
20. Gibel' Tsarskogo Petrograda in www.Statehistory.ru.
21. Globachev, *Pravda*, 87 (English translation, 70).
22. Globachev, *Pravda*, 90 (English translation, 72).
23. Richard Pipes, *The Russian Revolution* (New York: Alfred A. Knopf, 1991), 272.
24. Globachev, *Pravda*, 359–361.
25. Globachev, *Pravda*, 113 (English translation, 98).
26. Daly, *Watchful State*, 189–190.
27. Globachev, *Pravda*, 113 (English translation, 98–99).
28. Globachev, *Pravda*, 115 (English translation, 99–100).
29. Globachev's entire report of January 19 is published in Globachev, *Pravda*, 362–373.
30. Globachev's entire report of January 26 is published in Globachev, *Pravda*, 374–380.
31. Peregudova, *Pravda*, 36 (English translation, 119).

Chapter 7

1. Globachev's dispatch of February 27, 1917 to the director of the Department of Police, in *Pravda*, 407–408.

2. Globachev, *Pravda*, 122 (English translation, 105).

3. P. P. Zavarzin, *Zhandarmy i Revoliutsionery: Vospominania* (Paris: Izdania Avtora, 1930), 236.

4. Zavarzin, *Zhandarmy i Revoliutsionery*, 241.

5. Globachev, *Pravda*, 124 (English translation, 108).

6. Globachev, *Pravda*, 126 (English translation, 109).

7. Globachev, *Pravda*, 126 (English translation, 110).

8. A dacha was usually a summer home or a seasonal retreat. There were such dachas around the various country and vacation royal palaces.

9. Globachev, *Pravda*, 131 (English translation, 113–114).

10. Globachev, *Pravda*, 146 (English translation, 148).

11. Globachev, *Pravda*, 146 (English translation, 148).

12. Globachev, *Pravda*, 150 (English translation, 152–153).

Chapter 8

1. Globacheva, *Pravda*, 246 (English translation, 131).

2. Globacheva, *Pravda*, 251 (English translation, 136).

3. Globacheva, *Pravda*, 253 (English translation, 137–138).

4. Globacheva, *Pravda*, 255 (English translation, 139–140).

5. Globacheva, *Pravda*, 255 (English translation, 139–140).

6. Globachev, *Pravda*, 147 (English translation, 149–150).

Chapter 9

1. Globachev, *Pravda*, 151 (English translation, 153).

2. Globachev, *Pravda*, 153–154 (English translation, 156–157).

3. Bernard Pares, *The Fall of the Russian Monarchy* (New York: Alfred A. Knopf, 1939), 13.

4. The original notarized document is part of the Marinich collection.

5. Globachev, *Pravda*, 157 (English translation, 159).

6. Globachev, *Pravda*, 160–161 (English translation, 161–162).

7. Transcript of Globachev testimony, August 6, 1917. GARF, Fond 1467, Op. 1, D. 39, L 23–26.

8. Globachev, *Pravda*, 166 (English translation, 166).

9. GARF, f. 1467, op.1 d.44.1, pp. 241–243.

Chapter 10

1. Globachev, *Pravda*, 167 (English translation, 175).

2. Globachev, *Pravda*, 169 (English translation, 177).

3. Globachev, *Pravda*, 167 (English translation, 175).

4. Globacheva, *Pravda*, 259 (English translation, 168).

5. Globacheva, *Pravda*, 259 (English translation, 168).

6. Globachev, *Pravda*. 173 (English translation, 180), and Nikol'skii in *Pravda*, 439.

7. Globacheva, *Pravda*, 261 (English translation, 169).

8. Kolokolov, *Zhandarm s Tsarem v Golove*, 494.

9. Globachev, *Pravda*, 177 (English translation, 182).

10. Globachev, *Pravda*, 176–177 (English translation, 182–183).

11. Globacheva, *Pravda*, 266 (English translation, 186).

12. Globachev, *Pravda*, 266–267 (English translation, 186–187).

13. Globachev, *Pravda*, 268 (English translation, 187–188).

14. Globachev, *Pravda*, 270 (English translation, 189).

15. Cited in W. Bruce Lincoln, *Red Victory: A History of the Russian Civil War* (New York: Simon and Schuster, 1989), 313.

16. Globachev, *Pravda*, 181 (English translation, 200), although Lincoln, *Red Victory*, 316, suggests that Petliura entered Kiev around August 30, 1919.

17. Globacheva, *Pravda*, 273 (English translation, 193).

18. Globachev, *Pravda*, 181 (English translation, 200).

19. Globacheva, *Pravda*, 275–276 (English translation, 195).

Chapter 11

1. Lincoln, *Red Victory*, 213.

2. Globachev, *Pravda*, 189 (English translation, 207).

3. Globachev, *Pravda*, 189 (English translation, 207).

4. Globacheva, *Pravda*, 276 (English translation, 210).

5. Michael Glenny and Norman Stone, *The Other Russia: The Experience of Exile* (New York: Viking Press, 1991), 165.

6. Globacheva, *Pravda*, 278–279 (English translation, 212).

7. Vladimir Marinich, private collection.

8. Globacheva, *Pravda*, 284 (English translation, 217).

9. Globachev, *Pravda*, 202 (English translation, 238).

10. Globachev, *Pravda*, 208 (English translation, 242).

11. Globacheva, *Pravda*, 286–287 (English translation, 220).

12. Globacheva, *Pravda*, 286–287 (English translation, 220).

Chapter 12

1. Lincoln, *Red Victory*, 449. See also "The Russian Refugee Crisis of the 1920s," https://blogs.bl.uk/european/2015/12/the-russian-refugee-crisis-of-the-1920s.html.

Chapter 13

1. https://en.wikipedia.org./demographics of Istanbul.

2. Alexander Vertinskii, *Chetvert' Veka Bez Rodiny* [A quarter of a century without a homeland] (Kiev: Muzichnaia Ukraina, 1989), 24.

3. Globachev, *Pravda*, 295 (English translation, 262–263).

4. V. G. Babenko, *Artist Alexander Vertinskii* (Sverdlovsk: Ural University Publisher, 1989), 50. See also Vladimir Alexandrov, *The Black Russian* (London: Head of Zeus, 2013).

5. Vertinskii, *Chetvert' Veka Bez Rodiny*, 21.

6. Globachev, *Pravda*, 222 (English translation, 269–270).

7. Letter of Major General A. A. vonLampe to V. Marinich, February 21, 1961. Marinich private collection.

8. Globachev, *Pravda*, 212 (English translation, 254).

9. General Baron Peter N. Wrangel, *Always with Honor* (New York: Robert Speller & Sons, 1957), 113.

10. Globacheva, *Pravda*, 393 (English translation, 259).

11. Globachev, *Pravda*, 5 (English translation, xxiii).

12. Globachev, *Pravda*, 51 (English translation, 1).

13. General V. F. Dzhunkovskii clearly blamed the "intelligentsia" and the Socialist Revolutionaries as having been the most dangerous groups in Russia and the main cause of turmoil. See Dunaeva, *Reformy politsii v Rossii Nachala XX Veka i Vladimir Fedorovich Dzhunkovskii*, 304.

Chapter 14

1. Russkii Obshche-Voinskii Soiuz. St. Petersburg, 1994, www.izput.narod.ru.

2. James E. Hassell, "Russian Refugees in France and the United States between the World Wars," *Transactions of the American Philosophical Society* 8, part 7 (1991).

3. Herman Bernstein, "Komissarov, 'The Terror,'" *New York Times*, October 12, 1924.

Chapter 15

1. www.Bigenc.ru. Bol'shaia Rossiiskaia Entsiklopedia.

2. Alexander Solzhenitsyn, "200 Years of Russo-Jewish History." www.Alor.org.

3. Martynov, *Moia Sluzhba v Otdel'nom Korpuse Zhandarmov*, 53.

4. Blok, *Poslednie Dni Imperatorskoi Vlasti*, 216.

5. Letter, Dragomirov to Globachev, August 18, 1930.

6. Robert H. Johnston, *New Mecca, New Babylon: Paris and the Russian Exiles, 1920–1945* (Montreal: McGill-Queen's University Press, 1988), 25.

7. Pavel Nikolaevich Shatilov, *Memoirs*. Bakhmeteff Archives, Columbia University, New York, Box 9, 10, p. 1736.

8. Paul Robinson, *The White Russian Army in Exile 1920–1941* (Oxford: Oxford University Press, 2002), 162.

9. Robinson, *White Russian Army in Exile*, 162.

10. Shatilov, *Memoirs*, 1773.

11. Letter, Globachev to Kussonski, November 3, 1937.

Chapter 16

1. Hassell, "Russian Refugees in France and the United States between the World Wars," 33.

2. Letter, Globachev to Kussonski, November 3, 1937.

3. Letter, Kussonskii to Abramov, February 22, 1937.

4. The name Matchabelli is sometimes thought to be Italian. It is, in fact, a Georgian name. See the "Annotated List of Names" for more detail.

Chapter 17

1. Blok, *Poslednie Dni Imperatorskoi Vlasti*, 16.

2. Globachev, *Pravda*, 74 (English translation, 56).

3. Bushnell, "Tsarist Officer Corps, 1881–1914."

4. Leon Trotsky, *The History of the Russian Revolution, Vol. 2* (New York: Simon and Schuster, 1932), 108.

5. Maurice Paleologue, *An Ambassador's Memoirs* (New York: Geo. Doran Co., 1925), vol. 1, 243.

6. Spiridovich, *Velikaia Voina i Fevral'skaia Revolutsia, 1914–1917*, 184.

7. Spiridovich, *Velikaia Voina I Fevral'skaia Revolutsia 1914–1917*, vol. 3, 79.

8. Kolokolov, *Zhandarm s Tsarem v Golove*, 416.

9. Globachev, *Pravda*, 60 (English translation, 41).

10. Globachev, *Pravda*, 135 (English translation, 128–129).

Appendix B

1. V. I. Gurko, *Features and Figures of the Past: Government and Opinion in the Reign of Nicholas II* (Stanford, Calif.: Stanford University Press, 1939), 624–638.

2. Robbins, *Overtaken by the Night*, 239.

3. Globachev, *Pravda*, 61 (English translation, 42).

4. Peregudova, *Pravda*, 58.

5. Peregudova, *Pravda*, 58.

6. Lauchan, *Russian Hide-and-Seek*, 112, and email from Professor Daly to V. Marinich, October 30, 2018.

7. Martynov, *Moia Sluzhba*, 216.

8. Spiridovich, *Velikaia Voina i Fevral'skaia Revolutsia, 1914–1917*, 184.

9. Peregudova, *Pravda*, 95.

10. A. T. Vassilyev, *The Ochrana: The Russian Secret Police* (London: J. B. Lippincott Company, 1930), 122.

11. Vassilyev, *Ochrana*, 64.

12. Daly, *Watchful State*, 172.

13. Transcript of Globachev's testimony to the Extraordinary Commission of the Provisional Government on August 6, 1917, in Globachev, *Pravda*, 411.

14. Lauchan, *Russian Hide-and-Seek*, 174.

15. Globacheva, *Pravda*, 240–241 (English translation, 34).

Bibliography

Alexandrov, Vladimir. *The Black Russian*. London: Head of Zeus, 2013.

Babenko, V. G. *Artist Alexander Vertinskii*. Sverdlovsk: Ural University Publisher, 1989.

Baksht, D. A. "Stat' Ten'iu Rasputina: Zhandarmskaia Kar'era Mihaila Komissarova." *Politicheskaia Istoria Rossii: Proshloe i Sovremennost'* ["Standing in Rasputin's shadow." The political history of Russia: Past and contemporary]. St. Petersburg, 2015.

Balk, A. P. *Poslednie Piat' Dnei Tsarskogo Petrograda (23–28 fevralia 1917): Dnevnik posledniago Petrogradskogo Gradonachal'nika*. [The last five days of Tsarist Petrograd (23–28 February 1917): Diary of the last city prefect of Petrograd]. Stanford, Calif.: Hoover Institution.

Baumgardner, Eugenia S. *Undaunted Exiles*. Staunton, Va.: McClure Company, 1925.

Blok, Alexander A. *Poslednie Dni Imperatorskoi Vlasti* [The last days of imperial power]. Moscow: Progres Pleiada, 2012.

Bortnevski, Viktor. *White Intelligence and Counter-Intelligence during the Russian Civil War*. Center for Russian and East European Studies no. 1108, August. Pittsburgh: University of Pittsburgh, 1995.

Bullock, David. *The Russian Civil War, 1918–1922*. Oxford: Osprey Publishing, 2008.

Burdzhalov, E. N. *Russia's Second Revolution: The February 1917 Uprising in Petrograd*. Translated by Donald J. Raleigh. Bloomington: University of Indiana Press, 1987.

Bushnell, John. "The Tsarist Officer Corps, 1881–1914: Customs, Duties, Inefficiency." *American Historical Review* 86, no. 2 (1981): 753–780.

Daly, Jonathan W. *The Watchful State: Security Police and Opposition in Russia, 1906–1917*. DeKalb: Northern Illinois University Press, 2004.

Dunaeva, A. Iu. *Reformy politsii v Rossii Nachala XX Veka i Vladimir Fedorovich Dzhunkovskii* [Police reforms in Russia at the beginning of the twentieth century and Vladimir Fedorovich Dzhunkovskii]. Moscow: MVD Russia, 2012.

Dzhunkovskii, V. F. *Vospominania*. [Memoirs]. Vol. 2. Moscow, 1997.

Gessen, I. V., ed. *Arkhiv Russkoi Revolutsii* [Archive of the Russian Revolution]. Vol. 7. Berlin, 1923.

"Gibel' Tsarskogo Petrograda: Fevral'skaia Revolutsia Glazami Gradonachal'nika A. P. Balka" [Downfall of Tsarist Petrograd: The February Revolution through the eyes of City Prefect A. P. Balk]. www.Statehistory.ru.

Glenny, Michael, and Norman Stone. *The Other Russia: The Experience of Exile*. New York: Viking Press, 1991.

Globachev, Konstantin Ivanovich, and Sofia Nikolaevna Globacheva. *The Truth of the Russian Revolution: The Memoirs of the Tsar's Chief of Security and His Wife*. Translated by Vladimir G. Marinich. New York: State University of New York Press, 2017.

Goldin, Vladislav I., and John W. Long. "Resistance and Retribution: The Life and Fate of General E. K. Miller." *Revolutionary Russia* 12, no. 2 (December 1999): 19–40.

Gurko, V. I. *Features and Figures of the Past: Government and Opinion in the Reign of Nicholas II*. Stanford, Calif.: Stanford University Press, 1939.

Hassell, James E. "Russian Refugees in France and the United States between the World Wars." *Transactions of the American Philosophical Society* 8, part 7 (1991).

Huntington, W. Chapin. *The Homesick Millions: Russia-out-of-Russia*. Boston: Alpine Press, 1933.

Johnston, Robert H. *New Mecca, New Babylon: Paris and the Russian Exiles, 1920–1945*. Montreal: McGill-Queen's University Press, 1988.

Kolokolov, Boris. *Zhandarm s Tsarem v Golove* [A gendarme with the Tsar on his mind]. Moscow: Molodaia Gvardia, 2009.

Kucherov, Samuel. *Courts, Lawyers, and Trials under the Last Three Tsars*. New York: Frederick A. Praeger, 1953.

Lauchlan, Iain. *Russian Hide-and-Seek: The Tsarist Secret Police in St. Petersburg, 1906–1914*. Helsinki: Studia Historica 67, 2002.

Lincoln, W. Bruce. *Red Victory: A History of the Russian Civil War*. New York: Simon and Schuster, 1989.

Luckett, Richard. *The White Generals: An Account of the White Movement and the Russian Civil War*. Harlow, England: Routledge, 1971.

Martynov, A. P. *Moia Sluzhba v Otdel'nom Korpuse Zhandarmov* [My service in the Special Corps of Gendarmes]. Stanford, Calif.: Stanford University Press, 1972.

Mawdsley, Evan. *The Russian Civil War*. Edinburgh: Birlinn, 2000.

Maylunas, Andrei, and Sergei Mironenko. *A Lifelong Passion: Nicholas and Alexandra, Their Own Story*. New York: Doubleday, 1997.

Paleologue, Maurice. *An Ambassador's Memoirs*. Vol. 1. New York: Geo. Doran Co., 1925.

Pares, Bernard. *The Fall of the Russian Monarchy: A Study of the Evidence*. New York: Alfred A. Knopf, 1939.

Peregudova, Z. I. "Okhrana: Memoirs of Security Bureau Leaders." *Novoe Literaturnoe Obozrenie*, vol. 1, 2004 (www.hrono.ru).

———. *Politicheskii sysk Rossii, 1880–1917* [Political investigation in Russia, 1880–1917]. Moscow: Rosspen, 2000.

———., ed. *Pravda o Russkoi Revolutsii* [The truth of the Russian Revolution]. Moscow: Rosspen, 2009.

Pipes, Richard. *The Russian Revolution*. New York: Alfred A. Knopf, 1991.

Purishkevich, V. M. *Iz Dnevnika V. M. Purishkevicha: Ubiistvo Rasputina* [From the diary of V. M. Purishkevich: Rasputin's murder]. Buenos Aires, 1944.

Robbins, Richard G., Jr. *Overtaken by the Night*. Pittsburgh: University of Pittsburgh Press, 2017.

Robinson, Paul. *The White Russian Army in Exile 1920–1941*. Oxford: Oxford University Press, 2002.

Ruud, Charles A., and Sergei A. Stepanov. *Fontanka 16: The Tsar's Secret Police*. Montreal: McGill-Queens University Press, 1999.

Sbornik Statei Posveshchennykh Pamiatsi Imperatoru Nikolaia II I ego Sem'i [Collection of essays dedicated to the memory of Emperor Nicholas II and his family]. Sofia, 1930.

Shatilov, Pavel Nikolaevich, *Memoirs*. Bakhmeteff Archives, Columbia University, New York, Box 9, 10.

Smele, Jonathan D. *Historical Dictionary of the Russian Civil Wars, 1916–1922*. New York: Rowman and Littlefield, 2015.

Smith, Douglas. *Rasputin: Faith, Power, and the Twilight of the Romanovs*. New York: Farrar, Straus and Giroux, 2016.

Spiridovich, A. I. *Velikaia Voina i Fevral'skaia Revolutsia, 1914–1917* [The Great War and the February Revolution]. Vol. 1. New York: All Slavic Publishing House, 1960.

Stewart, George. *The White Armies of Russia: A Chronicle of Counter-Revolution and Allied Intervention*. New York: Russell & Russell, 1933.

Trotsky, Leon. *The History of the Russian Revolution*. Vol. 2. New York: Simon and Schuster, 1932.

Vassilyev, A. T. *The Ochrana: The Russian Secret Police*. London: J. B. Lippincott Company, 1930.

Vertinskii, Alexander. *Chetvert' Veka Bez Rodiny* [A quarter of a century without a homeland]. Kiev: Muzichnaia Ukraina, 1989.

Wrangel, General Baron Peter N. *Always with Honor*. New York: Robert Speller & Sons, 1957.

Zavarzin, P. P. *Zhandarmy i Revoliutsionery: Vospominania* [Gendarmes and revolutionaries: Memoirs]. Paris: Izdania Avtora, 1930.

Zuckerman, Frederic S. *The Tsarist Secret Police in Russian Society, 1880–1917*. New York: New York University Press, 1996.

Index

Page numbers in *italics* indicate illustrations.

Working Musicians